100 THINGS SPIDER-MAN FANS SHOULD KNOW & DO BEFORE THEY DIE

Mark Ginocchio

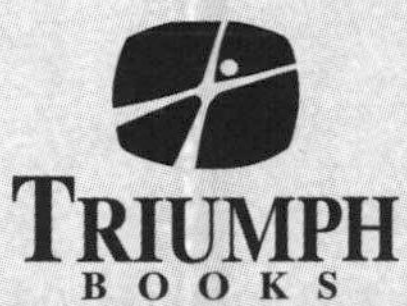

Library of Congress Cataloging-in-Publication Data

Names: Ginocchio, Mark, author.
Title: 100 things Spider-Man fans should know & do before they die / Mark Ginocchio.
Other titles: One hundred things Spider-Man fans should know & do before they die
Description: Chicago, Illinois : Triumph Books, [2017] | Series: 100 things...fans should know
Identifiers: LCCN 2017004501 | ISBN 9781629374024 (paperback)
Subjects: LCSH: Spider-Man (Fictitious character) | Marvel Comics Group. | Spider-Man (Comic strip) | Comic books, strips, etc.—United States—History and criticism. | BISAC: ART / Film & Video. | COMICS & GRAPHIC NOVELS / Nonfiction.
Classification: LCC PN6728.S6 G56 2017 | DDC 741.5/973—dc23 LC record available at https://lccn.loc.gov/2017004501

This book is available in quantity at special discounts for your group or organization. For further information, contact:

Triumph Books LLC
814 North Franklin Street
Chicago, Illinois 60610
(312) 337-0747
www.triumphbooks.com

Printed in U.S.A.
ISBN: 978-1-62937-402-4
Design by Patricia Frey
All photos are courtesy of the author's personal collection unless otherwise noted.

To my wife, Erin, for embracing
the superhero chaser in me.

Contents

Foreword

Peter Parker is an amazing guy. Like many of us, his parents once dropped him off with relatives and departed with the usual, "Be good for your aunt and uncle." Unlike many of us, Pete's parents never returned, so he stayed and grew up with his Aunt May and Uncle Ben.

That's only one of the things that differentiates Peter from the rest of us. He was also bitten by a radioactive spider while still in high school. Instead of dying an agonizing death from radiation poison, he gained the proportional strength, speed, and agility of a spider. He also developed a "spider-sense" that somehow warns him of danger. And he invented a pair of gizmos that shoot webbing strong enough to hold a rampaging Rhino. Like I said, Pete's an amazing guy.

I was about 11 years old when I first encountered Peter Parker on a spinner rack at the local candy store where I regularly bought my comic books. Already a fan of Marvel's *Fantastic Four* (which might have been up to the sixth or seventh issue at the time), I was intrigued by the new Spider-Man character introduced in *Amazing Fantasy #15*.

I became an instant fan when Pete was awarded his own title—*Amazing Spider-Man*—some months later. I faithfully followed Pete's adventures until I joined Marvel Comics in the late '70s—first as a writer and then in the '80s I became Pete's editor. A few years later I found myself writing *Amazing Spider-Man* (and paired with the equally amazing Ron Frenz) before becoming Marvel's editor-in-chief in 1987. I returned to writing Pete's adventures in the mid-90s and even co-created Spider-Girl with Ron Frenz (yes, I've often ridden on his shoulders) in 1998. Spider-Girl told the story of an aged Pete and his teenage daughter, who had inherited his powers and taken up the family webs. (Thanks to a brief stint as a scripter on *Untold Tales of Spider-Man,* I am one of the few writers who dealt with Pete as a teen, a young adult, and a middle-aged man.)

Enough about me! This book is about Pete. You are about to learn some intriguing things about everyone's favorite friendly neighborhood web-slinger—100 things to be exact, and your guide will be Mischievous Mark Ginocchio.

Mark is a professional writer and editor. He's also one of Spidey's biggest fans. Not only does he write a regular blog called *Chasing Amazing* which is devoted to our ever-amazing one, Mark also co-hosts *Amazing Spider-Talk* with Dapper Dan Gvozden—a podcast that used to invite Ron and me on for the occasional interview but has gotten too big and fancy for us.

Mark has scoured the pages of Spidey's adventures and annoyed quite a few past creators (the guy's relentless) in his hunt for facts that will enlighten you about our boy Pete. The time has now come for you to sit back and enjoy.

Thanks for being there!

—Tom D.

Introduction

My love for superhero comics was born from a weekly ritual with my older brother. When I was in elementary school, every week he and I would walk to the corner candy store in my small Long Island, New York, hometown with a dollar in our pockets to buy whatever treasures we could afford. I'd usually buy a snack (one time I bought 20 pieces of bubble gum just because that was the most efficient way to spend my dollar). However, one afternoon when I was about seven, I followed my brother over to a spinning rack of comic books. He picked up a copy of *Amazing Spider-Man #296*—I'll never forget that strange cover depicting a giant red-and-blue spider tormenting this nebbish man with glasses and four mechanical arms (it turned out to be Spidey's archnemesis, Doctor Octopus). And since this was my older brother, someone I looked up to and idolized, I decided I'd use my dollar to do the same. (I even got a quarter back in change!)

A few weeks later, I saw another Spider-Man comic on the spinner rack: *Amazing Spider-Man #297*. I once again used my weekly dollar to pick up a comic. And on the very first page was a visual that has stuck with me ever since: an illustration of a miserable-looking Spider-Man, sopping wet from being out in the rain. He had run out of fluid in his patented web shooters and was unable to swing across town to get home. I thought to myself, *What kind of superhero is depicted as such a loser in his very own comic?* As it turns out, it was the kind of hero that I would instantly gravitate toward. Superman, Batman, Captain America, Iron Man, etc., were all idealized grown-ups, doing grown-up things. Spider-Man, while certainly not a kid by the time I started reading his comics, was totally different. He was average. He had problems. He was someone I could relate to.

Since those days at the candy store, I've managed to stick with Spider-Man for nearly 30 years—enduring a slew of writers and artists, editorial mandates, and status quo upheavals. And while I'd be a liar if I said I never took a lengthy break from the character (a multi-year story involving clones can break the spirit of the most devoted fan), as time went on, I dreamt that someday I would own every single issue of *Amazing Spider-Man*. It was mostly fueled by my love for the character, but also my compulsive need to "collect" and have every single issue of the series. It was a crazy dream. One that required two things I had very little of: time and money. But it was something I stuck with for more than 25 years, scouring an assortment of local comic book shops, conventions, musty VFW halls, online auctions, and more, until October 2014, when I purchased a copy of *Amazing Spider-Man #3* (the first appearance of Doctor Octopus). That was the final piece to my collection. Only fitting that the first and last Spider-Man comic I purchased for my collection featured Doc Ock on the cover.

In the interim, I started a blog that chronicled my quest to collect every issue of *Amazing Spider-Man,* called *Chasing Amazing*. I also co-founded the *Amazing Spider-Talk* podcast to talk about Spider-Man comics past and present on a weekly basis. It was during these endeavors that I started talking to some of the creators who had scripted, illustrated, or edited *Spider-Man* and learned some of the stories behind my favorite stories. By discovering some of these anecdotes or behind-the-scenes machinations, I've come to appreciate Spider-Man even more than I did as a kid.

In taking you on a tour of 100 things every Spider-Man fan should know or do before they die, my goal is to share these stories and help you appreciate the world of Spider-Man as much as I do. These breakdowns of key stories, moments, creators, characters, and activities aim to both shepherd new fans into the flock of die-hards and provide some new insights to the hardcore fans. I love to think that I've written a book I would like to read over the course of every phase of my own fandom. I hope in reading this book you will make some fantastic new discoveries about a character who I have nothing but love and respect for.

1 Introducing Spider-Man

In the world of comic books, there are origin stories, and then there's *Amazing Fantasy #15*, arguably the most famous and expertly crafted superhero introduction the medium has ever produced. Even the most casual of fans knows Spider-Man's origin—high school bookworm gets super powers from a spider bite; dons a red-and-blue costume and mask—and Uncle Ben is probably second only to Bruce Wayne/Batman's parents when listing the most famous dead characters from the world of comics.

But beyond everyone's familiarity with the story, and the pop culture phenomenon that Spider-Man would become, *Amazing Fantasy #15* still warrants celebration more than 50 years after it was first published in August 1962. Stan Lee and Steve Ditko, Spider-Man's co-creators, needed just 11 pages to introduce Spider-Man to the world. That means the Spider-Man story (one of four tales to appear in the issue) is so tightly plotted and scripted, in the span of a mere 11 pages—half a comic by today's standards—the reader gets nearly every critical element of the Spider-Man mythos.

We are introduced to Peter Parker, an orphan who lives with his doting Aunt May and Uncle Ben. We learn that Peter is smart, but disliked by his classmates and socially aloof, aka "Midtown High's only professional wallflower!"[1] We witness the now iconic radioactive spider-bite that gives Peter his fantastic powers that include leaping high in the air, clinging to walls, and immense strength. We see Peter initially use these powers for personal financial gain, first as a masked wrestler and later as a recurring act on the *Ed Sullivan Show.* The comic also demonstrates Peter's ingenuity. He engineers his own mechanical web shooters to mimic the act

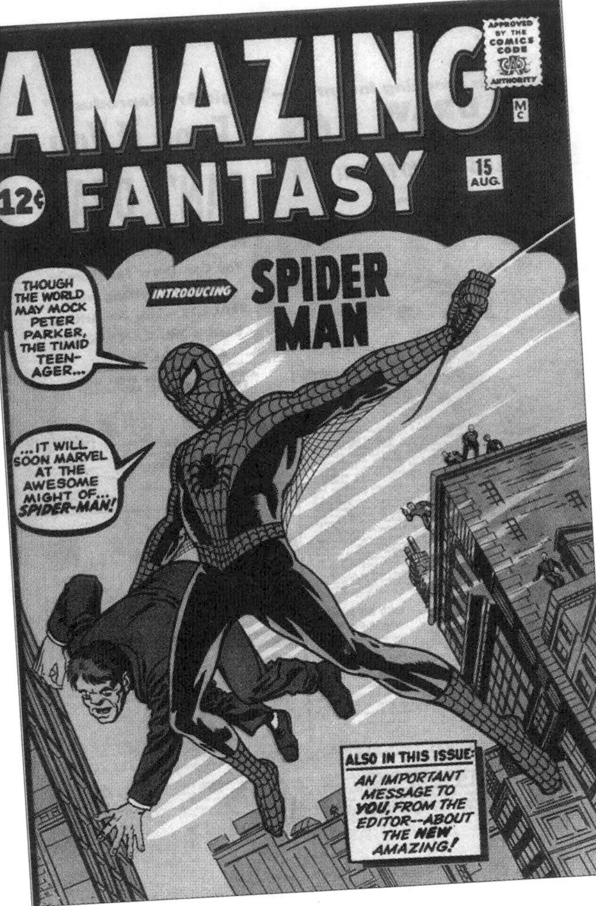

The cover of *Amazing Fantasy #15*, the first appearance of Spidey, which told the whole origin story in just 11 pages. (Newscom)

of a spider spinning its web. He also designs his own costume, and a name, Spiderman (the hyphen is added later).

Things are going great for Peter until there's a twist straight out of an O. Henry story. After performing on television, Spider-Man witnesses a petty thief being pursued by a cop. The cop begs Spider-Man to stop the crook, but he stands idly by, snidely telling the officer "That's your job!... From now on I just look out for number one—that means me!"[2]

Peter's selfishness would come back to haunt him. He comes home one night and sees a police cruiser in front of his aunt and uncle's house. He's told that his Uncle Ben has been murdered by a burglar. Peter dons his costume and seeks revenge on the criminal. He captures him and, as he descends upon the burglar, recognizes his face—it's the same small-time crook he let run by him at the television studio. The comic ends with Peter realizing the error of his ways, absorbing a lesson that would haunt him forever: "With great power, there must also come—great responsibility!"

Amazingly, despite its iconic status today, *Amazing Fantasy #15* almost never came to be. As Lee loves to tell it, fresh off creating the Fantastic Four and the Hulk, he pitched the idea of a teenaged hero named Spider-Man to Martin Goodman, publisher of the company that would later be known as Marvel Comics. Goodman dismissed it, claiming that teenagers could only be sidekicks in comics.[3] Plus, he thought the idea of a superhero based on a spider—one that could stick to walls and climb up them—was "grotesque."[4]

Still, Lee would get his opportunity to produce Spider-Man. The story was earmarked for the recently rebranded *Amazing Adult Fantasy*, which had changed its name to simply *Amazing Fantasy* and was on the verge of cancellation.[5] Lee first turned to his *Fantastic Four* collaborator, Jack Kirby, to develop the art for a Spider-Man story. Kirby produced a five-page sample about a teenager with a magic ring that transformed him into an adult hero named Spiderman (sans hyphen).[6] Lee immediately realized Kirby wasn't the right guy for the job. He wanted Spiderman to be vastly different in terms of look and physique than Marvel's other heroes. So Lee turned to Ditko.[7]

Rejecting Kirby's magic ring idea outright, Lee provided Ditko with a short synopsis of a teenage bookworm who develops spider-like powers after being bitten by a radioactive spider.[8] Ditko took Lee's direction of making this hero "different" to heart. In fact, Lee was initially worried that the Comics Code Authority—the entity that oversaw decency in comics—might misinterpret Ditko's illustrations and ban the story for showing a non-human spider-creature. Fortunately, Ditko pushed back, giving birth to Spider-Man's unique physicality, which continues to define the character to this day.[9]

With Lee's Shakespeare-esque narrative and Ditko's idiosyncratic interior artwork, the last piece to the puzzle was a dynamic cover. Ditko's cover design was rejected for something more traditional developed by Kirby—the instantly iconic image of Spider-Man swinging over the New York City landscape, telling the world it would soon "marvel at the awesome might of Spider-Man!" The rest, of course, is history. A comic so iconic, pages of Ditko's original artwork were donated to the Library of Congress in 2008.[10] A comic so desired, in 2011 a nearly flawless copy sold for a stunning $1.1 million, making it the most expensive Silver Age comic (published between the late 1950s and 1970) to ever be auctioned off.[11]

With so much time and money invested in this one comic, is it any surprise that almost the *entire story*—the spider-bite, the burglar, Uncle Ben's murder—has been recreated countless times over? We've seen variations of it in two blockbuster films, scores of cartoons, and even in the comics themselves. And in all of these iterations, changes to Lee and Ditko's masterwork have traditionally been very minor, for good reason. "Everything that takes place in that Spider-Man origin story resonates today," said Brian Michael Bendis, who scripted an updated version of Spider-Man's origin for Marvel's *Ultimate Spider-Man* series in 2000. "Every single theme, every single family thing, it's all human truths."[12]

2 Peter Parker

Peter Parker might not know a cha-cha from a waltz, but that doesn't change the fact that he's secretly the masked hero known across the globe as the "Amazing" Spider-Man. Don't let the cross-city web-slinging and the snazzy costume fool you, what has long set Spidey apart from most other superheroes is the fact that, at its core, Spider-Man is as much of a story about the human under the mask as it is a tale of a costumed vigilante.

"What really made Spidey unique wasn't so much his powers or his costume, sure those were cool things, but what really made him unique was that it was about the guy inside the costume and the soap opera that was his life," said Joe Quesada, Marvel's chief creative officer and a longtime Marvel editor-in-chief. "Peter could have had a whole different set of powers and it still would have been a ground-breaking comic because in the end, that's not what made Spider-Man stories different."[13]

Peter's co-creator, Stan Lee, wanted the character to be unique from the beginning. When describing Peter to non-fans, he would often say Spider-Man is an average teenager who "gets sinus attacks, he gets acne and allergy attacks while he's fighting."[14] While this rather glib description of Peter does touch upon his everyman status and relatability, there's far more to Peter Parker than just sinus attacks and acne.

Naturally, Peter was introduced in the same story where Spider-Man was—1962's *Amazing Fantasy #15*. The opening splash page of the comic, which depicts a sad-looking Peter standing alone while his classmates at Midtown High School mock and scorn him, cuts to the heart of one of the teenager's defining characteristics: his aloof personality. Some have mistakenly cast Peter as a geek or a nerd, but that's not exactly true. Yes, he's good at school and appreciates science, but he's more of a social outcast and a loner, instead of a nerd.

Amazing Fantasy #15's first few pages establish all of the pertinent information about Peter: he's 15, orphaned, and lives in Queens, New York, with his elderly aunt and uncle, May and Ben. The three of them have a loving relationship filled with smiles and May's trademark wheatcakes. Ben is a father figure to Peter, rustling his hair and joking about no longer being able to out-wrestle his nephew. While attending a science exhibition, Peter is bitten by a radioactive spider, making him feel ill. But as he's walking home, Peter discovers that the bite has given him strange powers: the ability to leap incredible heights, scale walls, and crush objects in his bare hands.[15]

Peter immediately thinks to use these new powers for financial gain. He enters himself into a wrestling competition against a brute named Crusher Hogan. But in a moment of self-doubt that would play a key part in Peter always wanting to keep his identity as Spider-Man a secret from the public, he puts a mask on in case he lost. The mask would later evolve into Spider-Man's trademark red and blue costume. And in a demonstration of his scientific ingenuity, Peter also develops a pair of mechanical "web shooters" that shoot a strand of fluid that mimics the properties of a spider's web. From there, the Spider-Man persona was officially born.[16]

The success of Spider-Man immediately goes to Peter's head, leading to the character's defining moment: one day while standing backstage at a television studio, Peter witnesses a police officer chasing down a burglar. Rather than stop him, Peter shrugs it off as not being his problem. That decision would soon haunt him when he comes home one night and learns that a burglar had shot and killed his Uncle Ben. A distraught Peter dons his Spider-Man costume and chases down the criminal to an abandoned warehouse.

Peter Who?

Blink and you'll miss it, but on the second page of the "Spider-Man vs. the Chameleon" story found in *Amazing Spider-Man #1*, there lies one of Stan Lee's biggest editorial gaffes ever. After referring to Peter by his proper last name, Parker, multiple times earlier in the issue, the narrative box on the page's first panel refers to the *Amazing Spider-Man's* main character as "Peter Palmer." Three panels later, there's another reference to this mysterious gentleman named "Peter Palmer."[19] Did Lee and Steve Ditko change gears and install a new hero in their comic without telling anyone? No, just a stilly typo that has shockingly found its way into the mainstream thanks to the fact that it hasn't been corrected in any reprints (including the digital version one can find in the Marvel Unlimited app).[20]

After defeating the burglar, Peter gets a good look at the man's face and realizes it is the same crook he let run by him at the television studio. Peter bemoans the fact that if he had only stopped him at the studio, his uncle would still be alive, teaching him that with "great power, must also come—great responsibility."[17]

Lee and Ditko continued to develop both Spider-Man and Peter as he became the titular character in his own series, *Amazing Spider-Man*. In the book's first issue, the reader is introduced to Spider-Man's most persistent antagonist, the loud-mouthed *Daily Bugle* publisher and editor, J. Jonah Jameson. Jameson is unique in that he has a relationship with both Spider-Man (he uses the power of the press to turn New Yorkers against the hero) and Peter (he would later hire the teenager as a freelance photographer to take photos of—who else?—Spider-Man).

The series also establishes another long-running theme that is unique to Peter and Spider-Man: his often tragically comical bad luck (also known as the "Parker Luck"). As Spidey, Peter would save the day and still find a nasty headline written about him in the *Daily Bugle*, or overhear his Aunt May talk disparagingly about that "awful" Spider-Man. As a result, Peter may very well be the first superhero whose life got substantially worse and more complicated after he received powers.

As other creators followed Lee and Ditko on the book, the complications of Peter's life, including his uncanny sense of responsibility to atone for his one major lapse of judgement, continued to be front and center. His social life was always in disarray as he futilely tried to balance being Peter and Spider-Man. And even when things seemed to be going right in Peter's life, a tragedy—usually caused by his secret double life as Spider-Man—was just around the corner. There's the time police captain George Stacy (father of his girlfriend, Gwen Stacy) was killed by falling debris during a battle between Spider-Man and Doctor Octopus, or when the Green Goblin—who knew Peter's secret identity—kidnapped Gwen and murdered her, despite Peter's failed attempt to save her.

Like all well-crafted comic book characters, the only constant in Peter's life has been change. He's quit as Spider-Man (only to pick up the webs again an issue or two later), married (to the red-headed supermodel, Mary Jane Watson, though that marriage was later mystically undone as part of 2007's "One More Day" storyline), watched other loved ones die (though in the case of Aunt May, he also witnessed her unlikely resurrection), and has even "died" himself. But in all these cases, Peter's core characteristics—his unyielding sense of responsibility, his scientific ingenuity, his social awkwardness, and his feelings of self-doubt and guilt—have remained constant.

Perhaps what makes Peter so special and so unique is best emblemized in 2011's "Spider-Island" storyline by Dan Slott. In it, Peter has to cope with the fact that everyone in New York has Spider-Man's powers (but none of his responsibilities). Still, he uses his intellect and perseverance to concoct a plan to cure the city from an infestation that threatens to take over the entire country. In the story's final chapter, Peter jokes with Mary Jane that the whole city "walked a mile in my shoes." However, he's only partly right.

"No, just the wall-crawling parts," Peter's ex-wife tells him. "Everything that *really* matters is still right here, Tiger."[18]

3 With Great Power Comes Great Misquotes

As Peter's Uncle Ben would say, "With great power comes great responsibility." Except that's not actually the way the quote goes. And despite pop culture's insistence in attributing it otherwise, the first person to espouse the mantra that would go on to define the moral code of one of the world's most famous superheroes was not really Uncle Ben.

The quote in question can be found on the 11th and final page of Spider-Man's origin story in *Amazing Fantasy #15*. After Peter Parker makes the stunning revelation that a burglar he could have easily stopped earlier in the story had gone on to murder his Uncle Ben, the dejected soon-to-be hero slumped off into the night, with the following narration over his head: "And a lean, silent figure slowly fades into the gathering darkness, aware at last that in this world, with great power there must also come—great responsibility!"

Okay, so while "with great power comes great responsibility," is very close to the actual quote, there's a subtle difference that's very important. More on that in a second.

"Power" and "responsibility" have played pivotal roles in nearly every major Spider-Man story since the quote first saw the light of day in 1962. While Peter is far from infallible, he has followed this mantra regardless of the circumstances: ignoring how the deck might be stacked against him when fighting a powerful villain like Doctor Octopus or the Juggernaut, or even the trivial inconveniences that come with being a super-powered teenager who aspires to have a social life. By staying true to these words, he is atoning for the one time he did not use his power responsibly while also demonstrating his capacity to grow and evolve as an individual.

As for the quote's frequent attribution to Peter's sage-like uncle, there are a number of explanations as to how that happened. Over the course of 50-plus years of Spider-Man comics, Uncle Ben has been consistently characterized as a wise, paternal figure who was a role model for Peter. "With great power there must also come great responsibility" certainly sounds like something he would say. However, the phrase had never been attributed to Uncle Ben until 1987's *Spider-Man vs. Wolverine* graphic novel by Jim Owsley (now known as Christopher Priest). The comic depicts Spider-Man reluctantly teaming up with the X-Men's Wolverine in Germany against the KGB. When the fight becomes too sticky, Peter debates leaving the country, only to think, "…I can't help remembering my Uncle Ben's words—with great power…comes great responsibility."[21]

From there, the expression was attached to Uncle Ben with increasing frequency. When Marvel reimagined Spider-Man's origin as part of its *Ultimate* universe in 2000, creators Brian Michael Bendis and Mark Bagley got their chance to teach Peter his "Uncle Ben lesson." In *Ultimate Spider-Man #4*, Ben actually cites Peter's father as the source of the power and responsibility mantra. Ben tells his nephew that his father long believed that a person with the ability to do great things had a responsibility to share those gifts with the world. Ben then tells Peter that he too is destined for great things, and "with that will come great responsibility."[22]

The mantra officially became a part of the pop culture zeitgeist as Uncle Ben's words in 2002's *Spider-Man* film. Similar to *Ultimate Spider-Man*, Uncle Ben (played by Cliff Robertson) notices that his nephew is changing. Warning that his decisions could impact what kind of man he would become, Ben concludes, "with great power comes great responsibility."[23] Considering how much larger the audience for a major blockbuster film like *Spider-Man* is compared to a comic book that was released in 1962, it's easy to see how this attribution has managed to stick as canon, regardless of the quote's actual origins.

How Lee actually came up with the narration that ended *Amazing Fantasy #15* is open to debate. Some historians have traced variations of this theme back to the French National Convention in 1793. And in 1906, British statesman Winston Churchill delivered a speech to the House of Commons that included the phrase, "where there is great power there is great responsibility."[24] Lee has frequently cited William Shakespeare's turn of phrase as an inspiration for his comic book writing, and "with great power..." certainly has a Shakespearean flair to it.[25]

But what about those words—namely the two words, "must also" that are frequently omitted from the full quote? While leaving out two words may seem inconsequential, for some comic book creators and historians, the "must also" found between "power" and "responsibility" is what gives the phrase its heft and power.

"'Must also come' changes the whole meaning of the statement," said Ron Frenz, a comic book artist who enjoyed a beloved run illustrating *Amazing Spider-Man* in the 1980s. "The world is filled with people with great power who victimize people.... You have to bring the responsibility to the table. The power itself doesn't give you the responsibility."[26]

4 Stan Lee: Excelsior!

Perhaps no name is more synonymous with Spider-Man than Stan Lee. As the man who came up with the "idea" of a superhero with spider powers named Spider-Man, Lee often gets the lion's share of credit for creating the character, despite the fact that without the contributions of artist Steve Ditko, who visually defined Spidey's look, costume, etc., Spider-Man arguably wouldn't have been such a hit. Still, even though some have called Lee's legacy into question, no man has put more energy, effort, and enthusiasm into ensuring the long-term success of the character than Stan "the Man."

Born Stanley Martin Lieber in New York City in 1922, he grew up in a working-class part of the "Big City" with parents Jack and Celia, and later his younger brother, Larry Lieber.[27] Lee credits his voracious love of reading as a child for his career in writing. His list of influences, which unquestionably informed many of his creations at Marvel Comics, included *Tarzan*, the *Hardy Boys,* and *Robin Hood*, as well as authors such as H.G. Wells, Charles Dickens, Emile Zola, and William Shakespeare.[28]

Lee broke into comics in 1940 at Timely, a predecessor of Marvel. There, he worked under editor Joe Simon and writer/artist Jack Kirby (Simon and Kirby would go on to create the iconic Captain America shortly after Lee joined up). Timely's publisher was Martin Goodman, who would later gain fame for being the man who almost rejected Lee's pitch for Spider-Man.[29]

Lieber debuted his iconic pen name, "Stan Lee," when scripting *Captain America Comics #3* in 1941, later joking that he used the pseudonym for comic books to protect his real name for the "great American novel" he planned to write one day.[30] Shortly after getting his big break at Timely, Lee enlisted in the U.S. Army

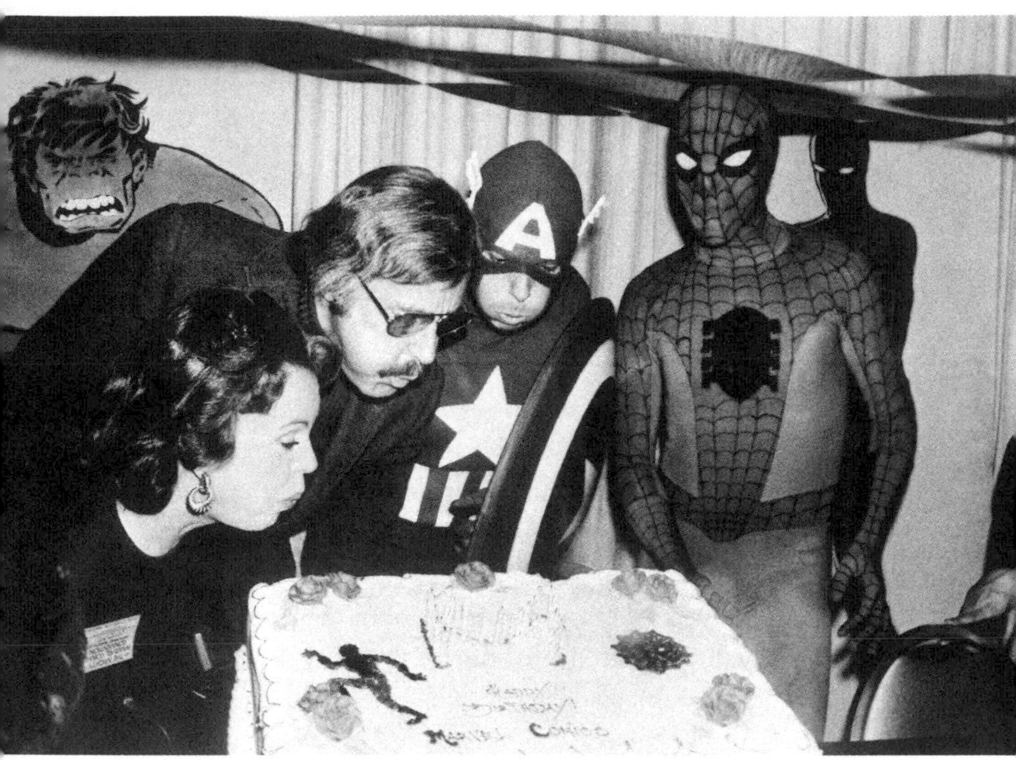

Stan Lee and his wife, Joan, blow out the candles at the opening ceremonies of the first Mighty Marvel Comic Book Convention in 1975 as Captain America and Spider-Man look on. (AP Photo)

during World War II and was assigned to the Signal Corps in New York, North Carolina, and Indiana. While in the service, he worked as an Army "playwright," writing how-to manuals in comic book format using a character named Fiscal Freddie. When the war ended in 1945, Lee returned to Timely as a full-time editor.[31]

During this era, Timely often followed the trends of other comic book companies. Like when romance titles were hot, Lee wrote books such as *Tessie the Typist* and *Millie the Model*, and once the Western genre took off a few years later, Lee scripted series such as *Rawhide Kid*. It was during this time period that Lee also met his wife, Joan, a beautiful blonde who has been described by others in the industry as being a dead ringer for Peter Parker's former girlfriend (now deceased) Gwen Stacy (which might explain why Lee had a particular attachment to the Peter and Gwen coupling).[32]

The mid-1950s marked a turbulent time for Timely (which was also being called Atlas Comics), and the comic book industry as a whole. First was the publication of psychiatrist Fredric Wertham's *Seduction of the Innocent*, which claimed that the perversity in comic books was adversely affecting children, leading to the creation of the Comics Code, which regulated the industry.[33] Shortly thereafter, Timely/Atlas almost went belly-up when Goodman decided to change his distribution model and signed on with the American News Company. Unfortunately, the American News Company went under a few weeks later, which left Atlas/Timely without a distributor for its library of more than 60 titles. The company actually cut a deal with one of their largest competitors, National Comics (aka, DC), to distribute a significantly reduced number of titles a month. After that, Timely/Atlas's long-term prospects were cast in grave doubt.[34]

Lee was one of the few personnel survivors from the American News Company fiasco when Kirby returned to the company in 1959. It was around this time that Lee had the idea to rebrand the company a bit, changing its name to "Marvel Comics." The name paid homage to Marvel Mystery Comics, the first title Timely ever published.[35] But even with a flashier new name, Lee actually debated quitting comics entirely. That's when Goodman famously came to him with a mandate: DC's new group of superheroes, the *Justice League*, was selling great, so it was time for Marvel to enter the superhero game with a group of their own. Still, Lee felt bored and tired with scripting comics. He wanted to write more realistic stories and Goodman wouldn't let him. When this new demand came along, Lee's wife, Joan, suggested her husband just write the comic the way he always wanted to. Lee did just that and the Fantastic Four were born—a group of heroes (like Goodman wanted) who bickered and fought each other like real-life people (like Lee wanted).[36]

Coincidentally, about a year later, another disagreement between Lee and Goodman went on to lead to the creation of everyone's favorite web-slinger. In 1962, Lee had an idea for a new superhero named Spider-Man. As a twist on the convention, Spider-Man would actually be a teenager. And like the Fantastic Four, he would have real-life problems like dealing with high school bullies and unpopularity with women. Goodman flatly rejected Spider-Man, telling Lee that people hate spiders, teenagers were only good for being cast as sidekicks, and people wouldn't want to read a story about an unpopular outcast. Undeterred, Lee planned on sticking Spider-Man into an issue of *Amazing Adult Fantasy* (soon to be renamed *Amazing Fantasy*). The magazine was on the verge of cancellation, so Lee figured Goodman wouldn't be paying close attention and he'd have his opportunity to get Spider-Man out of his system.[37]

After Kirby's first version of Spider-Man didn't work for Lee, he turned to another artist in the Marvel stable, Steve Ditko. Lee provided Ditko with a synopsis of what he wanted to have happen in the first story. He also mentioned that the hero, Peter, lived with his Aunt May and Uncle Ben. From there, Ditko took these ideas and ran with them, and Spider-Man was officially born, in time to be the featured story (in a cover illustrated by Kirby) in *Amazing Fantasy #15*.[38]

Like the Fantastic Four, Thor, and the Hulk before him, Spider-Man was an immediate success, and while *Amazing Fantasy* still ceased publication at issue *#15*, the character was soon earmarked for his very own series, *Amazing Spider-Man*. Lee sent Ditko some outlines for the first few issues, containing ideas for such characters as blustery newspaper publisher J. Jonah Jameson and villains Vulture, Sandman, and Doctor Octopus.[39] Lee's unique creative process, which is known around the comic book industry as "Marvel style," provided the penciler with a tremendous amount of artistic freedom.

For Spider-Man, Lee would provide Ditko with a very loose story synopsis or plot and then turned the reins over to the artist. After getting the finished pages back from Ditko, Lee filled in the dialogue and narration boxes. It was a style that lent itself to efficiency for Lee since he was working on scripting multiple books at once. Keep in mind that within just a few years of creating Spider-Man, Lee had also co-created the Avengers, X-Men, Doctor Strange, Nick Fury, the Silver Surfer, and Daredevil. But the "Marvel style" also helped the company distinguish itself from the competition, mainly DC, which Lee thought was far more controlling of its artists. "I feel the best rule is no rules at all," Lee said. "Just let an artist do it the way he wants."[40]

Ditko took this mantra to heart—so much so that by *Amazing Spider-Man #10*, the artist started to plot and illustrate the comic entirely by himself, rarely sharing his ideas with Lee until the finished pages were handed in. This lack of communication became problematic as Ditko became more deeply enmeshed in his Ayn Rand–inspired objectivist principles, which were seeping into the comics he worked on. Lee apparently felt like the comic was being held hostage by Ditko's whims.[41] However, after turning in his artwork for *Amazing Spider-Man #38*, Ditko quit Marvel. Years later, Lee still isn't sure why his mercurial artist up and left. "I even asked him about it and he just said that I should know," Lee said.[42]

In a series of essays he's published in the newsletter/zine *The Comics*, Ditko has described Lee as someone who takes far more credit for Marvel's success than what's deserved. And Ditko was particularly outraged over a letter Lee published where he said he "considered" Ditko the co-creator of Spider-Man, finding the use of the word "considered" to be condescending. When Lee was asked to further clarify the disagreement with Ditko in the

2007 BBC documentary *In Search of Steve Ditko*, "Stan the Man," smiling but clearly exasperated, said, "I really think the guy who dreams the thing up created it. If Steve wants to be called the co-creator, he deserves to be called the co-creator."[43]

Still, Spider-Man soldiered on after Ditko left. For his replacement, Lee tapped the versatile veteran John Romita Sr. The two had a far more symbiotic relationship than Lee/Ditko. The two rarely argued over plot points, with the lone exception of one of the all-time great debates in Spidey history: which girl should Peter date? Gwen Stacy (Lee's pick) or Mary Jane Watson (Romita's pick)?[44] Before eventually leaving *Amazing Spider-Man* in 1973, Lee managed to make history with the character one more time. In 1971, he challenged the strict Comics Code with a three-part story that detailed Peter's friend Harry Osborn using recreational drugs—a major no-no for the comic authority. Lee pushed Goodman to let Marvel allow the story, even though the issue (*Amazing Spider-Man #96*) was published without the Comic Code "stamp" on the front issue, which impacted its distribution.[45]

Lee obviously did not fade into obscurity after leaving *Amazing Spider-Man*. As Goodman's replacement as Marvel's publisher, he was still very active, often consulting with writers and editors on major stories and events. He once caused a bit of a stir in this capacity when he was asked by *Amazing's* creative team about an idea to kill off Peter's girlfriend, Gwen Stacy. Lee reportedly okayed the storyline, but later backtracked a bit and claimed he didn't realize how serious the creators were about murdering Spider-Man's true love. Whoops.[46]

By the late '70s, Lee leveraged his relationship with Spidey to take on a more traditional comic book project with the launch of the *Spider-Man* daily newspaper strip. Lee reunited with his one-time collaborator, Romita, to bring Spider-Man to syndicated newspapers around the country seven days a week. For years, Lee kept the storylines in the strip in their own universe, separate from the mainstream comics until 1987, when he and Marvel's then-editor-in-chief, Jim Shooter, decided to marry off Peter and Mary Jane in both the newspaper strip and the regular comics.[47]

Throughout the '80s, Lee was also heavily involved in trying to get his Marvel properties onto the big screen. He moved to Southern California and was placed in charge of the creation and development of new projects at Marvel Productions. When this venture was in its infancy, Lee described his work in very enthusiastic terms: "It's as though I'm once again reliving those exciting days of the early '60s when we were building Marvel Comics," he said in a 1981 interview.[48]

Except the romanticism of what Lee described and the reality didn't match up. By the mid-80s, superhero movies were falling out of a favor in Hollywood, and Lee didn't have the right experience to seal any significant deals with the studio heads.[49] At one point in the early '90s, director James Cameron shared a "scriptment" for a new Spider-Man movie with Lee, but the film was embroiled in legal issues for nearly two decades and the version that finally made the big screen in 2002 (directed by Sam Raimi) was dramatically different from Cameron's conception.[50]

In the '90s, with the dreams of Marvel Productions in the rear-view mirror, Lee was relegated to being Marvel's unofficial mascot, albeit a well-compensated one. Every few years, Lee would sign a new contract with Marvel so he would receive, on top of a six-figure salary, about 10 percent of all revenue generated by the use of his characters in television and movies—even when Marvel was in dire financial straits by the mid-to-late '90s. The only hiccup in this arrangement came in 2002, when Lee sued Marvel, claiming they'd failed to pay him his contracted percentage of the profits from the first *Spider-Man* movie. But it was only a temporary blip. Lee even managed to cash in when Disney purchased Marvel in 2009. Part of the deal involved a Disney subsidiary buying a small piece of POW! Entertainment, a media production company Lee co-founded in 2001, and paying him a little more than $1 million a year as a consultant.[51]

Over the past decade, Lee's legacy has become further muddied thanks to all of the highly successful Marvel properties making bank on the big screen. Lee traditionally has a cameo in all of these films, keeping him in the limelight, leading even some of his closest allies to question whether or not the artists, Kirby and Ditko, get enough credit for Marvel's explosion in Hollywood. Still, even with these criticisms, Lee has plenty of adoring fans and defenders. For example, in 2012, current *Amazing Spider-Man* writer Dan Slott tweeted a happy birthday message to Lee for his 90th, days after the controversial *Amazing Spider-Man #700* came out that resulted in the death of Peter Parker. Lee retorted, "What a gift, some guys give a nice cigar, a watch, but no not you, I get a dead Peter Parker." Slott, hip to the joke responded, "Ha! Printing that out now. THAT'S goin' up on the fridge. I'm NEVER taking that down!!!!"[52]

5 The Quiet One, Steve Ditko

Stan Lee has long been the face of the "Marvel Age of Comics," while the legendary artist Jack Kirby has typically been credited for breathing life into Marvel's aesthetic by creating the visuals behind characters such as the Fantastic Four, Captain America, and Thor. However, Steve Ditko deserves a spot on the comic book industry's Mount Rushmore as one of the greatest artists the medium has ever seen. It's just that his quiet, reclusive nature has often contributed to Ditko's legacy getting lost in the shuffle behind Lee and Kirby.

Born in Johnstown, Pennsylvania, in 1927, Ditko grew up in a working-class family, going to a school that would later serve as a source of inspiration for Peter Parker's Midtown High School (Ditko's class even had a bully like Eugene "Flash" Thompson).[53] Some early artistic influences on Ditko included Hal Foster's *Prince Valiant*, and later Will Eisner's *The Spirit*, which he would read with regularity in the pages of the *Philadelphia Inquirer*.[54]

Ditko moved to New York City in 1950 to study at The Cartoonists & Illustrators School (now known as the School of Visual Arts).[55] After working in the comic book industry for a few years, Ditko contracted tuberculosis and returned to Johnstown. There were doubts he would even survive the disease. Still, he managed to persevere and he returned to New York in 1955, where he met up with Stan Lee and Atlas Comics, a predecessor to Marvel Comics. From there, Ditko's legend started to grow.[56]

The bulk of Ditko's early work at Atlas included monster stories and surrealist tales in books like *Strange Tales*, *Journey Into Mystery*, *Strange Worlds*, *Tales of Suspense*, and *Tales to Astonish*. Ditko evolved from a workhorse artist into a true industry superstar in 1962 when Lee came to Ditko with a brief synopsis for a new hero dubbed Spider-Man. Lee had originally given the idea to Kirby, but was unsatisfied with Kirby's creation—which Lee dubbed too "heroic."[57]

Ditko's take on Spider-Man was vastly different. One of his biggest artistic choices was to place the teenaged character in a full mask as Spider-Man. Ditko felt a mask would better conceal the fact that Spider-Man was a teenager, thereby allowing the criminal he was apprehending to believe it could be anyone in the costume. However, there were also psychological reasons for the mask: "A mask can generate anxiety, fear. A clearly 'unreadable' expression from strangers in close contact [building lobby, elevator, etc.] can make a person uncomfortable. And spiders, with their crawling bodies, make people more than uncomfortable."[58] Ditko's unique visual spin was ultimately realized in Spidey's debut in *Amazing Fantasy #15*, and thus began one of the more complicated writer/artist relationships in comic book history.

In interviews, Lee often describes his relationship with Ditko as being fine, until it one day just wasn't; and even then he says he would work with the artist again if the opportunity ever came along.[59] But Ditko's account paints a far more confrontational picture. He notoriously doesn't grant interviews, but in a series of essays he penned in the fan zine *The Comics!*, Ditko describes how he frequently pushed back against Lee for his insistence to insert what he found to be outrageous and unrealistic plot ideas into stories, like Spider-Man chasing after a falling space rocket in *Amazing Spider-Man #1.* Ditko also bristled at Lee's insistence to feature guest appearances from other heroes like Fantastic Four as well as the introduction of new spinoff characters like a Spider-Woman or Spider-Girl. And Ditko loathed the fact that Lee would seemingly change a story in response to negative feedback from readers.

Despite the disagreements, Lee and Ditko quickly created a dynamic supporting cast of friends, family, and adversaries for Spider-Man: Aunt May, Uncle Ben, J. Jonah Jameson, Betty Brant, Flash Thompson, Liz Allan, Vulture, Doctor Octopus, Sandman, the Lizard, and Electro. By *Amazing Spider-Man #10*, Lee ceded almost total control of the book and the character to Ditko, allowing the artist to plot and illustrate an entire issue before returning the finished work to Lee at the end for dialogue.[60] It was during these issues that Ditko's artistic prowess was on full display as he created such iconic characters as the Green Goblin, Kraven the Hunter, Mysterio, Gwen Stacy, and Norman and Harry Osborn, while also fleshing out the characterizations for Liz, Flash, and others.

The pinnacle of Ditko's storytelling came in the three-part "Master Planner Trilogy" found in *Amazing Spider-Man #31–33*.

Considered by many fans and historians as the greatest Spider-Man story ever, the saga follows Peter as he attempts to get a serum for his dying aunt (who has taken ill because she accepted a blood transfusion of Peter's tainted, radioactive blood). During a battle with Doctor Octopus, Peter is crushed by tons of steel and debris. The serum he needs is just out of reach and Peter is resigned to the fact that he failed his aunt and he is destined to die. But instead of giving up, he uses those emotions to steel his nerve long enough to lift the wreckage over his head and escape.

It was one of Ditko's finer moments, and he was outraged when Lee would later take credit for the idea during an interview with an industry magazine in the late '90s. Ditko wrote the magazine, claiming Lee had zero input on the memorable sequence.[61] It wasn't the first—or last—time Ditko struck back against what he thought was Lee taking credit for an idea.

The relationship between Lee and Ditko had clearly become strained during the latter stages of their creative run together on *Amazing*. Ditko had developed a fondness for philosopher and writer Ayn Rand, whose objectivist philosophy places the rights of the individual as being paramount to anything else. Rand's ideology emboldened Ditko to demand published credit as both plotter and artist in *Amazing Spider-Man #25*, a distinction that even Kirby and his 20 years of experience could never wrestle away from Lee.[62] Meanwhile, the two barely spoke to each other. Instead, Ditko would just swing by the Marvel offices every month and drop off his pages without saying a word to Lee. Some described the situation as Lee being "held hostage" to Ditko's whims for Spider-Man.[63] Lee was apparently unhappy with some of Ditko's decisions. Then one day, after years of building tension, Ditko dropped off his pages for *Amazing Spider-Man #38* and quit.

Beyond Spider-Man, Ditko's other famous contribution to Marvel history is Doctor Stephen Strange, a mystic and "sorcerer supreme." The book's trippy, almost psychedelic landscapes are considered among the most influential visuals from the comic book industry's Silver Age. Of course, when Ditko quit Spider-Man, he left Strange too. Following his exit from Marvel, Ditko reportedly took less money to work for Charlton and DC comics, where he was able to indulge his objectivism with characters such as the Question, Creeper, and Hawk and Dove.

In 1967, Ditko created Mr. A. for an independent publisher. The character was the ultimate love letter to Rand and the objectivist movement. Readers who are curious to read about some of Ditko's experiences at Marvel and elsewhere in the industry can do so by sifting through some of his essays on objectivism published in *The Comics!*, which still publishes and has some back issues available online. One anecdote that Ditko returns to frequently is his response to an interview Lee gave where he said he "considers Ditko a co-creator of Spider-Man." Ditko writes that Lee's choice of the word "considers" is demeaning, savaging the writer for only providing a synopsis and nothing more: "the synopsis does not tell/show the way, how, and why for every panel and exactly how each character should, must, be seen, act, react, in art in every situation."[64]

6 Ben and May Parker

As the patriarch and matriarch of the Spider-Man universe, Ben and May Parker (aka Uncle Ben and Aunt May) are arguably two of the most important members of Spider-Man's rich supporting cast. The two are first introduced by Stan Lee and Steve Ditko in Spider-Man's origin story, *Amazing Fantasy #15*, as Peter Parker's caretakers and parental figures. After Peter's biological parents, Richard and Mary—both secret agents/spies—are presumed dead on a mission gone awry, Ben (Richard's brother) and May raise Peter as if he were their own child. And Peter has always appreciated them for it. When Peter first acquires his spider-powers in *Amazing Fantasy*, he thinks to himself: *They're the only ones who've ever been kind to me! I'll see to it that they're always happy, but the rest of the world can go hang for all I care!*[65]

Ben and May are depicted as having first met in Brooklyn, New York, during the Great Depression. Ben, a carnival barker at Coney Island, was helplessly in love with May Reilly. Unfortunately, Reilly had eyes for a well-to-do man named Johnny Jerome, who was later revealed to be a criminal. May rebuffs Jerome's advances, ends up with Ben, and they went off to live happily ever after… until the night that changed Ben, May, and Peter's lives forever.[66]

You've probably seen some variation of the next part of this story, whether it be in the comics, cartoons, or movies: Peter, as Spider-Man, lets a burglar run by him inside a television studio, thinking it wasn't his job to stop a petty thief. Sometime later, Peter comes home and finds that his uncle has been murdered. When he tracks down the thief, he realizes the same man he let run by him at the studio killed Uncle Ben. From that point on—known aptly enough as Spider-Man's "Uncle Ben moment"—Peter vowed to live by the mantra, "with great power there must also come great responsibility." And because Peter felt directly responsible for his uncle's death, he, in turn, felt responsible for taking care of his Aunt May, who is frequently depicted in the comics as being on the verge of death. As a result, pretty much everything Peter does as Spider-Man is inspired or fueled by his guilt over the death of his Uncle Ben and his responsibility to protect Aunt May.

Miraculously, in an era where no comic book character stays dead and buried forever (Marvel even resurrected Captain America's old World War II buddy, Bucky), Ben Parker is one of the few where dead has meant dead. Sure, numerous creators have attempted to expand on Ben's otherwise limited backstory (that's what happens when you're introduced in a story and killed off 11 pages later) via flashbacks and alternative universe tales. Writer Paul Jenkins, while scripting *Peter Parker: Spider-Man* in the early 2000s, frequently honed in on Peter's relationship with his uncle.

In one Jenkins-scripted issue (*Peter Parker #33*) titled "Maybe Next Year," the reader learns that Peter had an ongoing tradition with his uncle of attending a New York Mets baseball game. While at the game, the Mets would always lose in some absurd, unbelievable fashion, but Ben would always use the games as an opportunity to share some kind of paternal moment with his nephew. Jenkins later acknowledged that it's one of the more popular Spider-Man stories he ever wrote, despite the fact that Peter only appears in costume on one page.[67] As part of the revamping of Spider-Man for the *Ultimate Spider-Man* comic book series in 2000, writer Brian Michael Bendis utilized the extra issues he was allowed to write to reimagine Spidey's origins to further flesh out Ben's character, even attributing the "with great power…" life lesson to Peter's uncle.

As for Aunt May, despite some great character moments, more often than not, the character has been used by creators as a plot device; someone who would be dropped into a story as a means to add more misery and drama to Peter's life. She openly despises Spider-Man and frequently turns up on the verge of death whenever Peter is busy being a masked superhero. By the 1980s, Aunt May's ailing health had become such a trope, Jim Shooter, Marvel's editor-in-chief, mandated that his writers were not allowed to kill her.[68]

Of course, Shooter was eventually fired, paving the way for J.M. DeMatteis and Mark Bagley to do the unthinkable in 1995's *Amazing #400.* They were going to kill Aunt May! During the build-up to *#400*, DeMatteis recalled a funny conversation he had with another Spider-Man writer, Howard Mackie, about May's fate: "It was like two Mafia guys saying, 'This old lady...she's got to die! It's good for the book, she's got to die!'" DeMatteis said.[69]

Except, May's death was short-lived, even by comic book standards, and the explanation for her return was even more bizarre. As part of the 1998 storyline "The Final Chapter," it was revealed that Peter's archnemesis, Norman Osborn (aka the Green Goblin) hired an actress to pretend to be Aunt May and die. Osborn then kidnapped the real May and held her hostage by implanting a micro-bomb in her brain.

Ladies and gentlemen...comics!!!

Sensing an opportunity to reinvigorate the character, in 2001, J. Michael Straczynski (of *Babylon 5* fame) wrote a number of stories that focused on Peter and May's relationship. His most famous being *Amazing Spider-Man vol. 2 #38,* aka "The Conversation." In it, May finally confronts her nephew about his double life as Spider-Man. Sadly, the storyline was later erased by the events of "One More Day," which implemented a universe-wide "mind wipe," causing everyone that knew Peter's secret identity to magically unlearn it. But in terms of great single issue Spider-Man stories, "The Conversation" is among the very best.

In the *Ultimate* universe, rather than make Aunt May a sickly "fuddy duddy," Bendis modeled the matriarch after his mother. "She's a scary woman," he joked.[70]

Considering how pivotal both characters have been to the Spider-Man mythos, it's no surprise that a number of respected actors have portrayed Ben and May in all of Spider-Man's cinematic adaptations. In Sam Raimi's *Spider-Man* trilogy, Ben was played by Cliff Robertson and May was played by Rosemary Harris (who truly was the spitting-image of Lee/Ditko's Aunt May). For the two *The Amazing Spider-Man* films, some higher-profile "names" were cast in Martin Sheen and Sally Field.

And in a move that gives new meaning to the word "bombshell," for the most recent film iteration, Marvel Studios/Sony went against type and cast Academy Award–winner Marisa Tomei as May. Tomei, known best for her work in romantic comedies and other film dramas, is the youngest actress to play May. She has already appeared in *Captain America: Civil War* and even showed some chemistry with former flame Robert Downey Jr. (Tony Stark/ Iron Man). That should make for an interesting Thanksgiving in the Parker apartment.

7 Spider-Man Becomes "Amazing"

Any concerns that Spider-Man would be a one-hit wonder were cast aside following the success of his first appearance in *Amazing Fantasy #15*. Readers responded so positively to Spider-Man that, despite the fact that *Amazing Fantasy* had been canceled as planned, Spidey went on to star in his very own series, *Amazing Spider-Man,* which debuted in March 1963. In addition to having him interact with Marvel's flagship superhero team, the Fantastic Four, Spider-Man's first solo comic immediately expanded his supporting cast with the introduction of arguably his most important (and persistent) antagonist, newspaper editor/publisher J. Jonah Jameson. The issue also introduced Jameson's astronaut son, John, and the first of Spider-Man's true rogues, the Chameleon, a master of disguise who would evolve into a mainstay in Marvel's criminal underworld in later years. Within four issues, the title was successful enough to increase from a bi-monthly to a monthly publishing schedule.

Amazing Spider-Man's first 38 issues, and two jumbo-sized annual issues (aka the entire Lee/Ditko creative run), are considered by many fans and historians to be essential to the character's history, and are among the most important comics produced in the Silver Age (not to mention the most coveted by collectors). Nearly every character of consequence in Spider-Man's orbit is introduced

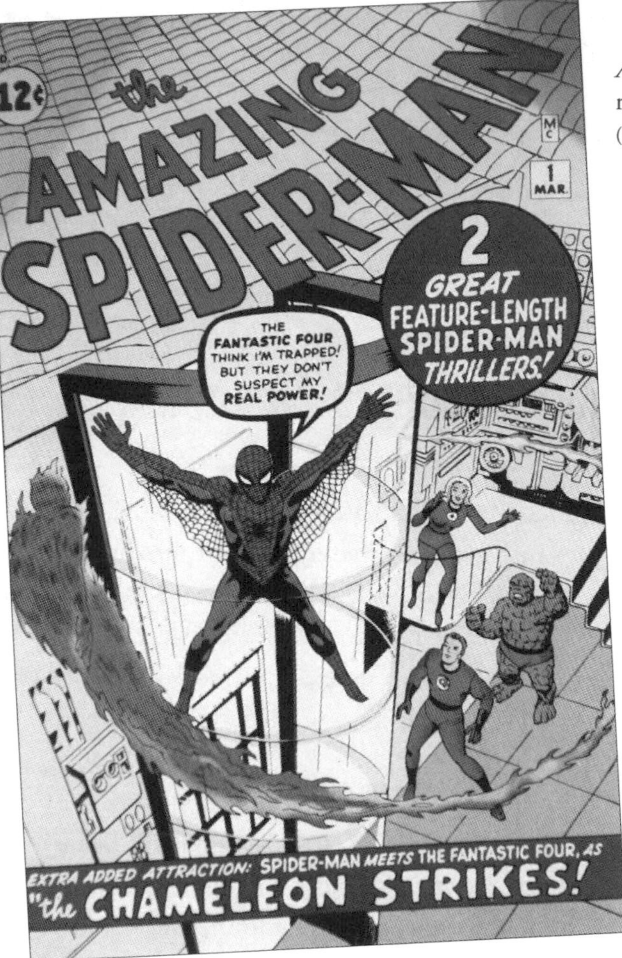

Amazing Spider-Man #1, released in March 1963. (Frances M. Roberts/Newscom)

during this period: the Vulture (first appearance: *Amazing #2*); Doctor Octopus (*Amazing #3*); Sandman, and Peter's first girlfriend, Betty Brant (*Amazing #4*); the Lizard (*Amazing #6*); Electro (*Amazing #9*); Mysterio (*Amazing #11*); Green Goblin (*Amazing #14*); Kraven the Hunter (*Amazing #15*); the Sinister Six (*Amazing Annual #1*); the Scorpion (*Amazing #20*); the Spider-Slayers (*Amazing #25*); the Molten Man (*Amazing #28*); and Gwen Stacy and Harry Osborn (*Amazing #31*). Additionally, these issues depict a number of major milestones in Peter Parker's world, such as his first job taking photos for the *Daily Bugle* (*Amazing #2*) and his graduation from high school (*Amazing #28*).

When Ditko abruptly left the book following *Amazing #38*, art duties were picked up by John Romita Sr. In short order, Romita established more of a stylish sense of realism in the series compared to his artistic predecessor. This was especially apparent with Romita's women, most notably Gwen Stacy and Mary Jane Watson who, thanks to the artist's distinct pencils, resembled glamorous supermodels and actresses. Meanwhile, following Lee's departure from the book in 1973, there were a number of writers and artists who unquestionably made a career for themselves working on what was considered Marvel's premier series.

Gerry Conway, Lee's immediate successor, was barely 20 years old when he started on the book, not fully understanding the magnitude of what was in front of him: "At that age, I had a sense of capacity and self-confidence that was untempered by reality," Conway said.[71] For Ron Frenz, the artist who collaborated with writer Tom DeFalco on a number of *Amazing* issues in the 1980s, the call to join the book was initially met with awe-induced trepidation: "I realized I'd just have to bust my hump and do the best work I could," Frenz said. "*Amazing* was THE JOB to me, how could I turn it down?"[72]

Furthering the narrative that *Amazing* was THE Spider-Man book, starting in the 1970s, Marvel started publishing other Spider-Man titles such as *Marvel Team-Up* and *Peter Parker: The Spectacular Spider-Man* to broaden the scope and appeal of the character. But even with these books, any creator involved in the Spider-office knew that *Amazing* was the gig to have. Roger Stern, who scripted both *Spectacular* and *Amazing*, has often referred to his time on the former as a "tryout" for his stint on the main book.

Amazing published continuously for nearly 50 years until issue *#700* (Marvel's first series to reach this number of installments)

Five Best Spider-Man Creator Runs

Stan Lee/Steve Ditko (*Amazing Spider-Man #1–38, Annuals #1–2*): *Amazing Spider-Man's* first creative run remains the benchmark against which all others will always be compared. These issues introduced nearly every single essential member of Spider-Man's supporting cast and rogues' gallery, and also featured numerous famous stories like "The Master Planner Trilogy" (*Amazing Spider-Man #31–33*).

Roger Stern/John Romita Jr. (*Amazing Spider-Man #224–227, #229–236, #238–250*): This duo churned out many famous stories, such as "Nothing Can Stop the Juggernaut" (*Amazing #229–230*) and the "Origin of the Hobgoblin" (*Amazing #238–239*). The team also played with the Spider-Man/Black Cat romance, and brought Mary Jane Watson back to the book.

Tom DeFalco/Ron Frenz: (*Amazing Spider-Man #251–52, #255–261, #263, #265, #268–271, #273–77*): DeFalco and Frenz brought something for every kind of Spider-Man fan—dialogue and visuals that harkened back to the Lee/Ditko days, and modern sensibilities and storylines that were designed for more modern audiences. Plus Spider-Man got to beat up a herald of Galactus's with his bare hands (*Amazing #270*).

Lee/John Romita Sr.: (*Amazing Spider-Man #39–75, #77, #80–81, #82–88, #93–95, #97*): In the wake of Ditko's departure from the book, Lee and Romita focused more on Peter Parker's love life while also introducing such memorable rogues as the Kingpin, Rhino, and Shocker. This run even marked the debut of Black Widow's iconic Emma Peel–inspired black jumpsuit.

J. Michael Straczynski/Romita Jr. (*Amazing Spider-Man vol. 2 #30–58, 500–508*): JMS and JRJR brought a cinematic quality to Spider-Man. Straczynski's mystical approach put a new spin on Spidey's origins and powers. The run also featured plenty of big moments like Spider-Man vs. the vampiric Morlun (*Amazing #30–35*), the September 11th issue (*Amazing #36*), Peter revealing his secret identity to Aunt May (*Amazing #38*), and the romantic reunion of Peter and Mary Jane (*Amazing #50*).

when it was replaced with a new series, the *Superior Spider-Man*, starring Spider-Man's nemesis, Doctor Octopus, masquerading as the hero after swapping brains and bodies with him. Peter, of course, would return after 18 months. And when *Amazing* was rebooted with a brand new #1 issue in March 2014, the book reaffirmed its dominance by selling 532,000 copies, the most by a single issue since the height of the comic book industry's popularity in the mid-90s.[73]

In retrospect, when Lee is asked about the longevity of a series like *Amazing*, he's at a loss to explain its popularity: "I was just happy that Spider-Man sold well enough for us to continue publishing it. Believe me, we never thought that any of these titles would last as long as they have."[74]

8 Spider-sense

Do you feel a certain tingling at the base of your skull that seems to be warning you of some kind of danger or bad news on the horizon? Well, perhaps you, like Spider-Man, have acquired the extraordinary superpower of "spider-sense" (and if it's not spider-sense, you might want to get that tingling checked out by a medical professional).

Spidey's spider-sense is arguably his most distinctive power. Other heroes have super-strength, or lightning-quick reflexes/agility, but few have Spidey's almost-innate ability to sense danger, such as an imminent strike from an opponent, or a supervillain waiting to pounce in the dark. He even uses this ability to assist him while web-slinging from building to building, or to warn him if a civilian is nearby while he's changing in or out of his costume (which helps keep his identity a secret).

And to think, "spider-sense" first manifested itself in a truly random way. While the reader got a fairly straightforward demonstration of all of Spider-Man's superhuman powers in his *Amazing Fantasy #15* origin story—his enhanced strength, speed, and ability to climb walls—his spider-sense was completely absent, with nary a suggestion in the text that he harbored such a skill. Then, while penciling the first issue of *Amazing Spider-Man*, the character's co-creator and original artist, Steve Ditko, had an impulse to draw squiggly lines radiating from Spider-Man's head. When he discussed the illustration with Spider-Man's other co-creator, Stan Lee, Ditko said that the hero "has 'spider-senses,' the way bats can detect, sense insects, objects at night." Lee, seemingly pleased with the explanation, allowed the lines to stay and the spider-sense was officially born.[75]

The power would naturally evolve over the years. For example, after using a radio transmitter to track the frequency of his "spider-tracer" devices, Spidey honed his abilities to the point that he could just rely on his innate "tingling" to find the tracers. In stories where major, world-ending threats were on the horizon, like the original *Secret Wars* (where a cosmic deity kidnaps all of Marvel's heroes and villains and makes them fight in another dimension for fun), or the *Infinity Gauntlet* (where a death-worshipping demigod named Thanos received infinite power), Spidey's senses would tingle with such force and ferocity, Spider-Man would be in pain from the sensation.

Naturally, villains would also often learn to game plan against the power. In *Amazing Spider-Man #39* the Green Goblin develops a special smoke bomb that disarms Spidey's spider-sense, allowing him to catch him off guard and learn his civilian identity.[76] Years later, another goblin villain, the Hobgoblin, would improve upon his predecessor's formula to wreak further havoc on Spidey's patented defense mechanism. Then there are villains like Venom, who, because he is powered by an alien symbiote costume that had once possessed Spider-Man, never set off his spider-sense.

In 2011, *Amazing Spider-Man* writer Dan Slott took things one step further for Spider-Man when he concocted a way to disable his spider-sense for nearly 20 issues. This new status quo allowed Slott to explore just how difficult life could be for Spider-Man without his special power: "It's very much as if one of us lost our sense of hearing, or smell, or sight," Slott said in an interview after the storyline kicked off, which featured such scenes as Spidey falling while web-slinging after unknowingly shooting his webbing at a broken piece of building facade. "In some ways, he's kind of spider-sense blind, or spider-sense deaf. And he hasn't had to operate that way since he was 15."[77]

9 J. Jonah Jameson

Here's the headline: J. Jonah Jameson Jostles Joke of a Superhero!

Seriously, Spider-Man has dealt with the many arms of Doctor Octopus, and numerous pumpkin bomb attacks from the Green Goblin, but there's been no bigger thorn in his side than "Jolly Jonah," the loud-mouthed, hot-tempered publisher of the fictional *Daily Bugle* newspaper. Going back to his very first appearance in *Amazing Spider-Man #1*, Jameson has made it his mission to defame Spider-Man's name and sway public opinion against him, regardless of how noble the "Web-Slinger's" actions may appear.

Jameson's mad-on for masked costume vigilantes has long been a defining character trait and he's been remarkably consistent, even if the evidence before him suggests he should change his opinion. When Spider-Man saved Jameson's astronaut son in *Amazing #1*,

Jonah still took it upon himself to portray Spidey as the villain in one of his rage-fueled *Bugle* editorials. And in adding yet another wrinkle to JJJ's character, unlike most members of Spider-Man's rogues' gallery, Jameson can easily wreak havoc on the "masked menace's" civilian alter-ego, Peter Parker, who is a freelance photographer for the *Bugle*, snapping photos of Spidey that the publisher, in turn, uses to smear Spider-Man.

Still, even though Jameson is a bit of a jerk, he's also a fan favorite, and arguably one of Marvel's greatest supporting characters. Jameson's role has evolved over the years, from newspaper publisher, to New York City mayor, to cable television news host, but he's always been a prominent fixture in Spider-Man comics. Removing the character from the world of Spider-Man would almost be as catastrophic as removing Peter Parker from the comics (and even when Peter's brain and body were taken over by Doctor Octopus during *Superior Spider-Man* in 2013–14, Jameson was still there causing trouble for the man in the red and blue costume).

Created by Stan Lee and Steve Ditko, Jameson has naturally long been a favorite of Lee's, who has often compared himself to the character. "I don't really know where I got him…maybe a combination of everybody I've ever known," Lee said about Jonah in a 1981 interview. However, immediately after creating him and giving Peter a job at the *Bugle* as a photographer, Lee realized that he was following a similar script to DC's *Superman* and its Clark Kent/Perry White dynamic. However, Lee clearly prefers Jameson because "He's much more irascible, he's very reactionary…. I thought it would be funny to get a guy like that and show he isn't really a villain."[78]

The character certainly has had plenty of moments of depth and self-reflection, like in *Amazing Spider-Man #10* when he concluded that he hates Spider-Man because he secretly envies him.[79] Or when he used the power of the press to take a stand against Wilson Fisk, aka the "Kingpin" of crime in Frank Miller/Klaus

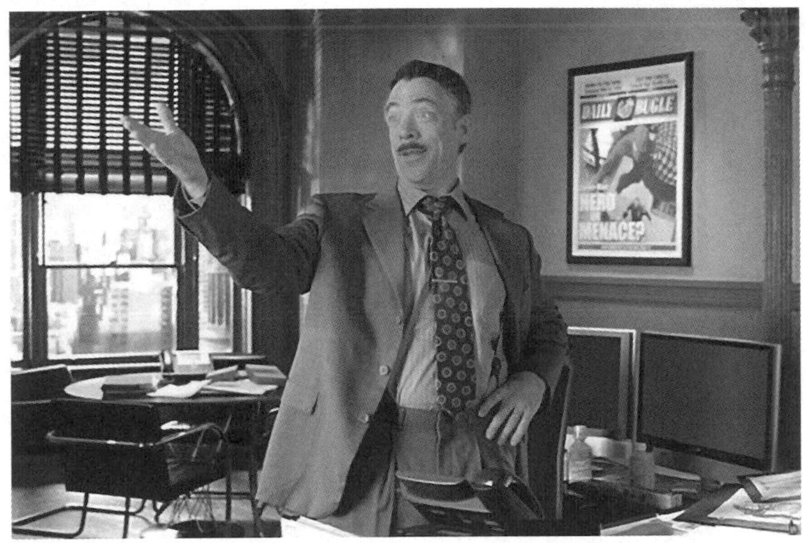

J.K. Simmons brings J. Jonah Jameson to life in 2004's *Spider-Man 2.*
(Columbia Pictures/Marvel Entertainment/Melissa Moseley/Newscom)

Janson's landmark run on *Daredevil.* But for the most part, JJJ is a class "A" weasel. He's worked closely with mad scientists and super-villains like Spencer and Alistair Smythe and their Spider-Slayers to put Spider-Man down for the count, and has even bankrolled the development of new Spider-adversaries like the Scorpion and the Human Fly.

In one 2016 interview, Kurt Busiek, writer of the mid-90s flashback series *Untold Tales of Spider-Man* and the 1994 miniseries *Marvels* (both featured JJJ in some capacity), said of Jameson: "I think he's a fascinating character, a study in contradictions. As a newspaperman, he does something good, something that's often heroic, but his hatred of Spider-Man makes him small and petty. He's a blowhard, but also a staunch believer in the First Amendment, and he'll stand up to generals to protect the freedom of press."[80]

The richness of the Jameson character extends well beyond the comics. During the mid-90s *Spider-Man: The Animated Series*, JJJ was voiced by veteran television and film actor Ed Asner (after Lee was originally considered for the role).[81] Then, during the 2000s, playing Jameson on the big screen marked a star-making turn for Academy Award–winning actor J.K. Simmons during Sam Raimi's *Spider-Man* trilogy. Simmons, who was described by *New York Times* film critic A.O. Scott as playing Jameson with "maniacal gusto" (is there a better description of JJJ than that?) in a review of *Spider-Man 2*, has been asked to reprise the role many times over since the last Raimi movie in 2007.

And when the character was inexplicably absent (save for one angry e-mail message sent to Peter bearing his name) in Marc Webb's pair of *The Amazing Spider-Man* films, fans actually organized a petition for Simmons to be considered for some future Spider-Man flick[82] (though Simmons's recent casting as police commissioner James Gordon in Warner Brother's Batman films probably disqualifies him from any JJJ talk going forward). While these fan petitions tend to go nowhere, Simmons still felt compelled enough to respond to it when asked by *Entertainment Tonight*: "Being in those movies with Sam [Raimi] was one of the great joys of my career. It was a super fun character so I'll never close the door on anything."[83]

10 The Parker Luck

Peter Parker may be the unluckiest fella in the world. So much so that he even has his own brand of misfortune named after him—the "Parker Luck."

The phrase "Parker Luck" appears in print as early as 1966's *Amazing Spider-Man #34*, but Stan Lee and Steve Ditko started tormenting their prized comic book creation going back to the very beginning of Spider-Man. Lee, when describing what makes Peter so unique, has frequently said he's the kind of superhero who gets sinus attacks, gets acne, and allergy attacks while he's fighting.[84] These elements are certainly a part of what makes up the Parker Luck. But there's more to it than pimples and sneezes. Over time, the Parker Luck evolved into a Shakespearean style of tragic irony that would taunt Peter at the most inopportune times; like he'd be out on a date and the Green Goblin or Doctor Octopus would crash the place and he'd have to secretly duck out and reappear as Spider-Man, while his date was left wondering why Peter was such a coward for disappearing. Or like in 2004's *Spider-Man 2* film, when he was out making a pizza delivery and he had to stop everything and contend with Spider-Man business, causing him to miss the pizza joint's "30 Minutes or Free" deadline and lose his job.

In the first issue of Spider-Man's own comic book series, *Amazing Spider-Man*, Lee and Ditko throw a number of bad-luck scenarios at Peter, most of which are the handiwork of J. Jonah Jameson, the flat-topped publisher of the *Daily Bugle* newspaper. Rather than treat Spider-Man as the hero he is, Jameson labels him a "menace," turning public opinion against him and limiting Spidey's ability to make any cash as his costumed persona. And even after Spider-Man rescues Jameson's astronaut son from a falling space rocket, JJJ still turns the tables on Spidey by insisting that the masked man sabotaged the vessel in an attempt to boost his image. This leads to Spider-Man being listed as a "Wanted" man by the FBI.[85] If that luck wasn't bad enough, when Peter returns home after a day of superhero-ing as Spider-Man, even his lovely Aunt May refers to his alter-ego as being "horrible," giving Peter no place to escape the abuse: "Everything I do as Spider-Man seems to turn out wrong!"[86] he exclaims.

The Parker Luck has also manifested itself in humorous ways, like the time Peter lost his costume and had to rent a poor-fitting replacement from a costume shop.[87] In a similar wardrobe malfunction, Peter decided not to pack his threads while traveling to Germany for a *Bugle* assignment and ended up having to wear a German version of his suit ("Die Spinne").[88]

Heck, even miraculously coming back from the dead has caused a headache for Peter thanks to his horrendous luck. That's because Peter can't just simply die. Instead, one of his mortal enemies, Doctor Octopus, was able to swap his brain and body

Parker's Lady Luck

Sure, no one should think that Peter Parker's life is full of good fortune. But for someone who's gotten a pretty raw deal in life, Peter has demonstrated some shockingly good luck with the ladies. This phenomenon was best on display in the mid-1960s when the *Amazing Spider-Man* series evolved from a story about an angsty outsider to a tale of a lovable loser who just so happened to have two beautiful women—the blonde bombshell, Gwen Stacy, and the red-headed, hip-talking vixen, Mary Jane Watson—competing for his attention.

Peter's lady luck was so vexing, many of his male peers were often rendered incredulous by his good fortune. In the immortal words of Johnny Storm, aka the Human Torch, in 2005's Spider-Man/Human Torch miniseries: "The Babes! Man, the girls I've seen you with! God, how I envied you. You always had everything going for you!"[90]

with Spider-Man before killing him in *Amazing Spider-Man #700*. When Peter finally got his body back, he had to deal with all the havoc Doc Ock had wreaked on his life while masquerading as Spidey. Oh, by the way, the name of that storyline? "The Parker Luck." Natch.

The Parker Luck is so powerful, it has even been used to describe unfortunate circumstances that have befallen Spider-Man in the real world. A few weeks before Spidey's cinematic reboot, *The Amazing Spider-Man*, hit theaters in 2012, an article in *Time* magazine cited "the Parker Luck" when the new film's buzz was being overshadowed by people's excitement for other comic book movies being released that summer—namely *The Avengers* and *The Dark Knight Rises*. The article speculated about what might have been if the first *Spider-Man* movie flopped back in 2002; concluding that the character's cinematic rights probably would have reverted back to Marvel's control, allowing Spidey (as what happened to the Hulk after his 2003 big-screen debacle) to appear in the *Avengers* movie, and raising his profile in time for the celebration of the 50th anniversary of his first appearance in the comics that summer.[89]

11 Extra! Extra! The *Daily Bugle*

Stop the presses! When it comes to having a unique setting that organically grows Spider-Man's famously great supporting cast, the *Daily Bugle* newspaper has long been the source for such developments.

The *Bugle* was first introduced in name in 1962 in *Fantastic Four #2* and then appeared as a brick-and-mortar business in 1963 in the inaugural issue of Spidey's own series, *Amazing Spider-Man.* It has been a critical setting for the Spider-verse ever since, and has been featured prominently in nearly every iteration of Spider-Man, including comics, cartoons, and movies (with the landmark Flatiron Building in Manhattan serving as the exterior in Sam Raimi's *Spider-Man* trilogy in the 2000s).

Modeled after real-life New York City tabloids, *The Daily News* and *New York Post,* the paper's publisher, J. Jonah Jameson, is one of the most persistent and nagging antagonists to ever lock horns with Spider-Man. Beginning in *Amazing #1*, JJJ has used the power of the press to sway public opinion and convince readers that the masked Spider-Man is not a hero, but a menace. However, in one of the true twists of irony in comics, the *Bugle* is also the place of employment for Spidey's civilian alter-ego, Peter Parker, who works as a freelance photographer, snapping photos of himself fighting supervillains and selling them to Jameson.

Of course, the *Bugle* is not unique in terms of having a newspaper serve as a central backdrop for a superhero comic book series. Most famously, DC's *Superman* comics featured the *Daily Planet*, where the Man of Steel's alter-ego, Clark Kent, worked as a reporter alongside his love interest, Lois Lane. After realizing that the *Bugle* might be viewed as a two-bit rip-off of the *Planet*, Stan Lee, Spider-Man's co-creator, set out to make the cast of characters at Marvel's flagship periodical as different from the "distinguished competition" as possible. Lee accomplished these goals by creating some very distinct and unique characters within the *Bugle* offices. For example, the hot-headed Jameson was the polar opposite of the *Planet's* chief, the more stately Perry White.[91]

Beyond "Jolly Jonah," other key supporting cast members introduced via the *Bugle* include Betty Brant, Peter's first romantic love interest, who debuted in *Amazing #4* as Jameson's secretary. Ned Leeds, created by Lee/Ditko in *Amazing #18*, was the ace reporter of the *Bugle* and Peter's rival for Betty's affections (he went on to marry Betty in the 1970s). Leeds was later believed to be the masked supervillain the Hobgoblin (only to be revealed that he was brainwashed into thinking he was the Hobgoblin). Joe "Robbie" Robertson, the *Bugle's* city editor (and later, editor-in-chief) made history when he was introduced by Lee and John Romita Sr. in *Amazing #51* as one of superhero comics' first African American characters.

For many creators who worked on Spider-Man comics, the proper usage of the *Bugle's* cast of characters was a vital part of crafting a well-rounded Spidey story. "Many of us went through great pains to make Peter Parker a three-dimensional character," said former Spider-Man scribe Tom DeFalco, who often strived to hook readers by offering them compelling subplots around the likes of Leeds or Robertson. "To do that, we had to surround Peter Parker with three-dimensional characters."[92]

That premise was probably best evidenced during Gerry Conway's run scripting *Spectacular Spider-Man* and *Web of Spider-Man* in the late 1980s. Conway, who first became famous in comics in the '70s, scripting dramatic Spider-Man stories such as "The Night Gwen Stacy Died," came back to Spidey only on the condition that he would have free rein to focus on the supporting cast rather than the traditional superhero stuff.[93] As a result, Conway crafted a number of memorable long-running arcs: one featuring Robertson being forced to confront his childhood tormentor, the gang boss Lonnie "Tombstone" Lincoln, and the other involving *Bugle* secretary Glory Grant's love affair with the mobster-turned-werewolf, Eduardo Lobo.

Outside of the cozy confines of Spider-Man comics, the *Bugle* has also been prominently featured in a number of non-Spidey stories. The fearless, chain-smoking *Bugle* reporter Ben Urich, created by Roger McKenzie and Gene Colan in *Daredevil #153*, was the heart and soul of Frank Miller/Klaus Janson's critically acclaimed creative run on *Daredevil* in the late '70s/early '80s.

These comics depicted Urich as an unofficial partner of Daredevil's in the hero's war on Hell's Kitchen's criminal underworld. Additionally, in 1977, a *Bugle* subsidiary, *Woman Magazine*, was used as a venue to introduce the world to Carol Danvers, the superheroine originally known as Ms. Marvel, who is now known by the name Captain Marvel (and the subject of Marvel's upcoming *Captain Marvel* film).

12 Your Friendly Neighborhood Street-Fighting (Spider) Man

For many creators who have worked within the world of Spider-Man, the hero is at his best when he's taking it to the streets. By that, they mean battling villains and dealing with problems that are smaller and more realistic in scale, e.g., burglars, pickpockets, and the occasional crime boss or enforcer. Those big cosmic threats involving end-of-the-universe scenarios are better left to the Avengers or the Fantastic Four. But taking out thugs like Fancy Dan or Ox of the Enforcers? That's a job for your friendly neighborhood Spider-Man.

This mindset from creators goes back to the earliest days of Spider-Man. Steve Ditko, Spidey's original artist, has said on numerous occasions that he always looked to set Spider-Man in a "teenager's world." Outside of Electro and Sandman (who was later shuffled off to battle the Fantastic Four), very few of Spider-Man's first batch of villains exhibited extraordinary, supernatural-like powers. And even heavyweights like Doc Ock or the Green Goblin were only aided by technology and man-made weaponry. For Ditko, that approach helped make Spider-Man a more realistic kind of superhero. Sure, the idea of a teenager getting powers from a radioactive arachnid is fantasy, but the trials and tribulations he faced in taking on a master of disguise like the Chameleon or gang boss like the Crime Master seemed more tangible and grounded to the average reader. The term that most often gets tossed around as it related to Spider-Man's role in the Marvel Universe is "street level."

"He was a lighter creature of the night," said longtime Spider-Man writer Tom DeFalco of Spider-Man. During DeFalco's two runs on *Amazing Spider-Man* in the '80s and '90s, he created a number of criminal underworld rogues for Spidey to fight, like the Rose, Black Tarantula, and Black Fox. "That kind of stuff really worked better for Spider-Man...the guys who operated out of the shadows, because Spider-Man was a guy who operated out of the shadows."[94]

One of the big mysteries that fueled a number of stories during the Stan Lee/Ditko era of *Amazing Spider-Man* was the identity of the masked villain the Green Goblin. One of the pivotal chapters of this arc was a two-part story involving an underworld showdown between the Goblin and another masked villain, the Crime Master. At the end, the Crime Master is accidentally shot and killed, but before he dies, he is revealed as just a random guy—which was supposed to represent Ditko's philosophy that not every evil-doer or hero had to be some fantastical, over-the-top character.[95]

Even when Ditko left Marvel in 1966, Lee and his artistic collaborator, John Romita Sr., continued to create new crooks and criminals for Spidey to face off against, like Wilson "Kingpin" Fisk and Silvio "Silvermane" Manfredi. Creators who followed Lee on Spider-Man drew inspiration from these early rogues. Longtime Spidey scribe Gerry Conway compared the likes of the Crime Master and the Enforcers to bad guys found in the world of comic strip detective Dick Tracy. Conway would later add his own street-level thugs to Spider-Man's mythos, including Tombstone and Hammerhead, as well as the Punisher, the dark vigilante antihero who fought mobsters and drug dealers.[96]

Now, don't be mistaken in thinking that street level is the *only* way to write Spider-Man. The character has certainly been a part of many memorable stories when he's taken on larger threats like Doctor Doom, Magneto, and even Thanos. Still, over the years, every time Spider-Man appeared to stray further and further from the friendly neighborhood path, some creative team or Marvel initiative would invariably get him back to his street-level roots. No status quo shift was more representative of that idea than 2008's "Brand New Day" storyline in *Amazing Spider-Man,* which brought Peter Parker/Spidey unabashedly back to his old ways, fighting newly created street-level thugs like Mister Negative and Menace. In 2015, Conway was even tapped by Marvel again to write the more grounded Spidey tale "Spiral," a street-level story that included foes like Hammerhead, Tombstone, and a cop with questionable ethics named Yuri Wantanabe. "Spider-Man is most effective when he's cracking jokes and punching characters," Conway said of his story and Spidey's return to his roots. "'Spiral' was my nostalgic tip of the hat to an old Spidey."[97]

13 Doctor Octopus/Otto Octavius

Every superhero needs an archnemesis and for Spider-Man, his most nefarious villain is Otto Octavius, aka Doctor Octopus—unless you're one of those people who thinks Norman Osborn/Green Goblin is Spidey's greatest foe. But then you would be wrong.

Think about it: there's so much to suggest that Doc Ock is the Yin to Spider-Man's Yang, the North Pole to his South Pole. Both are men of science with great intellects who model themselves

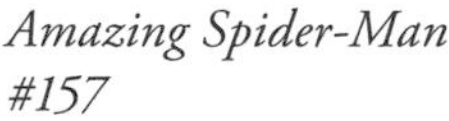
Amazing Spider-Man #157

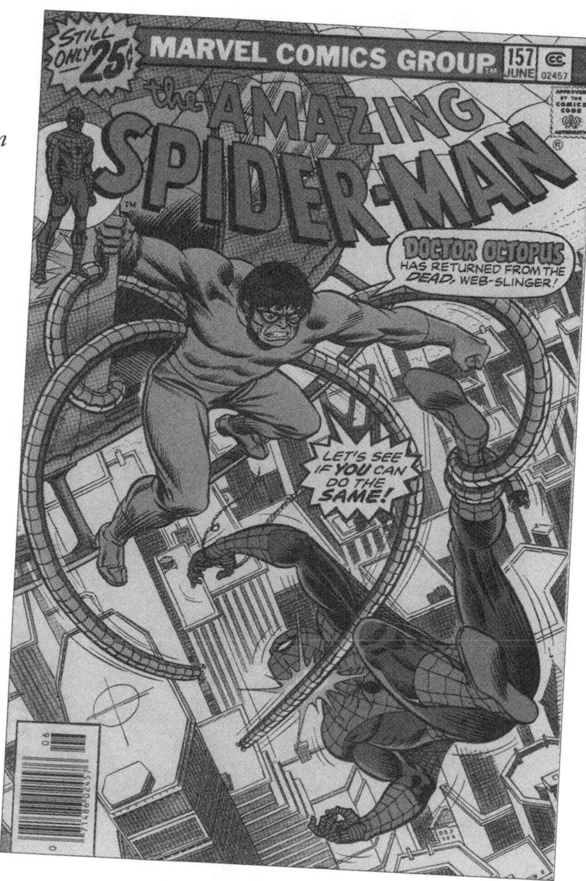

after creatures with eight arms/legs. But where the two characters diverge with their actions hits the core moral of Spider-Man comic books: "With great power, there must also come great responsibility." Peter Parker eventually understands that the great power he received from the radioactive spider that bit him must be used to help others and to make the world a better place, whereas Otto Octavius uses the great power he gets from a science experiment gone awry to become one of the most sinister villains on the planet, a man who has threatened to destroy the entire world if doing so serves his needs.

But don't take my word for it. Despite his potbelly and Elton John hairdo, Doctor Octopus has been treated as a very special attraction going back to his very first appearance and origin story in *Amazing Spider-Man #3*. In that issue, the reader learns that Octavius is a great nuclear physicist who uses a set of four mechanical arms to handle the sensitive materials that he works with. However, a radioactive explosion ultimately fuses Octavius to his arms, creating the murderous villain Doctor Octopus. Since then, the character has been the star of numerous comic book stories, cartoons, and video games. He was the featured villain in 2004's *Spider-Man 2* (played by Alfred Molina) and even had an entire comic book series based around him in 2013–14, the *Superior Spider-Man*, which captures Otto's ultimate victory: he manages to swap brains and bodies with Spider-Man and traps his foe in his dying body, allowing Doc Ock to become a "better" version of the "Web-Slinger."

His co-creators, Stan Lee and Steve Ditko, clearly had big things in mind for Otto, as he was presented as a threat early and often. He actually embarrasses and defeats Spider-Man in his debut story, and would go on to put a serious crimp in his adversary's romantic life a few issues later when the brother of Peter's girlfriend, Betty Brant, is killed in the crossfire of a battle between Spidey and Doc Ock. Shortly after that, he would emerge as the leader of the Sinister Six, a team of Spidey's deadliest rogues who fought the "Wall Crawler" in *Amazing Spider-Man Annual #1*. If that's not enough to convince the skeptics, keep in mind that during the Silver Age of comics, Doctor Octopus was the featured bad guy in what many considered to be the greatest Spider-Man story of all-time, the "Master Planner Trilogy" (*Amazing Spider-Man #31–33*). Naturally, Doc Ock is the master planner, and his desire to get his tentacles on a serum Peter needs to save his Aunt May almost leads to May's and Spider-Man's deaths in the issue.

Still think Norman Osborn is Spidey's archnemesis? How about that time one of Doc Ock's tentacles smashed into the side of a building, knocking rubble to the ground and killing police captain George Stacy, the father of Peter's girlfriend, Gwen? Or when, a few years later, Doc Ock attempted to marry Peter's Aunt May because he believed she was set to inherit a nuclear reactor that he wanted (granted, that was a pretty weird subplot)?

Then, of course, there was the whole *Superior Spider-Man* era, one of the most controversial and bizarre periods in Spider-Man comics' history. In the lead-up to *Superior Spider-Man #1* in early 2013, writer Dan Slott described his zany plot as, "This is: Oh, my God, John Wilkes Booth is inside Lincoln! It's Moriarty inside Sherlock Holmes!"[98]

Sure the character has had his setbacks. Like when he was reduced to a "simpering dishrag" according to Spider-Man writer David Michelinie, following his humiliating defeat at the hands of Spider-Man during the epic early '80s *Spectacular Spider-Man* tale "The Owl/Octopus Wars" (Spider-Man actually manages to rip Doc Ock's tentacles off of his body at the end of that storyline).[99] And having Spider-Man's deranged clone Kaine "kill" Doc Ock during the "Clone Saga" arc of the '90s never sat right with the guy who wrote the comic where it happened (*Spectacular Spider-Man #221)*, Tom DeFalco. "I thought it was a waste of a great character," DeFalco said.[100] But Otto would bounce back (or be resurrected, as the case may be) and prove again and again why he is Spider-Man's greatest adversary: "He's so much like Peter Parker," DeFalco added. "He's Peter Parker gone wrong."[101]

14 Norman Osborn

There's been one constant about Norman Osborn since he first appeared as the costumed supervillain the Green Goblin in *Amazing Spider-Man #14* in 1964: if something truly awful happened to Peter Parker/Spider-Man, Osborn was very likely the man behind it.

Created by Stan Lee and Steve Ditko, many people consider Osborn Spider-Man's indisputable archenemy, and with good reason: over the years, Osborn has tormented Peter by killing his first love, Gwen Stacy; kidnapping (and presumably killing) his newborn child; faking the death of his Aunt May; making him believe that he was a clone; and turning Peter's own best friend (and Osborn's son), Harry, against him. And that's just scratching the surface.

He's also the villain most closely associated with Spider-Man outside of the comics. Osborn and his associates have been featured prominently in two separate *Spider-Man* film series. Academy Award–nominee Willem Dafoe played the character in the Sam Raimi–directed *Spider-Man* trilogy that hit theaters between 2002 and 2007. When Spidey's cinematic world was rebooted as *The Amazing Spider-Man* in 2012, Osborn's company, Oscorp, was connected in some shape or form to nearly every significant moment of tragedy in Peter's life, including the receipt of his powers. Academy Award–winner Chris Cooper was cast as Norman in 2014's *The Amazing Spider-Man 2*, with Dale DeHaan playing his son Harry.

"Doc Ock, Sandman, and Vulture are all important [Spider-Man] villains," said longtime comic book scribe Gerry Conway, who scripted "The Night Gwen Stacy Died," one of the seminal Osborn/Goblin stories. "Peter had a personal relationship with

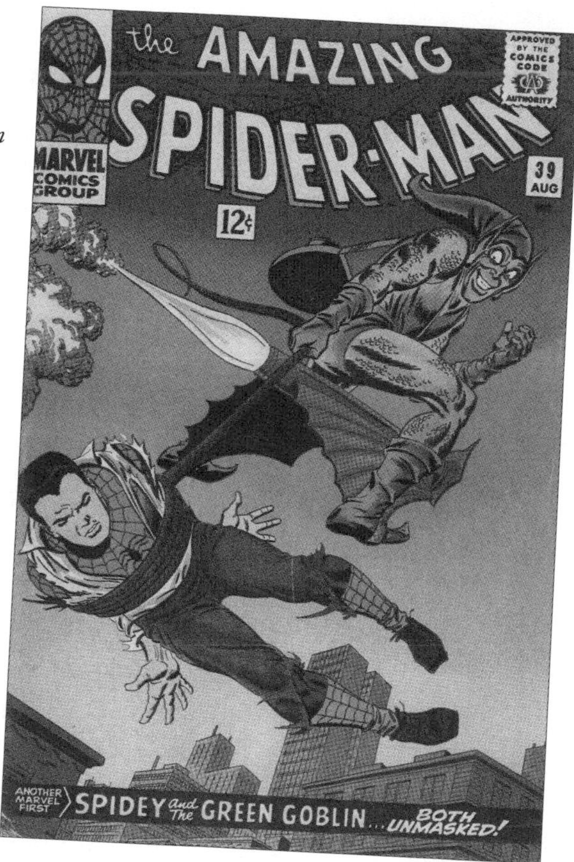

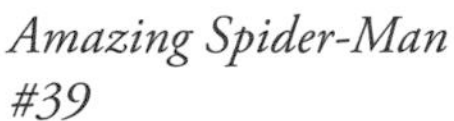
Amazing Spider-Man #39

Norman Osborn that he didn't have with other villains in his life. That's what made him his archenemy. His Joker."[102]

There has been a special aura surrounding Osborn dating all the way back to his debut as the Goblin in the comics. While the bulk of Lee/Ditko's newly introduced characters received some semblance of an origin story during their creative run on *Amazing Spider-Man*, the Goblin's identity and background remained a mystery. Nobody knew who was under the mercurial Halloween-esque mask. And the more the Goblin appeared, the more Lee and Ditko teased the mystery, so much so that when it finally came time to unmask the villain in *Amazing #39*, Marvel needed to deliver something momentous to pay off such a long-simmering storyline. The company did not disappoint. Ditko had quit Marvel, leaving veteran artist John Romita Sr. to collaborate with Lee and to settle this great mystery. In the story, the Goblin manages to unmask Spider-Man and learn his secret identity, only to then reveal himself as Osborn…the father of one of Peter's college friends, Harry.

Granted, at that point in time, Norman Osborn hadn't become *the* Norman Osborn. The character, outside of his costume, first appeared as a member of *Daily Bugle* publisher J. Jonah Jameson's social club in *Amazing #23*, and was named for the first time as Harry's curmudgeonly father in *Amazing #37*. But what Norman initially lacked in name recognition he quickly made up for in terms of his menace to Spider-Man's livelihood.

Lee and Romita crafted a fantastic origin story for how Osborn became the Goblin: the founder of the shady corporation Oscorp, Norman injects himself with a serum that enhances his strength but makes him paranoid and psychotic. Spider-Man triumphs against the Goblin in *Amazing #40* and at the end of the issue, Osborn develops amnesia and forgets that he was ever a supervillain. But he remains a threat to Peter every time he appears because he is the only Spider-Man villain who knows Peter's secret identity. And that fact was finally reinforced in 1973 with "The Night Gwen Stacy Died" when Osborn does the unthinkable: he kidnaps Peter's girlfriend, Gwen, in an effort to exact vengeance against his rival, and then kills her by tossing her off a bridge. In the very next issue, Norman himself is presumed dead when he is accidentally impaled by his own Goblin Glider flying device.

Even with his death, Norman would still find ways to haunt and disrupt Peter's life. Despite Norman's very key part in Gwen's death, Peter tormented himself for years over his inability to save her from the Goblin. Following Osborn's death, Spider-Man was pegged by the media and the police as being responsible. Then, thanks to Norman's toxic influence over his son Harry, the younger Osborn eventually turned on Peter/Spider-Man and became the second Green Goblin.

Finally, after nearly 20 years, Marvel's hierarchy decided it was time to bring Norman back from the grave and make him a prime-time player in Spider-Man's world again. Howard Mackie, who scripted Osborn's return, was initially opposed to the character's resurrection, feeling that his death was one of the few that "mattered" in comics. However, once he started writing Osborn in 1997's *Peter Parker: Spider-Man #75*, Mackie realized that he had a wonderful new toy to play with: "He's really an amazing character. Beyond the funny hair, Norman himself is just fascinating to write. I loved exploring the twisted relationship that existed not just between Spider-Man and the Green Goblin, but Norman and Peter."[103]

Norman 2.0 was depicted as a more diabolical power player in the Marvel universe, rather than the emotionally unhinged villain he was during the Silver Age era of comics. At one point, the character was even elevated to being one of the overarching big bads of the entire Marvel Universe, taking on "Earth's Mightiest Heroes," the Avengers, during the "Dark Reign" arc of the late 2000s. "We got a lot of great stories and mileage out of the fact that he was back," said Marvel's executive editor, Tom Brevoort, who described Osborn's reign of terror as the Marvel Universe getting "a taste of what it is to be Peter Parker. All of them are set in this underdog role where even doing the most basic thing becomes hard, becomes difficult because the world is against them."[104]

This turn for the character also informed how Norman was written as part of Marvel's alternative *Ultimate* universe throughout the 2000s. In the *Ultimate Spider-Man* series, Osborn is viewed as the central villain and adversary in Spider-Man's world, all the way up to each character's death in 2011's "Death of Spider-Man" storyline (they would later be resurrected).

15 The Burglar

Before there was Doctor Octopus or the Green Goblin, there was a simple burglar with a face that would haunt Peter Parker for the rest of his life. With no known powers to speak of, or high-tech gadgetry at his disposal, the Burglar is still considered Spider-Man's most nefarious foe primarily because, without the Burglar, there would be no Spider-Man. The character first appeared in Spider-Man's 1962 origin story, *Amazing Fantasy #15* when he sprinted past Peter Parker's masked alias inside a television studio. A cop shouted at Spider-Man to do something—*anything*—to stop the thief, but Spidey willfully ignored the request, believing that such grunt work was not his responsibility as an up-and-coming TV star.

Peter would live to regret that decision. And the Burglar would become a part of one of the biggest plot twists in comic book history when Peter returned to his Aunt May and Uncle Ben's house one night only to find that a crook had broken in and murdered his uncle. When Peter, as Spider-Man, catches up to the assailant he realizes, "It's the fugitive who ran past me! The one I didn't stop when I had the chance!"[105]

The Burglar's role in launching the career of Spider-Man has managed to be presented in almost every iteration of Spider-Man across all media, including both the *Spider-Man* and *The Amazing Spider-Man* film series. That's because it's the unquestioned turning point in Peter's life. From that moment on, Peter vows to use the great spider-powers with the utmost responsibility. And he would do that by always helping others when they were in danger, regardless of the odds or the inconvenience. Like in the comic *Amazing Spider-Man #50*, better known as "Spider-Man No More," when Peter temporarily gives up his superhero identity so he could pursue

Here's What Happened to Crusher Hogan

In addition to the Burglar, there was another character from *Amazing Fantasy #15* who years later became the focal point of a new story within the pages of *Amazing Spider-Man.* In 1985's "Whatever Happened to Crusher Hogan" (*Amazing Spider-Man #271*), Tom DeFalco and Ron Frenz revisit Crusher Hogan—the wrestler a masked Peter shockingly defeated the first time he took his new spider-powers out on a test drive. Years after Hogan was beating up geeks as part of a sideshow, he has become a simple janitor in a New York City gym. He also continues to talk about his relationship with Spider-Man as if the two regularly did lunch and shared workout tips with each other. However, Spidey being Spidey, when he learns about Hogan's braggadocios ways, he decides to corroborate the story in front of Crusher's co-workers at the gym.

Crusher Hogan would appear again in 2002's *Spider-Man Tangled Web #14* with a script written by Brian Azzarello and, interestingly enough, the professional wrestler Scott Levy (aka Raven).

a normal teenage life. At one point in the comic, Peter happens upon a night watchman who is being attacked by a couple of thugs. After rushing to the rescue, Peter realizes what drew him back to being a hero: the watchman reminded him of his Uncle Ben and his assailants of the Burglar who was there the night the teen "became Spider-Man for real!!"[106]

Despite the generally anonymous nature of the Burglar, the character would actually make a second appearance in the comics in 1980's *Amazing Spider-Man #200* by Marv Wolfman and Keith Pollard. Wolfman and Pollard used the comic to expand upon *Amazing Fantasy #15*'s mythology by providing the Burglar with more explicit incentive and motivation for breaking into Ben and May's house and murdering Ben. Apparently, the Burglar believes that a great treasure has been buried under the Parker's home in Forest Hills, Queens, so he breaks in hoping to strike it rich. When Ben interferes in the robbery, the Burglar shoots him in cold blood.

Amazing #200 ends with the Burglar dying from a heart attack after Peter angrily confronts him about his role in his uncle's death.

While it might have seemed controversial that *Amazing #200* retroactively changed certain plot points from one of the most historic comic book stories of all time, Wolfman contends that his story addresses one of the primary logic loopholes behind Stan Lee and Steve Ditko's great tale in *Amazing Fantasy #15*: "I always wondered why someone Peter accidentally ran into outside Madison Square Garden in Manhattan also appeared in Forest Hills, Queens," Wolfman said. "It seemed too coincidental to me. I decided there had to be a story there and therefore decided to go after the Burglar to explain why. Also it made issue *#200* special."[107]

16 Must Read: "The Master Planner Trilogy" (*Amazing Spider-Man #31–33*)

"If This Be My Destiny" blares the cover of this storyline's first chapter, which is undoubtedly the pinnacle of the Stan Lee/Steve Ditko's creative run of 38 issues (and two annuals) on *Amazing Spider-Man*. "The Master Planner Trilogy," which was published in 1965–66, perfectly encapsulates all of Spider-Man's most heroic qualities—his unyielding sense of responsibility, his perseverance, and his inner strength and resolve. Every storyline, regardless of the medium, that shows Spider-Man overcoming great odds, owes its inspiration one way or another to these comics. In many ways, the trilogy is as important to the greater Spider-Man mythos as his first appearance and origin story in *Amazing Fantasy #15*.

The story begins innocuously enough. Spider-Man crashes the party of a crime in progress that's being perpetrated by a bunch of anonymous goons. However, the drama escalates quickly when

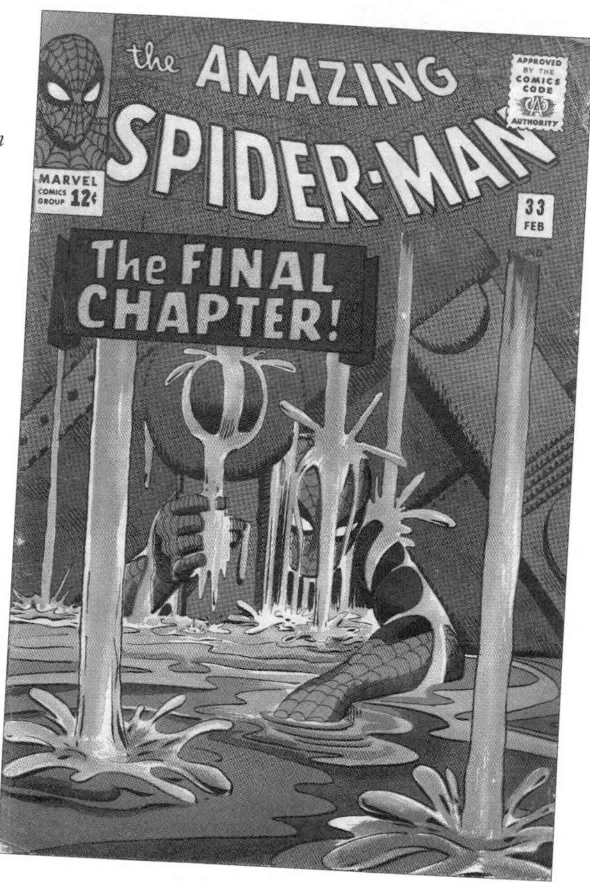

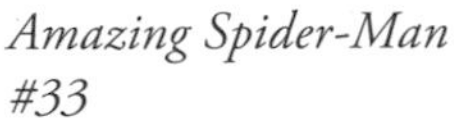
Amazing Spider-Man #33

things become deeply personal for Peter Parker. His elderly Aunt May has fallen ill—again. But this time the source of her sickness is the radioactive blood Peter donated to her in a preceding story. There's only one way to save Aunt May: obtaining a serum needed for an antidote that will cure her from radiation poisoning. However, the serum is also being chased down by Spider-Man's archnemesis, Doctor Octopus (aka the "Master Planner"). And that's when things really become harrowing.

In the storyline's most climatic scene—one that has been duplicated countless times over but never replicated—Spider-Man is buried under tons of steel and wreckage with the serum just out of reach. Spider-Man is resigned to failure. Aunt May will die. Until he remembers again how he failed his Uncle Ben in *Amazing Fantasy #15* when he arrogantly allowed a burglar to run by him and, in turn, that criminal went on to murder Ben.

Over the course of the next three pages, Ditko illustrated a brilliant sequence of Spider-Man struggling to lift the steel off his body, inch by agonizing inch. Every muscle in Spider-Man's body aches. His head is spinning. The weight is too much. But… "anyone can win a fight when the odds—are easy! It's when the going's tough—when there seems to be no chance—that's when—it counts!"[108]

Spider-Man overcomes these insurmountable odds and grabs the serum that saves the life of his aunt. Lee said the first time he saw this sequence illustrated on the page, he "almost shouted in triumph" from the excitement Ditko's visuals managed to project.[109]

But the significance of this story goes beyond how it demonstrates Spider-Man's peerless physical and emotional strength. *The Amazing Spider-Man* has continued to publish more than 50 years after this story was first published, but it still feels fitting that the title of the arc's last issue, *Amazing Spider-Man #33*, is dubbed "The Final Chapter." In many ways the story marks a culmination of the greater Spider-Man story that was being told by Lee and Ditko since the character had first debuted in 1962. From that moment on, Peter had evolved beyond a shy, socially awkward teenager who inadvertently fell into his extraordinary powers. He was a hero on the level of the Captain Americas and Supermans of the comic book world.

Additionally, it's worth noting that this comic is almost entirely Ditko's handiwork. As was the case with most issues of *Amazing Spider-Man* after *#10*, Ditko provided the pencils and plotted the whole thing, only handing off the pages to Lee at the end to provide the dialogue. Ditko was outraged when Lee attempted to take credit for the story's most famous scene—the lifting sequence—in a *Comic Book Marketplace* interview years later. The normally reclusive writer was compelled to write a rebuttal to the same magazine where he reminds readers that the work was entirely his.[110]

Regardless of the behind-the-scenes drama, the "Master Planner Trilogy" is as essential of a Spider-Man story as can be. For all the aforementioned reasons, if a reader is only going to check out one Lee/Ditko story, this is the one to track down. And even with its Silver Age sensibilities, nearly every facet of the story still holds up today. For further proof, just look to how the story inspired parts of 2004's *Spider-Man 2*, or even a 2016 issue of *Amazing Spider-Man* (*#16*, vol. 4).

17 The Mystery of the Green Goblin

Spider-Man and mysterious villains have gone hand in hand for decades. Over the years, a number of masked rogues and shadowy figures have been introduced in Spider-Man comics and have been attached to long-running arcs teasing their identities. And in almost every instance, these stories were drawing inspiration from Spider-Man's first mystery—the identity of the villainous Green Goblin—which stretched out over the span of 26 issues between 1964 and '66.

The Green Goblin was first introduced by Stan Lee and Steve Ditko in *Amazing Spider-Man #14*. Lee's original premise for the character was something more fantastical than what would eventually make it into the comics. Lee envisioned a movie crew coming across an Egyptian-like sarcophagus containing an ancient demon that would come to life. Ditko thought this idea was way too farfetched for a series that was supposed to have more grounded, realistic elements like *Amazing Spider-Man*, and instead came up with a mystery villain.[111]

Every Lee/Ditko story that featured the Goblin would further tease "who" was under the goblin mask. The creators would drop hints like in *Amazing #17*, when the reader is shown a lair filled with fancy and expensive machinery, implying the character is wealthy and has some mechanical know-how. Or in *Amazing #23,* when the character brags about wanting to take control of every criminal racket in New York City, indicating connections to Marvel's mobster underworld.

The mystery seemingly comes to a head in a two-part arc in *Amazing #25–26,* when the Goblin mystery is played off the introduction of another masked rogue, the Crime Master. Over the course of the story, both villains indicate they know the other's identity (but nobody is telling the reader!). But by the end, the Crime Master is unmasked as just a guy, a nobody. Meanwhile, the mystery of the Goblin lives on to fight another day.

Sadly, thanks to some behind-the-scenes turmoil involving Lee and Ditko, the Crime Master arc ended up being the very last Lee/Ditko Green Goblin story before the artist abruptly left the book about a year later. John Romita Sr. was brought over from *Daredevil* to pencil *Amazing #39* and in his very first issue, the Green Goblin was unmasked as Norman Osborn, the father of one of Peter's college friends, Harry. At the time, the reveal was a bit of a "so what" for some. Yes, Norman Osborn is infamously nefarious now, but back then, he had only been introduced in name a few issues earlier. And while anyone crazy enough to have a hairdo that looks like a Tootsie Roll should probably be considered a potential supervillain, it's not like Lee and Ditko ever truly established Norman as a potential Goblin suspect before making the reveal.

So then why the big mystery for such a tepid resolution? Apparently, at some point after Ditko's departure from Spider-Man, a rumor started circulating that the mercurial artist left the book because he was unhappy with the direction of the Goblin mystery. The story goes, Lee wanted Osborn to be the man under the mask because he believed it needed to be someone who had a personal connection to Peter. But Ditko, who was basically writing *Amazing Spider-Man* completely by himself at that point (Lee only provided dialogue for Ditko's finished pages), had planned on treating Norman as another red herring. Considering how Ditko anti-climatically revealed the Crime Master's identity as some random nobody in *Amazing #26*, Lee was apparently concerned the artist would attempt to do the same with the Goblin.

For decades, little has been done to dispel these rumors. Romita has been on the record saying he could never get a straight story from Lee regarding Ditko's departure and its connection to the Goblin story.[112] Then, in the 2007 BBC documentary *In Search of Steve Ditko*, both Ralph Macchio, a longtime Marvel editor, and Joe Quesada, Marvel's former editor-in-chief and current chief creative officer, speculated about Ditko's resignation being tied into the Goblin storyline.

Ditko vociferously disputes these claims in various essays he's penned in the industry fan zine *The Comics!* In one 2009 essay, he called rumors over the story's impact on his departure from Marvel as "made-up, fantasized issues." On the contrary, Ditko claimed he knew from Day One that Osborn was his guy, even citing that crazy Tootsie Roll hair that he and his son have as being one of the traits that helped make the character stand out and draw the reader's attention.[113] The artist absolutely sounds definitive in these essays, but perhaps because *The Comics!* has such a small audience, the urban legend about Ditko and the Goblin still manages to pop up from time to time in various fan histories and documentaries.

Regardless of any behind-the-scenes drama, the Green Goblin storyline is still one of the more influential arcs in Spider-Man history. It inspired 1983's Hobgoblin saga, which introduced a new goblin character, the Hobgoblin, and then proceeded to shroud the character in mystery for many years to follow. And then years later, the identity of the Green Goblin was once again a mystery as part of a long-running arc in the *Superior Spider-Man* comic book series. This time around the mystery man turned out to be...Norman Osborn...with a face transplant. Okay, so maybe that creative decision didn't set the world on fire like the Lee/Romita Goblin reveal. But that one story, written nearly 50 years earlier, served as the inspiration for a major Spider-Man arc.

18 John Romita Sr.: All That Jazz

While Steve Ditko gets credited for creating the visual world of Spider-Man, John Romita Sr. further refined it, and in many ways has been a bigger influence on the artists who came after him on Spider-Man. After first getting assigned to provide pencils for *Amazing Spider-Man* in 1966, Romita co-created a number of iconic characters, including Mary Jane Watson, Wilson "Kingpin" Fisk, Rhino, Prowler, and Shocker. But perhaps his greatest contribution to Spider-Man is how he helped change the tone of the Spider-Man universe by taking Ditko's tale of a teenage pariah and transforming it into a teenage soap opera, complete with beautiful girls in fashionable attire fighting for Peter Parker's affections. While some readers have gone on to bemoan Romita's brighter and cheerier landscape, his approach and sensibilities unquestionably helped make Spider-Man more accessible to a broader range of fans than Ditko's darker work on the character.

Like all good artists, Romita was bitten with the art bug at a very early age. Born in Brooklyn, New York, in 1930, he started drawing when he was five years old. At nine, he discovered newspaper comic strips and was immediately transfixed, drawing his own versions, complete with homemade logos and mastheads. Romita's characters were modeled after *Terry and the Pirates*, an action-adventure strip created by one of his biggest influences, cartoonist Milton Caniff.[114]

Romita was 19 when he started working for Stan Lee at Marvel's predecessor, Timely Comics—sort of. Unbeknownst to Lee, Romita had actually started "ghosting" (basically providing the drawings while letting another guy take the credit) for one of Timely's inkers. Romita's arrangement with an inker eventually hit sitcom levels of absurdity whenever Lee asked the artist for redos: the man would tell Lee he had to go somewhere "private" to work so he could coordinate the edits with Romita at a separate location. Finally, when Romita was looking for some work for himself, he went into Lee's office and told his secretary that while nobody would know his name, he'd actually been penciling for Timely for more than a year. The secretary disappeared for about a half hour and when she came back she was carrying an assignment from Lee for Romita.[115]

Romita left Timely in 1958 to work for the competition, DC. That's where he started making a name for himself in the industry as the master of illustrating romance comics.[116] He became highly regarded for the unique ways he made the talk-heavy genre visually interesting. Unfortunately, after eight years at DC, Romita was laid off, forcing him to reconsider his career prospects in comics. But at that time, Lee had started kicking the tires on a new wave of superhero comics over at Marvel. Lee looked up his old illustrator, leading to Romita's first full-time Marvel gig, illustrating the blind superhero, Daredevil. And it was through Daredevil that Romita found his way to Spider-Man.[117]

In 1966, Lee was growing concerned over his nonexistent relationship with Ditko and asked Romita to feature Spider-Man in *Daredevil #16* as an unofficial "tryout" for Spidey. When Ditko abruptly quit Marvel, Romita found himself being offered a spot on one of Marvel's most popular books, *Amazing Spider-Man*. Romita reluctantly accepted—he loved doing *Daredevil*—and only took the assignment because he was convinced Ditko would eventually come back to Marvel as quickly as he left.[118] In fact, Romita was so convinced the gig was temporary, he admittedly abandoned his own stylings for the character in favor of pencil-work that was an attempt to imitate Ditko.[119]

Romita's first issue was *Amazing Spider-Man* #39, arguably one of the most famous Spidey stories of all time. In it, Lee and Romita unmasked the Green Goblin, a character that had been introduced by Lee and Ditko a few years earlier and was subject to one of the most celebrated mystery angles in comic book history. Lee and Ditko reportedly disagreed over the villain's identity, making the choice to unveil the Goblin as businessman Norman Osborn in the issue immediately following Ditko's departure all the more curious.[120]

Three issues later, Romita breathed visual life into another character that was first facelessly introduced during the Lee/Ditko run on *Amazing*—the redheaded vixen and future Mrs. Peter Parker, Mary Jane Watson. As with the Goblin, Romita wondered if Lee had been holding off on introducing MJ while Ditko was on the book. In an effort to play off a long-running joke in the comics that Aunt May was trying to set Peter up on a blind date with a girl with a "great personality" (meaning she probably wasn't physically attractive), Lee had asked Romita to make Mary Jane a total bombshell. So Romita modeled her after 1960s teen queen Ann-Margret.[121]

After years of a chilly co-existence with Ditko, Lee found Romita to be far more amicable. The two collaborated face-to-face often, with Lee often acting out a story for the artist that Romita would then plot out on the page.[122] If the duo had one disagreement, it was related to one of the great debates in comic book history: Gwen Stacy or Mary Jane? Lee would sometimes accuse Romita of favoring Mary Jane over his preferred choice of Gwen, by making the redhead look more modern and glamourous. To put his boss at ease, Romita started make Gwen more fun and bouncy, dressing her in miniskirts and having her compete with MJ for Peter's affections. "They were like [*Archie's*] Betty and Veronica—the same girl except for the hair color," Romita said.[123]

After Lee left his perch as editor-in-chief in the early '70s to become Marvel's publisher, Romita was named art director. In this capacity, he oversaw all of the company's artists and had a hand in co-creating a number of iconic Marvel characters, like the Punisher, Wolverine, and Luke Cage. He also continued to provide editorial input on a number of major storylines the company was putting out, most famously "The Night Gwen Stacy Died," which saw the death of Gwen, much to Lee's shock and dismay.[124]

Lee and Romita joined forces again in 1977, when Marvel inked a deal with a newspaper syndicate to start distributing a daily *Spider-Man* comic strip. Like the good old days on *Amazing*, Lee would "script" while Romita provided pencils—except this time it was for a three-panel story that published seven days a week. The arrangement lasted about four years, when Romita trimmed back some of his managerial duties and was named Marvel's art director of special projects.[125]

It was around that point that the Romita legacy continued to grow via Romita's son, John Romita Jr., or JRJR, who followed in his father's footsteps and became an artist at Marvel. JRJR would enjoy two separate, long-term stints penciling *Amazing Spider-Man* in the mid-80s and early 2000s. Romita has long said he was proud of his son for making the leap, but wanted to emphasize that he never pressured him to follow the "family business."

Today, Romita is unofficially retired, since he still occasionally gets roped into providing some of his vintage pencil-work here and there. He's done a few special variant covers of *Amazing*

Spider-Man, and in the early 2000s, he even penciled four pages in *Amazing #500* (with JRJR providing the rest of the artwork). While he occasionally feels pangs of guilt when he turns down new work, "after fifty-years of late hours, short deadlines, and working seven days a week, I try to do as little as possible."[126] He's certainly earned that right.

19 Mary Jane Watson

Face it, Tiger…you just hit the Mary Jane Watson chapter.

Arguably comics' most famous redhead, Mary Jane has had a storied career dating back to her gobsmacking debut in *Amazing Spider-Man #42*. In that issue, Peter Parker, after months of dodging a blind date with his neighbor, Anna Watson's niece, is finally forced to meet the girl who was advertised as having a "great personality." When he opens the door and sees MJ in all of her kittenish glory, she tells the shell-shocked teenager, "Face it, Tiger… you just hit the jackpot!" The moment is considered so legendary, readers of the website *Comics Should Be Good* actually voted it the most iconic Marvel panel of all time.[127]

Despite the fact that Peter spent most of his early years dating the more demure Gwen Stacy, there was something clearly special about MJ from the beginning. Her co-creator, John Romita Sr., modeled her after *Bye Bye Birdie* actress Ann-Margret. Stan Lee, who first conceived of the character while he was still collaborating with artist Steve Ditko on *Amazing Spider-Man*, wanted a female who would resemble the then-modern ideal of beauty (and let's be honest, sexiness). She was an instant hit, so much so that MJ started to overshadow Gwen in the eyes of fans. And even when Peter started dating Gwen exclusively, "No matter what Stan and I did, the fans always liked Mary Jane better," Romita said[128]

Indeed, MJ just made an impression on fans. Gerry Conway, who replaced Lee as head writer of *Amazing Spider-Man* in the early '70s, read MJ's first appearance and was immediately floored by not only her looks, but her snappy, hip personality. "And then she just went away and I was devastated," Conway said. "The other girl was his girlfriend and I never understood that."[129]

Maybe that's why Conway killed Gwen in *Amazing Spider-Man #121* (just kidding—sorta). All joking aside, it is worth noting that in the final pages of *Amazing #122*, MJ greets Peter at his apartment and attempts to console him after Gwen's death. Peter initially rebuffs MJ, dismissing her as a shallow party girl, but MJ adamantly decides to stand by her friend and comfort him. "She grows up on those two pages," Conway said of Mary Jane.[130]

Peter and Mary Jane finally started dating a few years after Gwen's death. But the romance led to an ongoing struggle between various creative teams over how close Peter and MJ should ultimately get. Conway might have loved Mary Jane, but the idea of ever marrying them off would have been a "disastrous mistake."[131] And when Marv Wolfman took over scripting *Amazing Spider-Man* in the late '70s, one of his first storylines had MJ reject Peter's marriage proposal, allowing him to write her out of the book.[132]

But you can't keep a great character away forever, and by the time Mary Jane returned to the books in the mid-80s, she had yet another new attitude. Tom DeFalco and Ron Frenz provided MJ with her own "origin" story in *Amazing #259* that showed how her fun and silly personality was, in reality, an overcompensation for feelings of doubt and guilt over her estranged relationships with her father and sister. Then DeFalco and Frenz crafted a story where they reveal that Mary Jane actually knew that Peter was secretly Spider-Man. "We wanted to get her to a point where the reader could admire her as a character," Frenz said.

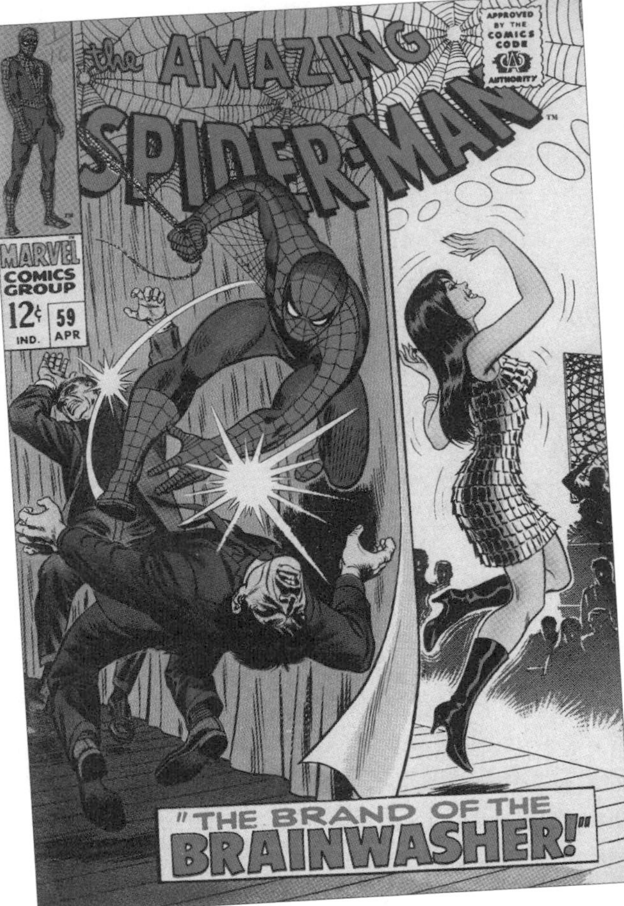

Amazing Spider-Man #59

Still, marrying Peter and MJ was not in the cards until 1986, when Marvel's editor-in-chief, Jim Shooter, mandated a special event where Peter and MJ would tie the knot. The story was going to coincide with the daily newspaper comic strip that was written by Lee. The only catch was that Peter and Mary Jane were actually a couple in the strip, making their marriage a logical next step. In the mainstream comic book universe, Peter was still technically dating the Black Cat, so he broke things off with her in favor of "someone to talk to, someone who knows me as well as I know myself. And someone I can talk to about Spider-Man!"[133]

Creators manning the Spider-Man ship had a new frontier in front of them: how to write a married superhero. Writer David Michelinie, who was opposed to the wedding, figured he'd make the best of it by depicting MJ as being level-headed and reasonable about her husband's superhero double life.[134] But others weren't so open-minded. Following Michelinie's departure from *Amazing* in the early '90s, there was an overwhelming concern throughout Marvel that a married Peter/MJ would age Spider-Man and make him less relatable.

As part of the "Clone Saga" in the mid-90s, Mary Jane became pregnant and Marvel planned on having her and Peter leave the books to start their family, while Peter's long-lost clone would return and assume the mantel of being Spider-Man. However, that storyline was later scrapped and the Parker child was kidnapped (and presumably killed off) putting Marvel back in the same situation it was trying to avoid. A few years later, Mary Jane was seemingly killed off in a plane crash, but even the creators working on the various Spider-books didn't truly believe that Marvel would stick to that status quo. "The death of Mary Jane, it's an event, it's a thing that happens," said Paul Jenkins, who scripted *Peter Parker: Spider-Man* in the early 2000s when MJ was still initially presumed dead. "You can't really get rid of [Peter's] wife because you will need her at some point…so the death has no meaning."[135]

Beyond the difficulties in breaking the two up for the long-term, Marvel also had to contend with Mary Jane being depicted as Peter's one true love in other comic book series and related media. In Marvel's *Ultimate Spider-Man* series, which takes place on a different timeline, MJ is presented as Peter's high school best friend and later girlfriend, with whom he shares everything. Then in Sam Raimi's *Spider-Man* trilogy in the 2000s, which was loosely adapted from *Ultimate*, Peter's affection for MJ (played by Kirsten Dunst) was a driving force behind the film series' narrative. Raimi went so far as to say that even if Peter wasn't a superhero, his movies still would have worked as "just a love story with Mary Jane Watson."[136]

Marvel finally had a way out in the mid-2000s thanks to the machinations developed by its then-editor-in-chief, Joe Quesada, along with a number of other editors, writers, and executives. In 2007, Marvel published "One More Day," which saw Peter and Mary Jane agree to have the devilish Mephisto eliminate their marriage from existence (as if it never happened) in exchange for saving the life of Peter's Aunt May. By this point of the character's existence, it was obviously an unpopular choice to take Mary Jane away from Peter. However, outside of a few cameos, she and Peter remained separate until 2009's *Amazing Spider-Man #600*. For the years that followed, Marvel teased a few reunions and even released a series set in an "alternative" timeline where Peter and MJ were still married with a child, but in terms of the company's "mainstream" continuity, Quesada's "One More Day" mandate has held firm.

20 Gwen Stacy

Spider-Man has been a part of many watershed moments in comic book history, but there are two in particular that have truly defined the character for readers: the death of Peter Parker/Spider-Man's Uncle Ben in *Amazing Fantasy #15*, and the death of Peter's college sweetheart, Gwen Stacy, in *Amazing Spider-Man #121*.

The impact of Uncle Ben's death is obvious: it's the seminal moment in Spider-Man's origin story that marked the main character's transformation from a guy with powers to an actual superhero when he learns the lesson, "with great power, there must also come great responsibility." But the ramifications of Gwen's

The Radioactive Spider-Gwen

After being relegated to being the ultimate damsel in distress for years, in 2014, Marvel decided to offer readers a new spin on Gwen Stacy by giving her the proportionate speed and strength of a spider and allowing her to kick butt as an alternative universe take on Spider-Woman.

This superheroine, dubbed by many fans as "Spider-Gwen," was first introduced in *Edge of Spider-Verse #2*, a miniseries featuring one-off stories that tied into a larger Spider-Man-centric event, "Spider-Verse." While planning the storyline—which depicts every Spider-Man from every universe/timeline joining together to fight a larger-than-life foe—Spider-office editor Nick Lowe and *Amazing Spider-Man* writer Dan Slott pitched the idea of a new version of Spider-Woman portrayed by Gwen. Writer Jason Latour and artist Robbi Rodriguez took the reins from there and transformed Gwen from the "girlfriend" to a slang-talking drummer in an all-girl rock band (called the Mary Janes), who dons a neo-punk-inspired white hoodie/mask combo to become Spider-Woman. The character was an instant success with a *Spider-Gwen* ongoing series launching in 2015. "Gwen had been a plot point," Latour said. "We wanted her to stand on her own two feet and have her own personality."[140]

death are rawer and cut deeper than Ben's. With Gwen—who was murdered when she was knocked off the top of a bridge by Spider-Man's mortal enemy, the Green Goblin—her death has come to represent a loss of innocence for Peter, and for superhero comics as a whole. Her death also marks the moment where Peter learned that, regardless of his great powers and responsibility, he was still capable of failing. As Gwen tumbled off the top of the bridge toward the water below, Spider-Man managed to snag her leg with his webbing before she made impact. However, the force of Spider-Man's webbing ensnaring Gwen while she was in free-fall also snapped her neck. There was no discernible way for Spider-Man to win and save the day, and it's a situation that would haunt Peter for years to come.

Gwen was first introduced in *Amazing Spider-Man #31* during the latter stages of the Stan Lee/Steve Ditko creative run on the book. In her first few appearances, Gwen was depicted as being more of an icy queen-bee type, but her character got both a physical and a personality makeover when Ditko left Marvel and John Romita Sr. took over on pencils on *Amazing*. Under Lee/Romita, Gwen become more glamorous and soon started dating Peter, a status quo that would last for a number of years, despite the fact that Peter was always juggling his secret superhero life with his social life. The couple briefly had a falling out after Gwen blamed Spider-Man for the death of her father—who was killed by falling debris from a fight between Spidey and Doc Ock. But Peter/Gwen were otherwise inseparable until a young writer in his early twenties named Gerry Conway conspired with Romita and editor Roy Thomas to change the industry forever.

Conway and Romita both felt that *Amazing Spider-Man* was getting stale and that the book desperately needed a shake-up. After tossing around a few ideas, Conway pitched killing off Gwen to "add an extra layer of horror to the life of a superhero." After getting Romita and Thomas's blessing and running the idea by Lee (who apparently approved it before walking the decision back and saying he didn't realize just how serious his creators were about killing off a major character), Gwen took her fatal tumble off a bridge in 1973.[137] Conway received an enormous amount of vitriol for the storyline, but more than 40 years later, he still stands by it: "Gwen was more memorable after she was killed," he said. Before her death, "she was a white bread, bland character."[138]

It's absolutely true that Gwen's death elevated the character. "The Night Gwen Stacy Died" storyline is considered so monumental, some comic book historians have dubbed it the unofficial "end" of the Silver Age of comics, which began in the late 1950s. Additionally, Gwen's final scene has been replayed or visually referenced numerous times over in comics, movies and other media.

The character has appeared in a whole score of flashback tales (and even appeared as a clone in a later Conway story in the '70s). Marvel even created an entire miniseries around the Peter/Gwen glory years of teen love with Jeph Loeb and Tim Sale's *Spider-Man: Blue* in the early 2000s.

Cinematically, the character was more of an afterthought during the Sam Raimi *Spider-Man* movie trilogy, with the red-headed Bryce Dallas Howard donning a blonde wig to play Gwen in a tertiary role in 2007's *Spider-Man 3*. However, the character reached a whole new audience starting in 2012, when rising Hollywood star Emma Stone brought a kittenish swagger to Gwen in Marc Webb's *The Amazing Spider-Man* franchise. Critics frequently highlighted Stone's performance as the best part of the two Webb movies, and the talented actress even made one longtime critic of Gwen heap some praise upon the character: "Emma Stone has made her an interesting character," Conway said. "She's witty. She's sharp. She's gorgeous but self-confident...she's Mary Jane!"[139]

21 Must Read: "The Night Gwen Stacy Died" (*Amazing Spider-Man* #121–122)

"The Night Gwen Stacy Died," is just a run-of-the-mill two-parter where nothing major happens—unless you count the death of a significant supporting character and the end of the age of innocence in superhero comics as something major.

Yeah, this 1973 story by Gerry Conway and Gil Kane is pretty important. In one fell swoop, Conway and Kane (with input from Marvel's art director John Romita and editor-in-chief Roy Thomas) effectively ended the "Silver Age" of comics by killing off Peter Parker/Spider-Man's love interest, Gwen Stacy, paving the road for the darker and grittier Bronze Age. Prior to this story, it was unthinkable to kill the hero's main love interest. And yet, in the final climactic pages of *Amazing Spider-Man #121*, Gwen is tossed off a bridge by Spidey's nemesis, the Green Goblin. If that's not bad enough, Spider-Man actually *fails* in trying to save her, when the fateful comic book panel suggests the webbing he shoots to break Gwen's fall and snag her actually inadvertently snaps her neck. A note from Thomas inserted in *Amazing #125*'s "The Spider's Web" letters page even confirms this horrible, horrible fact: "It saddens us to have to say that the whiplash effect she underwent when Spidey's webbing stopped her so suddenly was, in fact, what killed her."[141] Woof. Talk about a downer.

Such a story obviously caused quite the controversy for its creators. Interestingly, one of the people most upset by Gwen's death was Marvel's publisher (and Spider-Man's co-creator) Stan Lee. Conway, Romita, and Thomas have said on multiple occasions that they cleared the traumatic plot point with Lee before running with it, but Lee has always maintained an "I didn't know *that's* how they were going to do it" attitude about the whole thing, leading to some general awkwardness for everyone involved.[142] Readers were even less understanding. Conway got hate mail and threats at conventions for years following the story.[143]

Lost in the shuffle of this arc's controversy and historical significance for the industry is the fact that "The Night Gwen Stacy Died" is a really compelling story that shakes up Peter/Spider-Man's life in a way that few other stories had done before, or since. After absorbing the initial shock of his girlfriend's death, Spider-Man sets out to exact vengeance on the man responsible—Norman Osborn, aka the Green Goblin. During his epic confrontation with the Goblin, Spider-Man beats the villain within an inch of his life before pulling back at the last possible second and sparing him. It's a character-defining sequence that demonstrates how Peter's morality and his choice to always use his great power responsibly

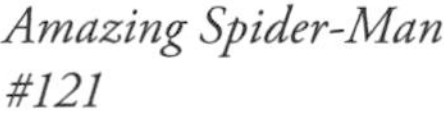

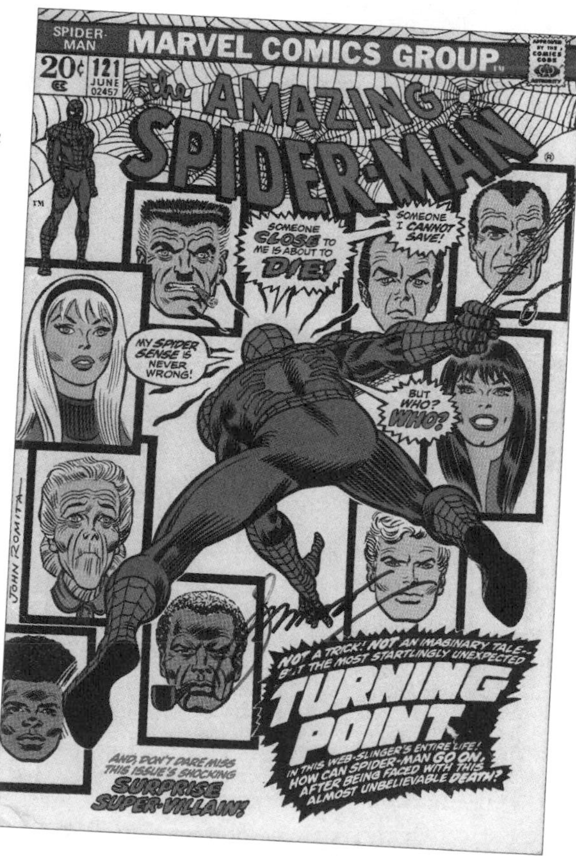

Amazing Spider-Man #121

can apply even when fueled with so much justifiable hate and desire for vengeance.

Still, in a cruel twist of irony, Osborn is apparently killed anyway when he is accidentally impaled by his glider device (the scene inspired a nearly note-for-note sequence in Sam Raimi's first *Spider-Man* film in 2002). Granted, Osborn would be resurrected years later as part of the '90's "Clone Saga" storyline (a development that still doesn't sit right with many at Marvel), but similar to what happened to Gwen, at the time this story was published, it was a total shock for a major villain to bite the dust with such seeming finality.

And then there's the "epilogue" page in *Amazing #122*, which set the table for another relationship that is critical to the Spider-Man mythos. Peter returns to his apartment after Osborn's death and finds Mary Jane Watson waiting for him. At this point, MJ was cast more as a party girl rather than someone the reader should take seriously. However, Mary Jane pledges to comfort Peter in his darkest hour, even after Peter initially tells her to go away and leave him alone.[144] While the two would eventually enter into a romantic relationship and even marry (well…until that whole thing gets washed away by the devil, but that's a story for another chapter), Conway has said that his intention wasn't to plant seeds for a new love for Peter, but rather, "I didn't want to leave this storyline with no hope for Peter."[145] In that regard, the scene hits its notes beautifully and also marks the beginning of MJ's transition from a shallow flirt to one of comics' most balanced and well-developed female characters.

Meanwhile, it's difficult for even modern readers of Spider-Man comics to get through an entire storyline without the events of *Amazing #121–122* being referenced in some fashion. Even cinematically, the arc is referenced in *Spider-Man* and is later repackaged as being essential to the events of 2014's *The Amazing Spider-Man 2* film. That's why there's no question as to why "The Night Gwen Stacy Died" is required reading for anyone looking to make that deep dive into Spider-Man fandom.

Now somebody get me a box of tissues.

22 Venom/Eddie Brock

Peter Parker was a bullied teenager who became Spider-Man. Venom was his dark and twisted opposite: a man who got Spider-Man's powers and became the ultimate Spider-bully.

Created by David Michelinie and Todd McFarlane, Venom first appeared in the landmark *Amazing Spider-Man #300* and was immensely popular from jump street. He marked the psychotic marriage of the black alien costume that Peter had rejected back in *Amazing Spider-Man #258* and a news reporter named Eddie Brock, who blamed Spider-Man for ruining his career and life.

Michelinie had actually been laying the groundwork for the character that would become Venom a few years earlier during his run writing *Web of Spider-Man*. In *Web of #18*, Peter was pushed in front of an oncoming subway train by a mysterious hand that didn't set off his danger-warning spider-sense. When Marvel's editorial group demanded a special new villain for *Amazing #300*, Michelinie talked with McFarlane, who let his wild imagination take hold: "I've always had an affinity for monsters, so I wondered if the alien costume was more like a shell that sort of swallowed the man," McFarlane said.[146]

Venom's debut included him showing up at Peter's home and scaring the bejeezus out of his wife, Mary Jane. In the same issue, the reader learns why Venom hates Spider-Man: the "Web-Slinger" destroyed Brock's journalism career by inadvertently discrediting a news story he wrote about the identity of a masked villain known as the Sin-Eater. When Brock debates suicide in a church, the alien symbiote swallows him and transforms him into the muscle-bound baddie.[147]

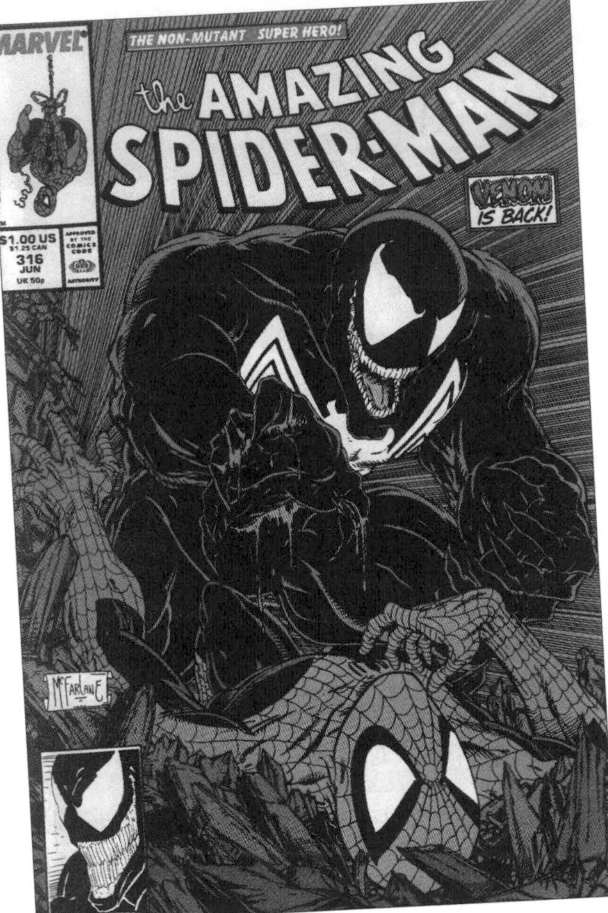

Amazing Spider-Man #316

Venom can do everything a spider can without setting off Spider-Man's spider-sense, making him extra difficult for Spidey to fight. And he even knows Spider-Man's civilian identity thanks to the alien symbiote, which had spent some time getting to know Peter. The villain's only weaknesses are high-frequency sounds like church bells, or fire.

However, as deranged as Venom might be, he also has a unique moral code that sets him apart from other villains. Venom often bemoans the death of "innocents" (e.g., security guards or other law

The Original Venom

Before he was all about brawn and eating brains, Venom was actually a she. When writer David Michelinie first started developing his Venom character in the '80s, he thought up an entirely different origin story from the one that would go on to be used for Eddie Brock. Michelinie's original Venom was a woman who was driven mad after she goes into labor and her husband is killed while hailing down a taxi cab to take her to the hospital. The woman has a miscarriage and goes into a catatonic state. Because the driver was distracted by a Spider-Man fight, the woman blames Spidey for all of her misfortune. She eventually bonds with the symbiote and Venom is created.[151]

Marvel's editors eventually shot down the idea in favor of a more "traditional" supervillain. But considering Marvel's current desire to reflect the diversity of its readership by featuring more female and minority characters in the comics, who knows what could have been if Venom had debuted today?

enforcement officials) who get caught in the crossfire of his battles with Spider-Man. He's even willing to join forces with Spider-Man to take on an even more sinister threat in Carnage, the result of Venom's symbiote "spawning" and merging with a serial killer, giving him super powers.

Venom's earliest appearances were treated as unique events by Marvel, who knew they had hit upon something special with the villain. However, once the industry entered the '90s, when sales often took priority over artistic merit, Venom was used everywhere. He even starred in his first of many solo books in 1993. "I was surprised by Venom's popularity," Michelinie said. "I just wrote a character that I thought would be a cool character that I would enjoy writing."[148] Michelinie knew that the character was becoming overexposed, but no one at Marvel seemed willing to reconsider saturating the market with Venom-centric content.[149] It also didn't help that Venom's character had started to change from a nuanced, moralistic monster to a two-dimensional caricature that had an odd fascination with devouring Spider-Man's brains and organs.

Marvel finally appeared ready to admit it had a Venom problem by the 2000s and a number of storylines intended to revamp the character followed suit. In '03, a *Spectacular Spider-Man* story arc that showed the alien symbiote had given Brock cancer, which was followed by a '04 *Marvel Knights: Spider-Man* story where, to pay for his treatments, Brock sells the symbiote to Mac Gargan, who had spent a number of years as the costumed villain known as the Scorpion. A few years after that, Brock reemerged as Anti-Venom, an antihero who used his "touch" to erase the powers of other supercharged characters. Meanwhile, after Gargan, the symbiote bounced around, eventually bonding to Peter's old high school bully, Flash Thompson, making him "Agent Venom," a government mercenary.

In other media, Venom has been a prominent part of numerous Spider-Man animated series and in 2007's *Spider-Man 3*, he got the big-screen treatment, being played by Topher Grace. More recently, Sony has toyed around with the idea of launching a Venom solo film, first announcing its intentions to do so prior to the release of 2014's *The Amazing Spider-Man 2* and then claiming it was still exploring the possibility of a Venom movie despite the fact that it had cut a deal with Marvel Studios to share Spider-Man as part of the Marvel Cinematic Universe.[150]

23 The Sinister Six

Things are bad enough for Spider-Man whenever he has to face one of his rogues. But six bloodthirsty, super-powered thugs at the same time? That's a truly sinister development for the "Web-Slinger."

In 1964's *Amazing Spider-Man Annual #1*, Stan Lee and Steve Ditko introduced one of comic's original supervillain supergroups:

The Superior Six

Like buffoonish yet lovable bad guys masquerading as one of the Marvel Universe's most notorious supergroups? Then look no further than the cult hit of 2013–14, *Superior Foes of Spider-Man.* Created by Nick Spencer and Steve Lieber as a spinoff to the *Superior Spider-Man* mega-hit, *Superior Foes* ran for 17 comedically sublime issues and featured lifetime loser Fred Meyers, aka Boomerang, leading a ragtag crew of Overdrive, Beetle, Shocker, and Speed Demon (yes, that's five people) in a "new and improved" version of the Sinister Six.

The book mostly functioned as an extended caper that saw Boomerang constantly trying to sabotage his teammates in the pursuit of absurd artifacts, like the disembodied head of crime-boss Silvio Manfredi and a portrait of Victor Von Doom's maskless face (Doom allegedly asked his artist to "draw Doom like one of your French girls").[155] Spencer's original pitch was for a series to be told from the perspective of Spider-Man's "working-class bad guys."[156] While some creators might have resisted taking on a book that intentionally featured less-popular, D-list characters, Spencer and Lieber relished having the artistic freedom to work on a series that Marvel's editorial powers frankly paid little attention to: "This was all about what's the weirdest thing I can think of, and bam, that's what I would turn in," Lieber said.[157]

the Sinister Six. In its original incarnation, this unholy alliance of a half dozen Spidey enemies included Doctor Octopus, Electro, Mysterio, Sandman, Kraven the Hunter, and the Vulture—all adversaries that were introduced by Lee and Ditko within the first 15 issues of *Amazing Spider-Man.* The assembly of evil proved to be the ultimate test for Marvel's most iconic underdog hero, even if the Sinister Six undermined its advantage by electing to fight Spider-Man one-on-one rather than all at once.

After Spider-Man's initial battle with the Six, it took nearly 30 years before Marvel revived the concept for a Spider-Man story. "The Return of the Sinister Six" was published in 1990 in *Amazing #334–339* (six issues, natch) with David Michelinie on scripts and Erik Larsen on pencils. Michelinie and Larsen introduced a couple of twists on the original Sinister Six story: for one, Kraven, who had committed suicide at the end of the legendary "Kraven's Last Hunt" arc a few years earlier, had been replaced with the Hobgoblin (Michelinie originally sought to use Harry Osborn's Green Goblin but was told he was unavailable).[152]

And this time around, the Sandman was an unwilling participant in Doc Ock's plans, since the character had evolved from just another rogue into a more reformed "hero for hire" who was employed by Silver Sable's Wild Pack, and even lasted one hot minute on the Avengers. The success of the Six's "return" led to another arc a few years later that was scripted and penciled by Larsen in the "adjective-less" *Spider-Man* series. This time around, Spidey teamed up with a hodgepodge of '90s-ified heroes including Ghost Rider, Nova, and Deathlok.

The team would transcend the "mainstream" Marvel universe and get a makeover for the alternative timeline *Ultimate* universe for the *Ultimate Six* miniseries. For this incarnation, Norman Osborn, aka the Green Goblin, led a team of villains that were birthed out of other Oscorp experiments. The series is also notable for being an early team-up between Spider-Man, S.H.I.E.L.D., and the *Ultimate* universe's version of the Avengers, the Ultimates (something to keep in mind for future big-screen fodder now that Spidey and the Avengers share a cinematic universe together).

Meanwhile, in regular Marvel continuity, the Six would grow into a Sinister 12 in the Mark Millar-scripted *Marvel Knights: Spider-Man* series, before current *Amazing Spider-Man* writer Dan Slott would bring a sense of stability to the team with a membership that included a dying Doctor Octopus, alongside Electro, Sandman, Mysterio, Rhino, and Chameleon. The arc for Slott's Sinister Six culminated with 2012's "Ends of the Earth," which depicted the team attempting to take over the world by speeding up the greenhouse effect and cooking the earth.

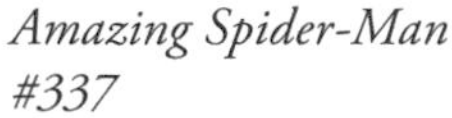
Amazing Spider-Man #337

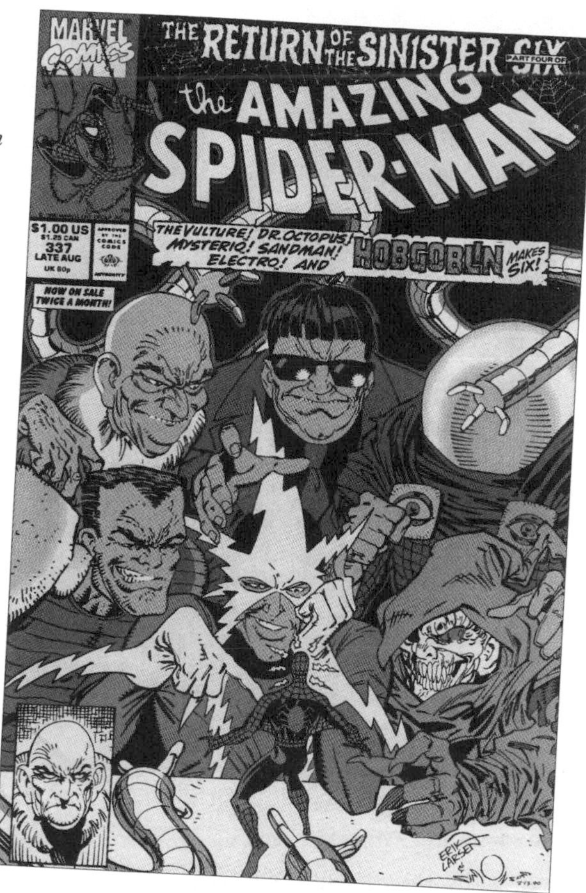

Demonstrating that it's difficult to resist such an awesome assembly of evil, the Sinister Six have played a prominent role in other elements of the Spider-Man Universe, namely television. In the mid-90s, *Spider-Man: The Animated Series* featured the "Insidious Six" with a lineup that included Doc Ock, Mysterio, Rhino, Scorpion, Shocker, and Chameleon (frequently recurring members Sandman and Electro were apparently off-limits for the show since both were being considered for James Cameron's never-to-be-seen Spider-Man film).[153] The Six also frequently antagonized Spider-Man in 2009's *Spectacular Spider-Man* and the recently concluded *Ultimate Spider-Man* series.

In 2013, Sony Pictures announced its intention to bring the Sinister Six to the big screen as a *The Amazing Spider-Man* spinoff project. *The Amazing Spider-Man 2* certainly lays the groundwork for the team to appear, with Easter eggs including visuals of the Vulture's wings and Doc Ock's mechanical arms. Drew Goddard, who wrote the screenplay for the 2015 film *The Martian* and is the lead writer and showrunner for Marvel's *Daredevil* series on Netflix, was tapped to direct the *Sinister Six* film. However, once Marvel Studios and Sony cut a deal to bring Spider-Man into the shared cinematic universe with the Avengers, any forward momentum for a Sinister Six film came to a halt.[154]

24 Harry Osborn

With friends like Harry Osborn, who needs enemies? Created by Stan Lee and Steve Ditko in 1965's *Amazing Spider-Man #31*, Osborn has long been one of the most complicated and interesting supporting cast members in the Spider-Man universe. He is the son of Spider-Man's greatest enemy, Norman Osborn, the original Green Goblin. But he is also a close confidante of Spider-Man's civilian alter-ego, Peter Parker, and is often referred to as Peter's "best friend." They were even roommates for a number of years. However, after the death of Harry's father during a battle with Spider-Man, the character began his own descent into madness, which ended with him emerging as the second Green Goblin to do battle with his best-friend-turned-enemy, Peter/Spidey.

"That tension between those two things made such great stories," said longtime Spider-Man writer J.M. DeMatteis, who scripted a number of classic Peter/Harry tales, including the fan

How Green Are These Goblins?

Norman and Harry Osborn are the two characters most closely associated with being Spider-Man's greatest villain, the Green Goblin, but here are a few others who have donned the purple and green over the years:

Bart Hamilton: Harry's psychiatrist actually had aspirations of becoming a criminal kingpin, becoming Marvel's third Green Goblin in a run of issues found in *Amazing Spider-Man #174–180.*

Phil Urich: In the mid-90s, Urich, nephew of *Daily Bugle* reporter Ben Urich, becomes the Green Goblin as a way to serve New York City as a masked vigilante hero, à la Spider-Man. Urich later becomes the masked villain, the Hobgoblin.

Normie Osborn: While there was always something suspicious about Harry's toddler child, in the alternative universe *Spider-Girl* series, Normie fulfills his family's destiny by becoming the Green Goblin and vowing a war against all Parkers.

favorite "Best of Enemies" in *Spectacular Spider-Man #200,* which ended with Harry's (temporary) death.[158] Even Harry's earliest appearances in the comics were marked by his love/hate dynamic with Peter and his estranged relationship with his father. With Peter, Harry initially mistook his college classmate's shyness (not to mention his double life as a superhero) as snobbishness. Meanwhile, Norman resented his son when his wife died following Harry's birth.

Harry's emotional frailties were first put on display as part of the landmark storyline in *Amazing Spider-Man #96–98,* when he becomes addicted to psychedelic drugs. The arc is considered a major turning point in comic book history because the issues are the first mainstream comics to not feature a seal of approval from the Comics Code Authority, due to their depiction of drug use. Marvel took a major risk in publishing the stories without the code's seal, since it could have potentially limited the comic's distribution to vendors.

Marvel revisited Harry's drug issues in *Amazing #121* when his relapse triggers a sociopathic episode from his father, who then sets out to exact vengeance against Peter by killing his girlfriend, Gwen Stacy. Norman is killed one issue later. Harry immediately blames Spider-Man for his father's death, and when he discovers a Spidey costume in Peter's bedroom, he has all the evidence he needs to put two and two together and launch a full-on attack against his ex-best friend by becoming the new Green Goblin. "Relationships are complicated," said Gerry Conway, who wrote the death of Gwen/Norman, and then Harry's heel turn in *Amazing #136–137*. "People who are closest to you can be very threatening, because they know you and know how to hurt you."[159]

Harry's time as the Goblin is short-lived and, after a bout of amnesia, he gets back on the straight and narrow when he marries Peter's high school friend, Liz Allan, and the two have a child, Normie. But the peace was relatively short-lived. In the 1990s, DeMatteis scripted "The Child Within," which analyzed the psychological implications of Norman's abuse of Harry, while also exposing Peter's own self-esteem issues due to his feelings of abandonment from the deaths of his parents. This emotionally rich story climaxes in *Spectacular Spider-Man #200* when Harry, as the Green Goblin again, traps Spider-Man inside of a building rigged to explode, before having one last moral epiphany and saving Peter (and his own soul), sacrificing his life in the process.

Harry's death lasted more than a decade, before the character was mysteriously resurrected as part of the "Brand New Day" initiative in *Amazing Spider-Man* in 2008. As part of that arc, Peter's marriage to Mary Jane Watson was magically wiped from existence, which inexplicably led to Harry's return, coupled with a story that he didn't actually die, but was sent over to Europe by his father (who inexplicably returned in the comics in the mid-90s) to clean up his act. Harry's return to Spider-Man comics also saw a revival of his cold war with his father, though his feud with Peter/Spider-Man was seemingly put to bed.

Reflecting how important the character is to the Spider-Man mythos, over the years, Harry has frequently been featured as one of the main players in other Spidey media. Award-winning actor James Franco portrayed Harry in Sam Raimi's three *Spider-Man* movies in the 2000s, which tracked the trajectory of Osborn's path from friend to villain to friend again. When the film franchise was rebooted, Dale DeHaan played Harry in 2014's *The Amazing Spider-Man 2,* where the character became the Green Goblin.

25 Eugene "Flash" Thompson

Listen up, ya wimps. It's time to stop hearing all about "Puny Parker" and instead focus on the real star (in his own mind) of the Spider-Man universe, Eugene "Flash" Thompson. Flash is the classic high school bully antagonist, who was apparently even modeled after some jerk that Spider-Man's original artist, Steve Ditko, knew from childhood.[160] Created by Stan Lee and Ditko, Flash appears on the very first page of the very first appearance of Spider-Man, *Amazing Fantasy #15*. In the iconic splash page, Thompson mocks the lonely outcast Peter for not knowing a "cha cha from a waltz."[161] Even then, the burns were sick.

Flash would continue to taunt Peter all through the Lee/Ditko run on *Amazing Spider-Man*. Making things even more complicated for the hero was the fact that Flash was just a mouthy kid and Peter could never get his revenge for fear of his spider-powers sending his classmate to the hospital. Still, in a twist of irony, despite his animosity for Peter, Flash was also Spider-Man's biggest champion and was even self-proclaimed president of the Spider-Man Fan Club. "He's just the greatest guy in the world!" Flash would tell any of his classmates who thought otherwise of the masked "Wall Crawler."[162]

As was the case with most of Peter's relationships with his high school and college peers, Flash and Peter started to get along a bit better once Ditko left *Amazing Spider-Man* and John Romita Sr. started collaborating with Lee. At that point, the series read more like a teen dramedy a la *Archie*. In a sign of how comics were starting to better reflect the events from the real world, Flash enlisted in the U.S. Army and was deployed to Vietnam during the late 1960s. By the time Thompson returned from his tour of duty, he and Peter had evolved from adversaries to frenemies to legitimate friends.

Flash remained a tertiary character in Spider-Man/Peter's orbit throughout the most of the '70s and '80s, outside of a few brief runs of issues, like when he was mistakenly believed to be the supervillain the Hobgoblin in the mid-80s. In the '90s, writer J.M. DeMatteis decided to look "for a door into Flash's psyche" by writing a series of stories that explored Thompson's struggles with alcohol abuse. "It was a way to deepen and humanize him," DeMatteis said. This storyline has remained a key part of Flash's biography ever since.[163]

The character was humanized even further during the landmark 2008 issue of *Amazing Spider-Man*, "Flashbacks." Written by Marc Guggenheim with art by Barry Kitson, *Amazing #574* sets Flash back in the Army, this time as a soldier in the U.S.-Iraq war. Flash valiantly goes back to save an injured soldier while under heavy fire from insurgents. Drawing inspiration from his hero Spider-Man, Flash rescues his friend despite being in immense pain from the enemy's attack. At the end of the issue, the reader learns that Flash had lost his legs. While being interviewed for consideration for a prestigious Medal of Honor, Thompson tells the general, "I don't need a medal, sir. Not to remind me to do the right thing, at least. Truth is, I've been lucky to know people whose example reminds me every day."[164]

In an effort to make the story "feel real," Guggenheim actually worked with a soldier who had served in Iraq, so that comic was both authentic and respectful to the very real dangers and tragedies American troops were experiencing in the Middle East. The soldier, Jeff Guerin, received a special thank you from the Spider-office in *Amazing #574*'s letters page.[165]

Flash's plight and struggle served as the impetus for a very unexpected status quo shift for the character in 2011. Marvel had once again relaunched *Venom* in his own solo comic book series. But rather than having it star Eddie Brock or some other villain as the titular character, Flash was the focus. Thompson was bonded to the erratic alien symbiote as part of a covert government program. The symbiote (temporarily) gives Flash his legs back and augments his overall strength and agility. However, given Thompson's previous issues with substance abuse, he eventually starts using the symbiote like a drug, suiting up around the clock despite the fact that he's under orders to only use the alien costume for his missions.

Reflecting his importance to Spider-Man/Peter's story, Flash Thompson has been depicted in other media, covering comics, animation, and movies. In Sam Raimi's *Spider-Man* film series, the character was played by a young Joe Manganiello (of *True Blood* fame). Chris Zylka portrayed Flash in 2012's *The Amazing Spider-Man*, directed by Marc Webb, and Tony Revolori will bring Eugene to life in 2017's *Spider-Man: Homecoming*.

26 Must Read: "Spider-Man No More" (*Amazing Spider-Man #50*)

Stop me if you've heard this before (in this book alone, I'm about to make this reference for approximately the 26th time): the core moral of Spider-Man is how Peter Parker learns that with great power must also come great responsibility.

"Spider-Man No More," which was created by Stan Lee and John Romita Sr., and was published in 1967, is the comic book antidote to "power" and "responsibility." It's a story about Peter getting fed up with the responsibilities that come with his great power, so he decides to forget all about that being Spider-Man stuff and instead opts to live the life of a normal teenager—taking care of his sickly aunt, excelling in school (as he should), and catching the eye of his beautiful and brilliant classmate, Gwen Stacy.

Of course, this seismic shift in *Amazing Spider-Man's* status quo was short-lived. But what makes this issue such an essential read for any Spidey fan is how Lee and Romita chart Peter's journey from hero, to quitter, to hero again. It's a joyful ride that only helps drive the larger narrative that Peter/Spider-Man is the most relatable superhero in comics, while also containing a compelling lesson at the end that plays to that ol' power and responsibility theme.

From a purely procedural perspective, *Amazing #50* is also significant in that it marks the first appearance of one of comic's greatest rogues, the rotund Wilson Fisk, better known as the Kingpin. And who can forget that striking cover image of a dejected Peter Parker, walking toward the reader while an illustration of Spider-Man, back turned, ominously looks back at him in disappointment? Even the most casual of comic book readers will probably recognize the cover image since it's been referenced so

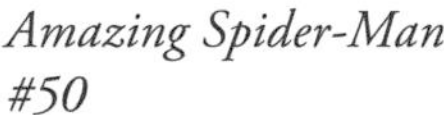
Amazing Spider-Man #50

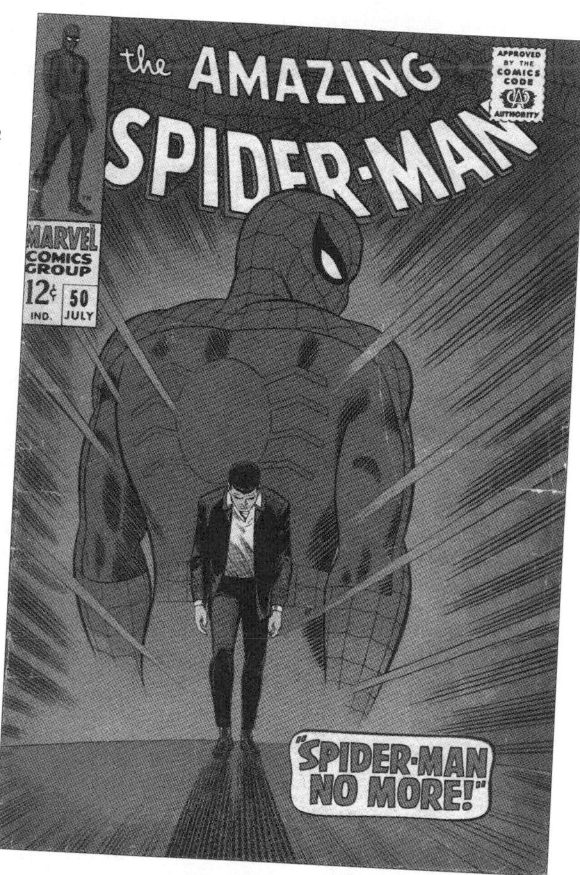

many times since *Amazing #50* was first published 50 years ago. It's easy to lose track of who paid homage to it last.

The comic marks Lee at his absolute schmaltziest—and that's a good thing. The story just wouldn't work without Lee's melodramatic script selling every one of Peter's Spider-Man-caused shortcomings as being similar to a shotgun blast to the chest. His Aunt May is sick, he doesn't have time for a real job, and he can't go to Gwen's party, all because he's too busy being Spider-Man. So he concludes that the only way he can make something out of himself is to just quit the superhero business cold turkey, responsibilities be damned. Peter stuffs his Spidey suit in a garbage can in an interior visual that's almost as famous as the cover. And with that, Spider-Man is "no more."

Naturally, for Peter, as Michael Corleone would say, "Just when I thought I was out, they pull me back in." Despite having the time of his life, doing things like taking Gwen for a spin on his motorbike, while walking by a warehouse, Peter hears those

Spider-Man No More, No More, No More...

Okay, Spider-Man might be known for his perseverance and unbreakable spirit, but the guy has quit more than your average hero. In addition to "Spider-Man No More," here are a few more memorable instances where Spidey hung up the webs:

"The Original End of Spider-Man" (*Amazing Spider-Man #17–19*): While fighting the Green Goblin, Peter overhears that his Aunt May has fallen ill, so he leaves mid-strike to look after her and is labeled a coward. He eventually becomes Spider-Man again after May gives an impassioned speech about Parkers having "gumption."

Amazing Spider-Man #100: In Spidey's first-ever special centennial issue, Peter decides that after his alter-ego is blamed for the death of Gwen Stacy's father, it's time to hang up the webs. He has his scientist friend/sometimes adversary Curt Connors (the Lizard) develop a serum that would remove his powers. Unfortunately, the serum transforms Peter into a six-armed "spider" man.

"The Clone Saga" (*Spectacular Spider-Man #229*): The original plan for this sprawling story was for Peter's clone from the 1970s to return and eventually be proven to be the real-deal Spider-Man. As a result, Peter and his pregnant wife, Mary Jane, head out to the West Coast to live a normal life and the clone, Ben Reilly, assumes the power and responsibility from Peter. This story was overturned about a year later and the clone was killed off.

"The Final Chapter" (*Spectacular Spider-Man #263*): Norman Osborn goes crazy again and while fighting Spider-Man, the *Daily Bugle* building collapses. Newspaper publisher/editor (and swell guy) J. Jonah Jameson blames Spider-Man for the whole thing and, in a fit of rage, Spidey quits. The entire line of spider-books is then rebooted and Peter is back to being Spider-Man by issue number two of the reboot.

tragically familiar cries for help that cause him to rush back into action. On the roof, he finds an old man getting hassled by crooks, who he realizes reminds him of his deceased Uncle Ben—someone Peter could have saved if he just acted selflessly and apprehended a thief that ran by him one day (the same crook who killed his uncle). And thus, Spider-Man is "back" and the world (and Wilson Fisk) better look out!

Winner of best supporting actor for this story is *Daily Bugle* publisher/editor J. Jonah Jameson. In many ways, "Spider-Man No More" is as much his story as Peter's. For years, Jameson has dogged Spider-Man as a masked menace who warrants vilification. When someone brings that discarded Spidey suit to Jameson's office, the man becomes overwhelmed by a euphoric sense of glee and accomplishment. He has *finally* defeated Spider-Man. This is a very personal victory for "Jolly Jonah," who has set out to tear down Spider-Man since the hero's earliest days. Then to watch that smug grin get knocked off Jameson's face when Spidey snatches his costume back from Jonah's office—let's just say it's pure joy.

This story is so emotionally rich (and don't forget funny) that Sam Raimi built most of his script for *Spider-Man 2* (considered by most critics to be the greatest of all the *Spider-Man* films) around "Spider-Man No More"—all the way down to Peter dumping his costume in a garbage can and Jameson finding it and hanging it in his office like a trophy. Considering how so many superhero movie directors tend to shy away from shot-for-shot adaptations from the comics, seeing so much of *Amazing #50* up on the big screen in *Spider-Man 2* is a real joy for fans of this timeless classic of a story.

27 Best Frenemies Forever: Spider-Man and Human Torch

When Stan Lee was laying the foundation of the Marvel Universe in the early 1960s, one of the criticisms he frequently heard was how teenagers could never be leading superheroes and were strictly sidekicks to the "adults." Lee bucked that convention when he and Jack Kirby co-created Johnny Storm, aka the Human Torch, as one-quarter of the "first family of comics," the *Fantastic Four*, in 1961. And then Lee would do one better in the teenage hero department when he and Steve Ditko co-created Spider-Man in 1962.

In Lee's world of interconnected heroes and villains, Spider-Man and Human Torch were to interact early and often. However, rather than have the two young guys celebrate their awesomeness together over some chocolate malts at the drug store, Lee bucked convention yet again by depicting Spider-Man and Johnny as being fierce rivals who reluctantly worked together for the common good—leading to a character dynamic that has helped define both heroes to this day.

Spider-Man and Human Torch first teamed up in 1963's *Strange Tales Annual #2* (which features the holy grail of creative teams: story by Lee, pencils by Kirby, and inks by Ditko), a comic that, among other things, established the official "meeting spot" for Spider-Man and Johnny—the top of the Statue of Liberty. In all of these early meet-ups, a common theme emerged: Spider-Man thought Johnny was an arrogant, brash hothead who had the world handed to him on a silver platter, while Johnny thought Spider-Man was aloof and stuck up. The two were constantly trying to one-up and embarrass each other, regardless of how childish or petty they might appear to others. In many ways, it reflected a similar dynamic that was established between Peter Parker and his high school classmate/nemesis, Flash Thompson.

Eventually, the cold war between Spidey and Torch would start to thaw when creators transformed the contentiousness into a more "friendly rivalry" type of affair. Marvel launched its *Marvel Team-Up* series in 1972, initially as a vehicle for Spidey and Johnny to pair off every issue against a random villain-of-the-month, before the Torch was swapped out in favor of a different hero with Spidey every issue. That didn't prevent Spider-Man and Human Torch from showing up in each other's books. One of the more memorable meet-ups came in the mid-80s, when Spider-Man, in an effort to figure out why the black suit he had acquired on another planet was alive and trying to take control of his body (spoiler alert: it was an alien symbiote), seeks advice from the Fantastic Four. After

Logan's Heroes

While the Spider-Man/Human Torch love/hate relationship was all the rage throughout the 1960s, '70s, and '80s, more recently, Spider-Man has been reluctantly paired off with another Marvel superhero that he hates to love: the curmudgeonly sour-pussed mutant, Wolverine.

At least Spidey and Johnny Storm were both teenagers when they first met up. Spider-Man and Wolverine have absolutely nothing in common. In fact, in 1987's *Spider-Man vs. Wolverine*, the two attempt to kill each other after teaming up against an army of KGB assassins in Germany. However, the Spider-Man/Wolverine "relationship" (if there ever was one) took a definitive turn in the mid-2000s when Marvel unexpectedly placed both heroes on the *New Avengers* team. Since Spider-Man and Wolverine were both unlikely selections for the "Earth's Mightiest Heroes," Marvel was able to generate some easy comedy out of playing up Spider-Man and Wolverine's polarizing personalities amongst a team of more "traditional" heroes, creating the ultimate comic book odd couple.

"They're completely different personalities, so they act different. They stand different, they walk different, they talk different, they look different. But in a weird way...they don't get along but they kinda have to get along," said Adam Kubert, who illustrated the *Astonishing Spider-Man & Wolverine* series, which paired the two characters off in a time-traveling adventure in 2010-11.[168]

successfully battling the costume, Spider-Man is rendered clothesless, so he asks Johnny if he has something he can borrow. Johnny does what any smart-alecky kid would do, which is grab an old Fantastic Four costume and fashions a new mask for Spider-Man… out of a paper bag. For the icing on the humility cake, Johnny also applies a well-hidden "kick me" sign to Spidey's back. And thus the Amazing Bag-Man (a favorite of many well-humored cosplayers) is born.

The decades of bickering, fighting and pranks served as a major source of inspiration for 2005's *Spider-Man/Human Torch* miniseries, written by Dan Slott with art from Ty Templeton. Each issue of the series captures a different decade from the life of Spidey and Johnny, culminating with a present-day tale that shows Spider-Man finally unmasking and revealing his secret identity to his longtime rival. The story is a fan favorite and is considered by many critics and readers to be the story that demonstrated how Slott—the current *Amazing Spider-Man* writer—was an obvious heir apparent to write Spidey comics full-time. For Slott, he has long called the mini a fulfilling experience, telling interviewers "I would have been set" if *Spider-Man/Human Torch* was the only Spidey story he ever got to write.[166]

In one of the most surprising twists on the relationship to date, Spider-Man actually replaced Johnny as a member of the newly formed "Future Foundation" after Storm's presumed death in a 2011 issue of *Fantastic Four*. For nearly a year, Spidey suited up (in a totally new suit, no less) with Johnny's old teammates, Sue, Reed Richards, and the Thing, as a member of the FF. And in a scene that undoubtedly typifies how Peter and Johnny's friendship has both grown and remained the same, when Storm returns from the Negative Zone alive and well, the first thing he asks Spider-Man when he sees him in the costume is, "Peter, what the heck are you wearing?"[167]

28 The Vulture

Adrian Toomes is an old man with a bad attitude. Created by Stan Lee and Steve Ditko, Toomes, better known as the Vulture, first appeared in 1963's *Amazing Spider-Man #2* and was the second supervillain Spider-Man fought while he was still getting his feet wet during the Silver Age of comics. Since their first showdown, the Vulture has grown into one of Spidey's key antagonists. He's a founding member of the Sinister Six supervillain supergroup and is the central villain in 2017's *Spider-Man: Homecoming* film. Not bad for a guy who looks like he should be using a walker and some Bengay when he's out of costume.

Despite his frail looks, the Vulture is unquestionably deadly. Prior to turning to a life of crime, Toomes was a brilliant engineer who developed a specialized harness that gave him the gift of flight and precise maneuverability. The device also augments Toomes's strength. Toomes originally wanted to sell his invention, but he turned to a life of crime after he was betrayed by his business partner, Gregory Bestman.[169]

The Vulture's aerial abilities are directly responsible for a key part of Peter Parker/Spider-Man's biography. In the Vulture's first appearance, the *Daily Bugle* newspaper calls on anyone who can get a photo of New York's newest supervillain. To earn some extra cash, Peter decides to leverage his web-slinging abilities to snap some pics of the Vulture mid-flight, leading to his long-standing arrangement as a *Bugle* freelance photographer.

While a number of creators have tackled the Vulture across all media over the years, nobody made him as compelling as Roger Stern, who wrote a number of *Amazing* and *Spectacular Spider-Man* issues in the early '80s. Stern has long maintained that the Vulture

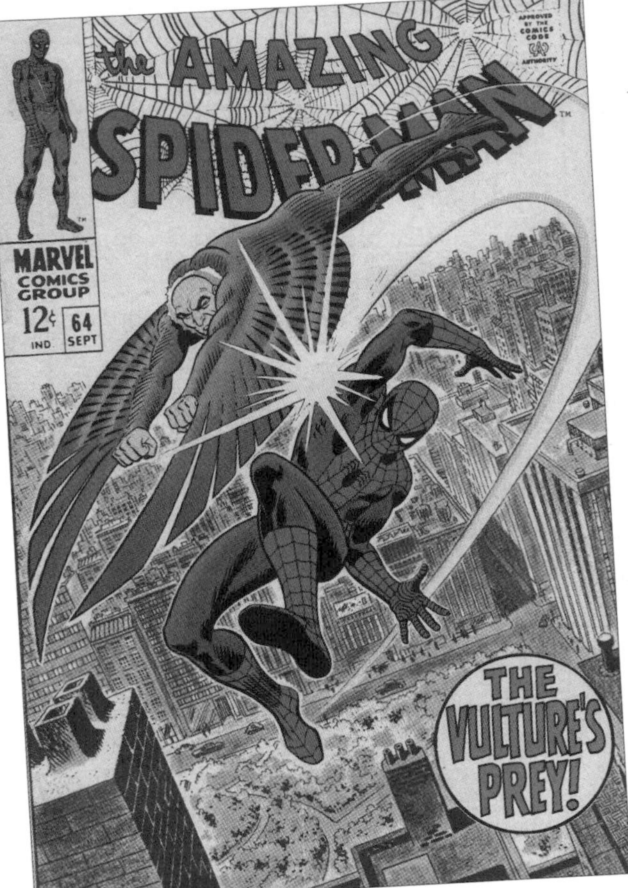

Amazing Spider-Man #64

is the perfect antagonist for Spider-Man: "It's old age and sneakiness versus youth and determination."[170] As a result, Stern provided Toomes with an origin story more than 20 years after the character was first introduced, while also adding a more personal touch to the Spider-Man/Vulture feud by having the villain interact with Peter's Aunt May and her geriatric boyfriend, Nathan Lubensky.

Beyond Toomes, a number of others have taken on the mantel of the Vulture at various points in Spider-Man history. Blackie Drago, a cellmate of Toomes's in prison, enjoyed a short stint as the Vulture in the mid-60s when he stole the original's costume and harness.[171] A third Vulture briefly appeared in a 1973 issue of *Amazing* when Empire State University professor Clifton Shallot went mad and experimented on himself, turning him into a supervillain.[172] During the "Brand New Day" era of *Amazing Spider-Man* in the late 2000s, a totally different kind of Vulture was created by Mark Waid and Mike McKone: Jimmy Natale was a lowly Maggia crime family goon who underwent a horrible experiment and was transformed into a grotesque half-vulture creature that could barely speak and who vomited acid into people's faces.[173] Talk about heartburn.

Years before the villain would make his big-screen debut in *Spider-Man: Homecoming*, the Vulture was the rumored big bad in the unmade *Spider-Man 4*. John Malkovich, who was also in the mix to play Norman Osborn/Green Goblin for the first *Spider-Man* film a decade earlier, would eventually confirm that he had signed on to play the Vulture, expressing disappointment that it never came to fruition.[174]

29 The Lizard

Dr. Curt Connors is proof that even the most brilliant people can sometimes have a monstrous side. Created by Stan Lee and Steve Ditko in 1964's *Amazing Spider-Man #6*, Connors is a well-meaning genetic biologist who, in an attempt to regenerate his missing arm, is temporarily transformed into the terrifying monster/supervillain known as the Lizard. This Jekyll and Hyde–inspired character has long presented a conundrum for the always-ethical Spider-Man: when Connors experiences one of his episodes and becomes the Lizard, he is a deadly force to be reckoned with. But because the

Lizard almost always changes back into Connors, Spider-Man has to find a way to stop the monster without hurting him so the man within will survive his inevitable transformation back to normalcy.

As such, over the course of the character's numerous appearances in comics, cartoons, video games, and other media, the Lizard has been depicted as the quintessentially tortured, complex villain. And just for one more layer of horror, whenever Connors changes into the Lizard, Spider-Man has to find a way to protect Curt's wife and son, Martha and Billy, from the villain's animalistic rampages. Unfortunately, Spider-Man has not always been successful in that regard. In the 2010 *Amazing Spider-Man* story "Shed," by Zeb Wells and Chris Bachalo, Connors, as the Lizard, finally gives in to his primal instincts and crosses that line and murders Billy, sapping the geneticist of his remaining humanity after years of transformations.

"I loved that idea as a way to let the readers know that this was a different Lizard story," Wells said. "We were taking the reptile further than we ever have. Then the challenge was to make the death have impact but not feel lurid. The reader had to feel the tragedy or it wouldn't work."[175]

The Lizard got the big-screen treatment as part of Spider-Man's 2012 cinematic reboot, *The Amazing Spider-Man*, played by Rhys Ifans. Connors had appeared in human form in the last two installments of Sam Raimi's *Spider-Man* films, but despite rumors of him one day making his transformation, it never came to pass in the original series.

30 Mysterio

Quentin Beck demands that you fear the fishbowl.

Sure, maybe Beck, better known as his supervillain persona, Mysterio, has a rather…unique appearance, consisting of green armor, a purple cape, and a domed helmet that sorta, kinda resembles a fishbowl. But that doesn't mean he's not one of the most nefarious evil-doers to ever go toe-to-toe with Spider-Man. Just ask Marv Wolfman, who scripted one of the more famous Mysterio stories in 1979, which saw him fake Peter Parker's Aunt May's death and conspire with the original burglar who killed Peter's Uncle Ben:

"I was never a huge Mysterio fan because I couldn't take his fishbowl helmet seriously," Wolfman said. "But his powers worked for my story so I went with him."[176]

Okay, never mind. The fishbowl *is* a tad ridiculous, but Mysterio truly is one of the most persistently troublesome villains in Spider-Man's colorful rogues' gallery. Created by Stan Lee and Steve Ditko in *Amazing Spider-Man #13*, he utilizes the power of deception and disorientation better than anyone. As explained in his origin story, Beck is actually a failed special effects wizard and stuntman from Hollywood. As a result, he has an endless number of tricks up his sleeve that have allowed him to take Spider-Man to the limit on numerous occasions. Such chicanery includes one Lee/Ditko story where Mysterio posed as a psychiatrist and almost convinced the "Wall Crawler" that he had gone crazy and should reveal his secret identity. For another great trick, during a two-part story in 1968, Mysterio warps Spidey's powers of perception, making him believe he's been shrunk down to the size of an actual spider. He even once found a way to send Spider-Man over to the

Mysterio's *Daredevil* Dance

One of Mysterio's most famous moments of the past 20 years actually came outside the confines of the Spider-Man comic universe, and instead transpired during the landmark Kevin Smith/Joe Quesada run on *Daredevil* in 1998. In the story, Mysterio is dying from cancer and wants to go out with a bang and destroy Spider-Man. However, because the Spider-books were embroiled in the "Clone Saga" at that point and it wasn't even certain who the "real" Spider-Man was, Mysterio instead turned his attention to Daredevil.

Seems benign enough, but the story did end up causing some problems for Marvel when Mysterio is seen committing suicide at the end of the *Daredevil* arc only to show up again soon after in an issue of *Amazing Spider-Man*. Apparently Smith never announced his plans to kill Mysterio when he sought permission from Marvel's editors to use the character in his story. And because Smith/Quesada's *Daredevil* was notoriously almost always behind its production schedule, this major editorial snafu managed to work its way into Marvel's continuity.[179]

alternative "Ultimate" universe, leading to 2012's *Spider-Men* event where Peter Parker meets his *Ultimate Spider-Man* counterpart, Miles Morales.

And when he can't do it alone, Mysterio has shown that he's not afraid to work with others. He's an inaugural member of the Sinister Six supervillain team and has appeared with the group through nearly all of its iterations.

Given his troublemaking longevity, Mysterio has been a mainstay of other Spider-Man-related media, including nearly every cartoon series and a slew of video games dating all the way back to the early '80s. However, the one medium where Mysterio has yet to make an appearance is on the big screen. According to Jeffrey Henderson, who worked on the storyboards for the never-made *Spider-Man 4* film, which would have been directed by Sam Raimi, the character was expected to appear and would have been played by Raimi's *Evil Dead* star Bruce Campbell.[177] Instead, when

Spider-Man was cinematically rebooted as *The Amazing Spider-Man* in 2012, the Lizard, Electro, and the Green Goblin were the main villains featured in the series. That's a shame since, as current *Amazing Spider-Man* writer Dan Slott noted in one interview, Mysterio would make for a great movie villain since he would provide a director with "free rein" to think of the most creative ways to utilize his special effects attacks against Spider-Man.[178]

In addition to Beck, other characters to don the fishbowl and cape as Mysterio include stuntman Daniel Berkhart, who took over as the villain after Beck was believed to be dead (but it was just a trick—go figure), and Francis Klum, who briefly appeared as the villain in the *Black Cat: The Evil That Men Do* miniseries (scripted by Hollywood director Kevin Smith).

31 Sandman

Not to be confused with Neil Gaiman's overlord of the dream realm, Marvel's Sandman, also known by his civilian alter-ego Flint Marko, is one of Spider-Man's most unique foes: a strangely physical behemoth who often outclasses Spidey in battle, while also demonstrating a complex, emotionally nuanced side that has led to him fighting on the sides of both evil and good.

In Marko's first appearance in *Amazing Spider-Man #4* (by Stan Lee and Steve Ditko), the character is seen escaping from prison where he ends up on a beach adjacent to a nuclear testing site. That's when the site is hit by a nuclear blast, transforming Marko into a half-sand, half-man creature that can shift and shape his body in countless ways. His new powers also allow him to change the density of his body from pillowy-soft to diamond-hard.

Elements of Marko's freak accident were masterfully captured on the big screen by filmmaker Sam Raimi in the 2007 blockbuster *Spider-Man 3*. Academy Award–nominated actor Thomas Haden Church was tapped to play the villain and had to play Sandman's origin scene opposite a centrifugal device built off of a Bell helicopter turbo engine that reportedly packed a wallop: "When it got up to full rev, the guys were like, 'Look, if you get hit it's like getting hit by a car at eighty miles an hour,'" Church said in a 2007 interview, adding that the "fear" his character shows during the accident was the actor's real-life terror of this special effect.[180]

In his earliest days in the comics, Sandman always managed to give Spider-Man a hard time, both as a solo act and as part of a larger group. He was an inaugural member of the Sinister Six supervillain stable that appeared in *Amazing Spider-Man Annual #1,* but after a few years of tormenting Spidey, Marvel's powers that be deemed the character too powerful to face off regularly against a "street level" hero like Spider-Man. As such, Sandman was transitioned over to the *Fantastic Four* series, where he fought Marvel's "first family" as a member of the Frightful Four group, before the character was updated again in the early '70s in the debut issue of the *Marvel Team-Up* comic series by Roy Thomas and Ross Andru. In the Christmas-themed issue, Spider-Man and Human Torch join forces to fight Sandman only to feel pity for the villain when he begs them to leave him alone so he can go visit his mother for the holidays. Overcome by the Christmas spirit, Spidey and Torch relent, and naturally Sandman escapes. Still, Thomas had succeeded in planting the seed for a kinder, gentler Sandman, and from that moment on, other creators started to approach Marko as more of an antihero/in-betweener rather than a straight-up villain.[181]

Sandman's full transition into a "good guy" was seemingly completed when he joined Spidey and Silver Sable against the Sinister Syndicate supervillain group in 1986's *Amazing Spider-Man #280.* Following the battle, Sable offered Marko a spot on her

Wildpack mercenary group. In an even bigger shock, a few years later, Marko served a very brief stint in the early '90s as a reserve member of "Earth's Mightiest Heroes," the Avengers.

Still, once a villain, always a villain. As slowly as Sandman evolved into a force of good, he started to regress back into being a thorn in Spider-Man's side. Marko's regression back into villainy was best captured in '09's "Keemia's Castle" story in *Amazing Spider-Man*, which depicts Sandman kidnapping a young girl who he believes to be his daughter. Spider-Man rescues the girl and hands her over to police thinking she would be given to her grandmother, only to learn that the child was instead put into the foster system. Spider-Man is overcome with guilt, while Sandman is enraged by having his daughter taken from him and arguably subjected to a worse situation in a foster home. Following "Keemia's Castle," Sandman makes amends with his villainous colleagues and rejoins the Sinister Six as part of *Amazing's* "Big Time" arc in 2010.

32 The Wedding

We are gathered here today to discuss one of the most problematic storylines in the history of Spider-Man. The wedding of Peter Parker and Mary Jane Watson has been anything but "happily ever after." Rather, it's been the source of countless headaches for Marvel. Barely moments after the big day transpired in 1987's *Amazing Spider-Man Annual #21*, creators, editors, and other executives started plotting ways to end the union before readers became too attached to it. And when none of those ideas worked, it took a storyline that had all the subtlety of a jackhammer on a quiet city street to undo it.

But that's a tale for another day (and another chapter). To understand how a storyline that was viewed by many as a bane to Spider-Man's creative existence came to be, it's best to first go back to the early days of Peter and Mary Jane.

Cue the Carpenters' "The Way We Were."

Mary Jane, the vivacious red-headed party girl, was a fan favorite going back to her very first appearance in *Amazing Spider-Man #42*, complete with one of the best first lines in comics' history, "Face it, Tiger, you just hit the jackpot!" However, to the confusion of many readers, shortly after MJ was introduced, Peter starting dating another woman, the beautiful, but more demure Gwen Stacy. And yet, in the wake of Gwen's tragic death in *Amazing #121*, the seeds for a possible union between Peter and MJ were first planted. Gerry Conway, the author of "The Night Gwen Stacy Died" and an unabashed MJ fan, had Mary Jane waiting for Peter in his apartment so she could comfort him following Gwen's death. Peter at first resists, but Mary Jane's insistence on being a friend made an impression on him, and a handful of issues later, they shared a passionate kiss at an airport and started dating.

So, should Conway get credit for being the first at Marvel to suggest that maybe Peter and MJ should be the ultimate couple? What does he have to say about their eventual nuptials?

"The marriage was a disastrous mistake," Conway said.[182]

Okay, so strike him off the list of conspirators. In reality, a lot of Conway's work of bringing Peter and MJ together was undone a few years later by writer Marv Wolfman, who thought it was silly for a "sad nebbish" guy like Peter to end up with a supermodel girlfriend.[183] Wolfman wrote MJ out of the books after Peter unsuccessfully proposes to her. Never to be heard from again…until the mid-80s when MJ returned to the comics in style: she got an origin story that added nuance to the character, and she even revealed that she knew Peter's secret identity as Spider-Man, which seemed to set the two characters on a path to a more permanent union.

And yet: "Being a Mary Jane fan, we had no real plans to marry them," said Ron Frenz, who provided pencils on a number of the aforementioned Peter/MJ stories in the '80s. "People who are still mourning the Peter/Mary Jane marriage, see [our stories] as an important turning point because it deepened the relationship.... We wanted to get her to a point where you could admire her as a character."[184] In fact, Frenz and writer Tom DeFalco actually pitched a story to Marvel's then-editor-in-chief Jim Shooter that would have had Mary Jane accept Peter's marriage proposal but ultimately leave him at the altar. But that pitch was rejected in favor of the story that brought them together without any caveats or compromises.[185]

The idea to marry off Peter and Mary Jane came out of a 1986 comic book convention panel that was attended by Shooter and Spidey's co-creator, Stan Lee. Lee, who was writing the daily *Spider-Man* newspaper strip, was asked by a fan about the prospects of Peter getting married to Mary Jane in the strip. Lee loved the idea and jokingly turned toward Shooter to put him on the spot about the request. Shooter, seeing a potential big event on the horizon, agreed to marry Peter and MJ off in both the strip *and* in the pages of *Amazing Spider-Man*.[186]

That left *Amazing's* creative team with minimal time to rebuild a romance and get Peter and Mary Jane to a point where they would realistically want to get married. Whether that was actually accomplished is subject to debate, but all the same, David Michelinie, who had just started scripting *Amazing* a few months before "The Wedding" was set to publish, was asked to submit a plot for the issue. Michelinie developed a rather complex plot involving Peter getting a concussion and being visited by all the people he had failed in his lifetime (like Uncle Ben and Gwen) on the eve of his nuptials, but the story was rejected in favor of something more straightforward written mostly by Shooter.[187]

Then came the problem of who was going to draw the comic. A number of artists were turned off by a storyline that was being "shoved down our throats," Frenz said. After getting rejected by a number of artists, Shooter found a taker in Paul Ryan, who later said he only accepted because was terrified of what the editor might do to him if he said no.[188]

That set the stage for the "big day." On June 5, 1987, Marvel hosted a wedding before a New York Mets game at Shea Stadium in Queens, New York. An actress dressed in a chic wedding gown played MJ, while an actor in a Spider-Man suit was there to marry the supermodel. Lee officiated the service. Captain America, Hulk, Iceman, and Firestar were also there to bear witness to this historic event.[189]

And thus began about 20 years of endless debates from creators and fans over the merits of this union. Lee said the event gave Peter "a bit more maturity" without changing him but others disagreed, thinking it made a character that was best known for his constant struggles into an indisputable winner. Michelinie set out to make a "happy marriage," free from predictable squabbles over Peter's superhero life. [190] But the happiness was not meant to last. Once Michelinie left *Amazing* in the early '90s, his successors worked to find ways to undo the marriage without uttering the two dreaded "D" words—divorce or death.

The first significant attempt came during the "Clone Saga" in the mid-90s. As part of this sprawling storyline, Peter was going to be revealed as a clone and his doppelganger would assume the mantel of Spider-Man, allowing Peter and a pregnant MJ to ride off into the sunset together, away from the comic book world until it was no longer inconvenient. When that idea failed, a few years later, Mary Jane was seemingly killed in a plane crash during an issue of *Amazing*. But after a year or so away, MJ showed up again alive and well.

That brings things to "One More Day" and the 20th anniversary of the marriage in 2007. Marvel's hierarchy, desperate to tell stories of a single Peter Parker again, had finally developed a foolproof way to end the marriage without resulting in death or divorce. Peter's Aunt May was going to get shot by a sniper bullet intended for Spider-Man. As she slowly died, Peter was going to be faced with a choice from Mephisto, Marvel's version of the devil: Peter could save Aunt May's life if his marriage to MJ was wiped from existence.

The only problem was, fans nearly revolted against the story. And *Amazing Spider-Man's* writer J. Michael Straczynski butted heads with Marvel's executives over the execution of "One More Day," leaving Marvel's editor-in-chief Joe Quesada to script the story to ensure it was done the way it needed to be done. Like Shooter before him, it took the head of Marvel to effectively drive a stake through the heart of fans—except this time it was getting rid of a storyline that everyone thought was a horrible, awful, terrible mistake 20 years earlier.[191]

33 Spider-Man's Little Black Suit

As many fashionistas will tell you, black goes with everything. In Spider-Man's case, the debut of his black costume in 1984 marked one of the most popular fashion change-ups in comic book history.

Oddly enough, Spidey's sleek black duds, which first appeared in *Amazing Spider-Man #252* (and coincided with the publication of Marvel's first-ever big event, *Secret Wars*), almost never saw the light of day. Years before Spidey was slated for his new look in *Secret Wars*, Marvel had received a solicitation from a fan for a new Spider-Man costume. Longtime Spidey scribe Tom DeFalco was tasked with sitting down with the fan and trying to make

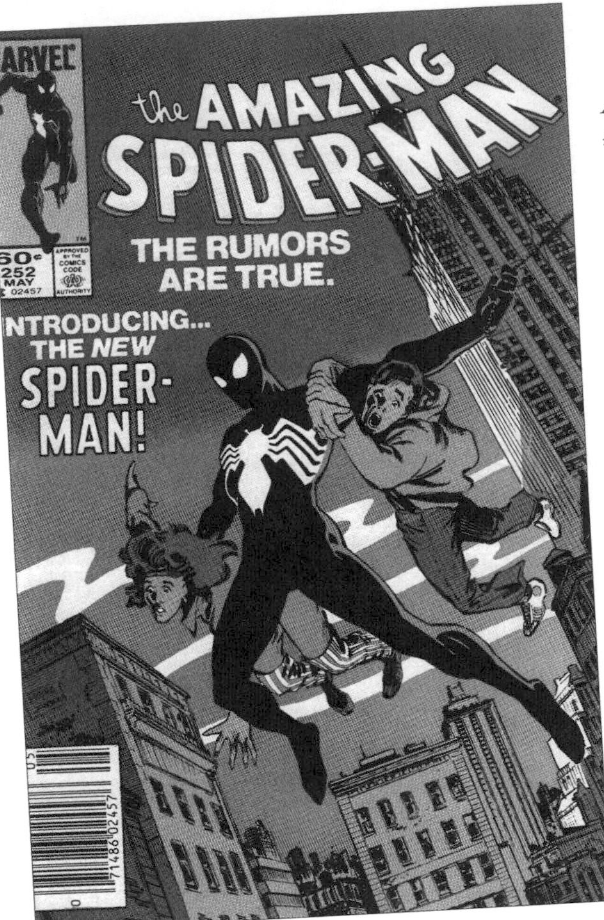

Amazing Spider-Man #252

this one-off idea into a substantive story, but was unsuccessful. However, a few months later, a Spidey makeover was back on the table after Marvel had signed a licensing agreement with Mattel Toys to produce a series of action figures based on *Secret Wars*. Marvel's editor-in-chief Jim Shooter suggested that one of the figures could be Spider-Man in his new costume, leaving it up to artists Mike Zeck, and later Rick Leonardi, to design the famous black attire for the comics.[192]

But all was not right in the black-costumed world. As rumors started to circulate about the "new" Spider-Man, Shooter's inbox was inundated with angry fan mail from readers who had decided they hated the change before they even got a chance to see it. Caving to pressure, Shooter asked DeFalco to ditch the duds as quickly as possible. However, because of the way *Amazing Spider-Man* and *Secret Wars* were supposed to cross over with each other, Spider-Man showed up in the costume in *Amazing #252* but wasn't seen receiving the costume for the first time until nearly eight months later in *Secret Wars #8*. That meant for everything to make sense in both books, Marvel had to ride it out until *Amazing #258*, fan reaction be damned.[193]

Then a funny thing happened. *Amazing #252* came out and the black costume was a sensation. "Days after the release of *#252*, I did a show up in Canada," said Ron Frenz, who provided the pencils for the issue. At the show, the comic "was selling at a ridiculous mark-up. People were selling it for $50." In fact, demand for the issue was so overwhelming, the fire marshal had to shut the show down because the convention hall was beyond capacity, according to Frenz.

Naturally, once Marvel realized it had a hit on its hands, *Amazing #258*, which showed Peter dumping the costume after it was revealed that it was an evil alien symbiote trying to control him, was off to the presses. So to satisfy the masses, over the next few years, Spider-Man would alternate between his traditional red-and-blue attire and a cloth version of the black costume before ditching it for good in *Amazing #300*. The comic is also notable for being the first appearance of the symbiote's new host: disgraced news reporter Eddie Brock, who used the power of the parasite to become the supervillain Venom.

In the aftermath of this behind-the-scenes drama, the "black costume saga" has gone on to become one of the most famous Spidey stories in the character's history. It's been notably adapted in the '90s *Spider-Man: The Animated Series*, the 2007 film *Spider-Man 3*, and the *Spectacular Spider-Man* animated series in '08, among others. And any time the character returns to the costume in the comics, like in '07's "Back in Black," it's always celebrated as a major event by Marvel and its readers.

34 Roger Stern: From the Kid to the Hobgoblin

Not every comic book creator is fortunate enough to be mentioned in the same breath as Stan Lee, but it is commonplace for Roger Stern when it comes to Spider-Man. Stern's stint scripting the *Amazing Spider-Man* in the early to mid-1980s is considered by fans and critics alike to be one of the all-time great creative runs immediately behind Lee's iconic stories with artists Steve Ditko and John Romita Sr. in the '60s. That's because Stern's Spider-Man featured snappy dialogue, unique villains, and compelling storylines that serviced not only the titular hero, but the book's entire supporting cast. Some of Stern's highlights include the creation of one of Spidey's best villains, the Hobgoblin, in the "Origin of the Hobgoblin" (*Amazing Spider-Man #238–239*); one of Spider-Man's most dramatic battles ever in "Nothing Can Stop the Juggernaut" (*Amazing #229–230*); and the Will Eisner-esque "The Kid Who Collects Spider-Man" (*Amazing #248*).

But those stories are really just the tip of the iceberg when it comes to Stern. Other fans talk passionately about some of the tales Stern has spun about the Vulture, J. Jonah Jameson, and the Black Cat. In short, you can't go wrong when it comes to Stern and Spider-Man.

A native of Indiana, Stern was born in 1950 and was a key member of Marvel's third wave of creative talent that included the likes of Frank Miller, John Byrne, and Mark Gruenwald. As a child, he purchased his first comics for a dime off the spinner rack at a drug store in Indiana. Come high school, he got hooked on Marvel Comics and Spider-Man after purchasing *Amazing #40*—the origin of Spider-Man's nemesis, the Green Goblin.[194]

Stern started to squeeze his way into the comic book industry in college when he produced a number of fanzines, including *CPL (Contemporary Pictorial Literature)* with longtime comic artist Bob Layton. Stern was also a contributor to Marvel's fanzine *FOOM* (Friends of Old Marvel). His work eventually earned him a call from Marvel and he was offered a staff position as an assistant editor, and later an editor.[195]

The job provided Stern with job security, but his passion was in writing. In an effort to keep him engaged, Marvel's editor-in-chief Jim Shooter offered Stern an exclusive contract to write full-time. That's when he crossed paths creatively with Spider-Man for the first time, being assigned to write *Peter Parker: The Spectacular Spider-Man*.[196]

Stern was initially intimidated by writing Spider-Man in any capacity, thinking he wasn't ready to take on one of Marvel's legacy characters. However, he accepted the *Spectacular* assignment because he felt "it wasn't *really* Spider-Man," since *Amazing* was considered the flagship title. So he took the challenge on and saw it as the ultimate on-the-job learning experience.[197] His early stories were heavily focused on Spider-Man's supporting cast, like many of Peter's graduate school colleagues, as well as new characters he created such as the George Burns-esque Nathan Lubensky (who later became a love interest for Peter's Aunt May) and the effeminate small-time crook/fashion designer Roderick Kingsley, who, years later, was revealed to be the Hobgoblin. Stern also quickly grasped Spider-Man's voice and learned to balance the character's "wisenheimer" personality with some of his down-to-earth, everyman problems. He developed the mantra: "No matter how bad my day was, Pete's was worse."[198]

After about a year and a half on *Spectacular*, Stern finally "graduated" to *Amazing,* where he was paired with young, up-and-coming artist John Romita Jr. (son of Marvel's one-time art director, John Romita Sr.). That's when Stern's talents and aptitude for writing some of the most revered Spidey stories ever became apparent. With a few exceptions, one of Stern's most notable contributions to the book was his focus on numerous new and non-traditional Spider-Man villains like Cobra, Mister Hyde, and Thunderball. And then there's arguably the greatest Spider-Man story ever, "Nothing Can Stop the Juggernaut," which pitted Spider-Man in an impossible-to-win fight against longtime X-Men villain Juggernaut.

Shortly after "Juggernaut," Stern co-created a new cosmically powered Captain Marvel, Monica Rambeau, in *Amazing Spider-Man Annual #16*. Rambeau would go on to play a key role in another book Stern was famous for scripting, *The Avengers*.

Stern also used his time on *Amazing* to harken back to the Silver Age era of Spider-Man when he created a long-running mystery around the newly created Hobgoblin. Stern had envisioned teasing the identity of the villain for as long as Stan Lee and Steve Ditko strung along the mystery behind the Green Goblin in the '60s. Unfortunately, Stern had long left the book by the time Marvel finally decided to pay off the storyline and it was botched terribly. But Stern was later allowed to right the wrongs of his successors when he pitched the *Hobgoblin Lives* miniseries in the late '90s as a "cold case just waiting to be solved," and scripted the story's appropriate resolution involving Roderick Kingsley and his lookalike (not a twin) brother, Daniel.[199]

The last of Stern's "big three" stories from his stint on *Amazing* was "The Kid Who Collects Spider-Man" with artist Ron Frenz, which was published as a backup tale in *Amazing #248*. Stern's quietly tragic story about a young boy with terminal cancer getting an opportunity to meet his idol, Spider-Man, remains one of the most moving comic book stories to ever be published. When Stern first dreamt "Kid" up, he was actually convinced that he was remembering someone else's story: "I was afraid that my sleeping brain had half-recalled a Superman story that I'd read as a boy and substituted Spider-Man into the mix."[200]

Stern left *Amazing* shortly after "Kid" was published, continuing to script *Avengers* full-time. He would later move to DC, where he enjoyed a sustained run writing Superman comics, including parts of the landmark "Death of Superman" saga. During the interim, he reportedly lost interest in Spider-Man following Peter's controversial marriage to supermodel Mary Jane Watson. He still contributed a story here and there, like *Hobgoblin Lives*, but his passion for the character didn't return in full until the marriage was undone as part of Marvel's "One More Day" event in 2007. Now that Peter was no longer married, Stern happily penned a number of Spider-Man stories during the "Brand New Day" era of the late 2000s. "For my money," he said, "Pete, Spider-Man, and the whole cast are finally acting like themselves again."[201]

35 Must Read: "Nothing Can Stop the Juggernaut" (*Amazing Spider-Man #229–230*)

If you're a big fan of dramatic battles between underdog heroes and unstoppable villains, then look no further than "Nothing Can Stop the Juggernaut," by Roger Stern and John Romita Jr. "Juggernaut" is a classic David vs. Goliath story. In it, Juggernaut plows through the streets of New York City, crushing everything that comes in his path and Spider-Man—and *only* Spider-Man—is around to stop him.

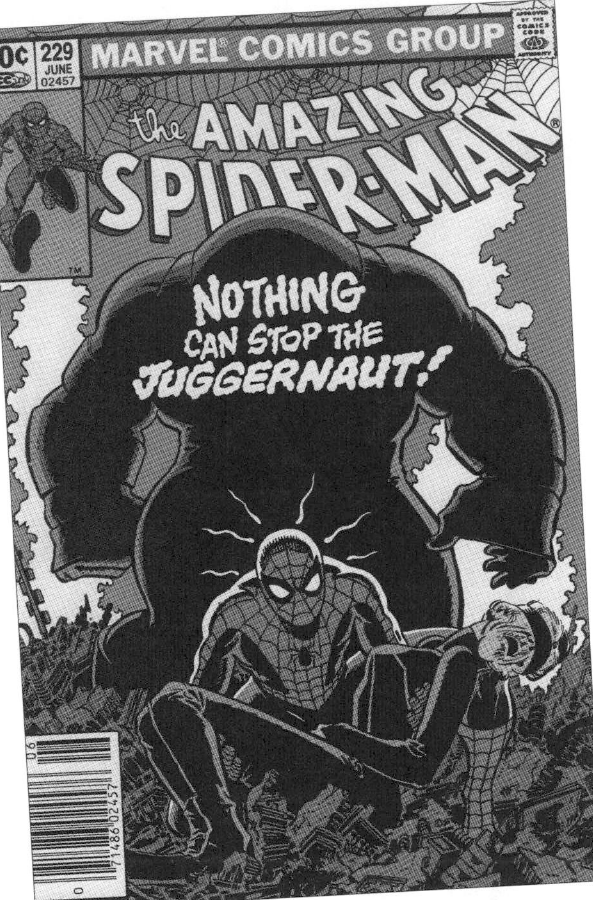

Amazing Spider-Man #229

While Spidey is no lightweight, the deck is clearly stacked against him in this one. Prior to Stern's story, Juggernaut had been traditionally used as a villain for the X-Men—the *entire* X-Men team. Still, thanks to Spider-Man's perseverance and refusal to quit, he busts out every trick in the book to slow down this unstoppable foe, before finally emerging victorious by using his brains instead of his brawn.

Additionally, since its publication in 1982, "Juggernaut" has served as a template for pretty much every "Spider-Man is over-matched and outclassed by a villain, but he'll never quit" story that has followed. Spider-Man vs. the Phoenix-powered X-Men in 2012's *Avengers vs. X-Men* miniseries? Spider-Man taking on the ultra-powerful Morlun during the "Coming Home" storyline in 2001? Both of these, and many, many others, have all been inspired by the Stern/JRJR story.

Adding to its legend is just how perfectly "Juggernaut" captures many of Spider-Man's core characteristics: his dedication to protecting his friends and family, his ingenuity, and his unstoppable spirit. Spider-Man only leaps into battle against Juggernaut when the villian critically injures his good friend, the psychic Madame Web. But even when the Juggernaut swats him away like a fly, Spider-Man accepts his responsibility as being the only person capable of stopping this monster, even if it means he might die trying.

Spidey stops at nothing to slow the Juggernaut down—even driving a loaded oil tanker directly into the villain, igniting a fiery explosion (and then, in a smartly written character moment, bemoaning that fact that his exuberance to beat the Juggernaut might have caused the villain's death). Yet, nothing works for Spidey, and Juggernaut's only getting angrier and angrier. That's when Spider-Man busts out one last trick: he leaps onto the Juggernaut's back and covers his eyeholes with his arms. During the struggle, Juggernaut accidentally steps into a newly poured building foundation in Lower Manhattan. And then the villain sinks, sinks, and sinks some more, and is finally…stopped. Sure, the villain is going to eventually break out of that cement, but when he does, either the authorities, the military, or some other superhero group is going to have to deal with capturing and holding him. So with that in mind, Spider-Man has "won," even if winning just means stopping his adversary in his tracks for a couple of hours.

In addition to the numerous Spider-Man stories that pay homage to "Juggernaut," the story even has inspired a few proper sequels, including a fairly recent offering from Stern in 2010's

"Something Can Stop the Juggernaut" (which highlights one individual who was adversely affected by Spider-Man and Juggernaut's battle back in the day). And the love affair for this tale seems to be fairly consistent across the board. Stern has called it one of his all-time favorites that he wrote, while the *Comics Should Be Good* blog, which is part of the *Comic Book Resources* network, declared it a "Comic You Should Own," in 2008.[202]

36 Kingpin/Wilson Fisk

Pound for pound, Wilson Fisk might be the deadliest Spider-Man villain in the "Web-Slinger's" much-ballyhooed rogues' gallery. That's because Fisk, better known around the Marvel Universe as the Kingpin (just don't call him that name to his face), weighs many, many pounds.

Okay, that was a cheap shot (though it's never been below Spider-Man to make a crack about Fisk's girth—just check out the *Ultimate Spider-Man* storyline "Learning Curve" for a few great zingers). And beyond that, some of you young whippersnappers might be asking yourself why a book about Spider-Man is focusing on Daredevil's archnemesis. But years before Fisk was tormenting Matthew Murdock, he was actually a very prominent nemesis of Spider-Man's.

Created by Stan Lee and John Romita Sr. in 1967, Kingpin first appeared in the landmark *Amazing Spider-Man #50* (aka, "Spider-Man No More"). For years, Kingpin exclusively tormented Spidey until Fisk semi-retired per the urging of his wife, Vanessa, only to reappear as part of the grim and gritty world of *Daredevil* during Frank Miller's iconic run scripting/penciling the "Man

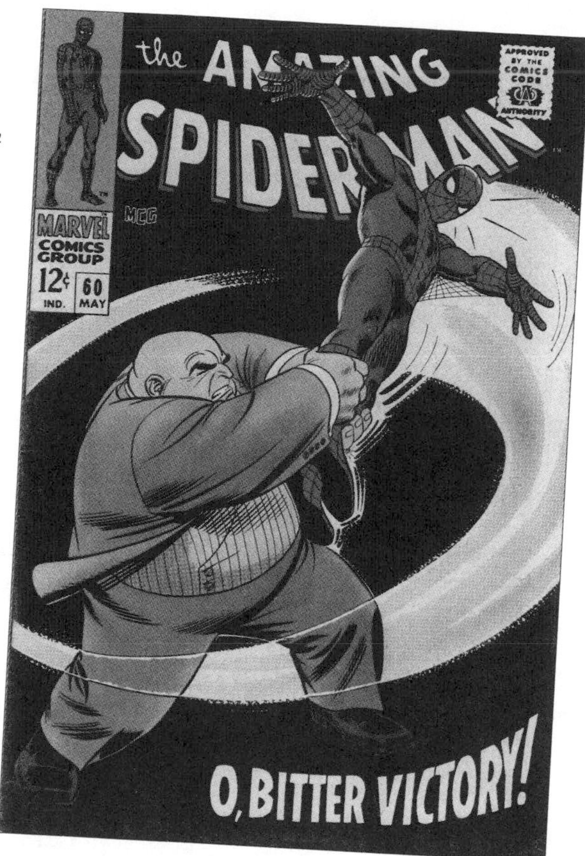

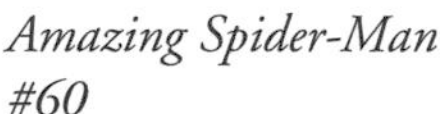
Amazing Spider-Man #60

Without Fear" in the 1970s and '80s. Today, Fisk antagonizes both characters, and also has drawn the ire of the ultimate vigilante, the Punisher.

When Lee first pitched Romita to design a "Kingpin of crime," the artist considered ways to make this new character quite different from the stereotypical criminal underworld boss. "I didn't want to do the standard guy with a mustache and scar, so I made him look like the furthest thing from that," Romita said in one interview. For Romita, that meant a guy the size of an elephant, who was also extraordinarily muscular and powerful. He also added some distinct costume items like a white topcoat, a stickpin, and a cravat, using actors Edward Arnold and Robert Middleton as visual references.[203]

Since the "street-level" criminal underworld was such a key part of *Amazing Spider-Man's* narrative during the '60s, Fisk was a series regular. Kingpin remained a thorn in Spider-Man's side until *Amazing #197* by Marv Wolfman and Keith Pollard, when the character is issued an ultimatum from Vanessa: quit crime and live a normal life with her or she'll leave. And Kingpin was just about to defeat Spider-Man too, but in a unique twist designed to make Kingpin "something special," Wolfman scripted the character to choose a normal life with his wife.[204]

After a few years, Fisk was repackaged in far more sinister fashion by Miller for *Daredevil.* While Fisk still made sporadic appearances in Spider-Man comics—even his son, Richard, got into the criminal game and appeared as the villain the Rose in the '80s—many of his most-famous moments from the last 30-plus years transpired in the pages of *Daredevil.* Still, Kingpin found ways to strike at Spider-Man personally, like during the *Civil War* event in 2007, when Fisk, like the rest of the world, learns Spider-Man's civilian identity after he unmasks, and he hires a sniper to kill him. When the assassin's bullet mistakenly hits Peter's Aunt May, Spider-Man gets retribution by attacking Kingpin in the most humiliating way possible—making him submit to Spider-Man in front of all the other prisoners in his cellblock.[205]

Over in the alternative *Ultimate* universe, the Kingpin was an equally persistent and deadly Spidey foe, though with one distinction: Fisk was depicted as being a far more "legitimate" member of society when compared to his more criminal representation in the mainstream Marvel timeline. In Fisk's very first *Ultimate* storyline, the character is shown to be a socialite with an iron grip on New York City thanks to his political clout and criminal connections. The presentation of the character ended up working as a wonderful foil to the high school–aged Spider-Man. "Kingpin represents injustice and how it can really thrive in this world," said Brian Michael Bendis, writer of *Ultimate Spider-Man*. "The 'greed is good' of it all. That [Spider-Man] will not win against this."[206]

37 Electro

And now for a word about the most electrifying villain in Spider-Man history.

Max Dillon, better known by his supervillain persona, Electro, was created by Stan Lee and Steve Ditko in *Amazing Spider-Man #9*. The character is one of Spider-Man's most enduring foes, having been a part of the original Sinister Six supervillain group, and was featured as the primary antagonist in 2014's *The Amazing Spider-Man 2* film, being portrayed by Academy Award–winner Jamie Foxx.

Electro's origin story is a simple one: blue-collared lineman gets electrified by a live wire and develops the power to harness electricity. In contrast to Peter Parker and great power/great responsibility, Electro chooses to use his abilities to rob banks. His shocking powerset initially caused problems for Spider-Man, but the "Webhead" has always managed to stay one step ahead of Electro, usually engineering some kind of special webbing that could defend against Dillon's electricity attacks.

After decades of being depicted as a shallow noob who would pop up in a story here and there only to get his comeuppance within an issue or two, in 1997, longtime Spider-Man writer Tom DeFalco attempted to add a little more depth and intrigue to Electro's character. In the "Rebirth of Electro" arc in *Amazing Spider-Man*, which saw Dillon get a power enhancement courtesy of the crime boss the Rose, DeFalco explored the villain's childhood, establishing that he was abused by his parents. Over the course of the story, a super-charged Electro confronts Spidey and gets his longtime tormentor to beg for mercy, marking a dramatic change of direction for the villain.

"I want my hero to be a three dimensional character and I want him to be surrounded by three dimensional characters and that includes his villains," DeFalco said of the "Rebirth of Electro" arc. "A lot of times I look at a character and think how [he's] been around for 30 years and nobody ever told us who he is. All we know is that he uses his powers every once in a while to steal or gain more power, but we don't know what's behind any of that. I try to find out why these guys do the things that they do."[207]

The character received yet another supercharged reinvention in the late-00s as part of the "Power to the People" story, which saw Electro return to his blue-collar roots by inciting violence and crime by parroting some of the talking points associated with the "Occupy Wall Street" anti-millionaire/billionaire movement. "I think Electro's always been pretty cool, but he was created at a time when his powers were a lot more unique than they are today, so the [creative team] decided he could use some amping up," said Mark Waid, who wrote "Power to the People."

Max Dillon, everyman villain, was a key part of Electro's characterization in Marc Webb's *The Amazing Spider-Man 2.* Foxx portrays the character as a mercurial loner who obsesses over Spider-Man before a laboratory accident involving some mutated eels gives him his electricity powers. "I wanted people to understand that he's a broken man and when he meets Spider-Man he sort of goes off," Foxx said about his character during a promotional interview hyping the film. "You sort of see how shy he is and things like that, so that when he does turn into Electro, he still has that in his mind that 'People will never notice me, now I need to be noticed.' And that's an emotion that everyone can recognize."[208]

38 Kraven the Hunter

Ignoring his obsession with leopard-print attire and loincloths, Sergei Kravinoff, or, more ominously, Kraven the Hunter, is considered by many to be one of Spider-Man's deadliest enemies.

Except it wasn't always that way. Introduced by Stan Lee and Steve Ditko in *Amazing Spider-Man #15*, Kraven, in his early days, was a bit of goof. A big-game hunter who came to the conclusion that Spider-Man was the greatest prize possible. Kraven frequently came up well short when pursuing his ultimate goal of defeating "the Spider." He was an inaugural member of the famed Sinister Six supervillain group, but that still didn't change the perception that Kraven was never a major threat to Spider-Man...until 1987's "Kraven's Last Hunt."

"Kraven's Last Hunt" is the definitive Kraven the Hunter story and is considered by many fans and critics to be one of the greatest Spider-Man tales of all time. Written by J.M. DeMatteis, with art from Mike Zeck, the six-part storyline depicts Kraven finally succeeding against Spider-Man—drugging him, shooting him, and burying him alive in a grave, where he remained for two weeks. While Spider-Man was "dead," Kraven assumed his identity, violently attacking criminals and even murdering in the "the Spider's" name. Then, after Spider-Man pulled himself out of his grave, Kraven committed suicide, not allowing his adversary to get the vengeance he so desperately sought.

With just one story—granted an all-time great one—Kraven was elevated to the upper, tippy-top echelon of Spidey's rogues because he definitively defeated the "Wall Crawler." Unfortunately, because of his suicide, there was never much of an opportunity of a follow-up story, so creators have had to make do with expanding

The Half-Kravinoff

The faceless Chameleon, the very first villain to face off against Spider-Man in 1963's the *Amazing Spider-Man #1*, is actually Kraven's half-brother, making him yet another member of the Kravinoff family tree. In the comics, the Chameleon is responsible for recruiting Kraven to the United States over from Russia in order to hunt Spider-Man in the Hunter's very first appearance in *Amazing #15*. Chameleon's obsession with Spider-Man becomes even more sadistic following Kraven's suicide in "Kraven's Last Hunt." As part of his revenge plot against the "Wall Crawler," Chameleon receives a power upgrade so that his face can become malleable, allowing him to seamlessly transform his appearance.

Separate from Kraven, Chameleon has frequently been depicted as a troublesome villain for Spider-Man to overcome, both as a boss in Marvel's criminal underworld and also as a member of the most recent incarnation of the Sinister Six villain team. He was even part of a plot to make Peter believe his long-dead parents had returned from the grave (only to be revealed as androids). In an '09 story, Chameleon unsuccessfully tried to kill Peter by drowning him in a pool of acid so he could steal his identity (he had no idea Peter was also Spider-Man). "I always saw him as a sociopath like a Batman villain," said that story's writer, Fred Van Lente.[211]

Kraven's biography via the use of flashbacks and the introduction of new members of the Kravinoff clan. In the mid-90s, Kraven's sons, Vladimir and Aloysha, were introduced and sought to carry on their father's work as hunters of and antagonists to Spider-Man. DeMatteis, who wrote a number of stories that expanded the Kravinoff legacy following "Kraven's Last Hunt," said something about the family "fascinated" him. "Kraven himself is so full of Dostoyevskian duality, something that always attracts me; and I guess I wanted to see how this profoundly flawed, yet strangely admirable, character impacted those around him."[209]

In the late 2000s, yet another Kravinoff was introduced in *Amazing Spider-Man #565*: Kraven's daughter, Ana. As part of the long-simmering storyline "the Gauntlet," Ana plots a way to resurrect her father by spilling "the Spider's" blood as part of a ritual. Of course, when Kraven comes back from the dead, he's none too pleased: apparently none of his children got the memo about the fact that he had killed himself because he wanted to die knowing he had conquered Spider-Man and no one could ever take that away from him.

In other media, as part of the *Ultimate Spider-Man* comic series, Kraven is depicted as a reality television star who seeks to hunt Spider-Man. He's also been featured in a number of Spider-Man animated television series. However, despite some legitimate interest from *The Amazing Spider-Man* series director Marc Webb, Kraven is yet to see his legacy captured on the big screen.[210]

39 Must Read: "Kraven's Last Hunt" (*Web of Spider-Man #31–32, Amazing Spider-Man #293–294, Spectacular Spider-Man #131–132*)

Most people associate Spider-Man with the bright and cheery superhero who patrols the "friendly neighborhood," catching crooks and fighting supervillains while uttering quippy jokes and barbs. But certain creators have proven over time that Spider-Man can also be cast as a grim and dark superhero—or at the very least, have to overcome grim and dark circumstances. And that edgier, dourer version of Spider-Man is best evidenced by J.M. DeMatteis and Mike Zeck's 1987 story "Kraven's Last Hunt."

"Kraven" easily stakes a claim to being the darkest and most twisted Spider-Man story of all. In it, Spidey's longtime adversary, Kraven the Hunter, is elevated from loin-clothed punchline to one of Marvel's most calculating and sinister villains ever, when he drugs, shoots, and buries alive a recently married

Spider-Man, and then sets out to prove his superiority by assuming his identity.

While the story is filled with powerful and enduring imagery, including Spider-Man pulling himself out of his grave while declaring his love for his wife, Mary Jane Watson, it also serves to function as Spider-Man's greatest nightmare being realized. Even "The Night of Gwen Stacy Died," which featured the death of Peter Parker's girlfriend, Gwen Stacy, at the hands of the Green Goblin, ended with an epilogue that hinted that Peter's wounds would eventually be able to heal. But "Kraven" ends with Spider-Man failing to exact his revenge. Kraven is so satisfied by his victory against Spider-Man, he commits suicide so he can never be robbed of that moment again.

The Hunt Before Kraven

Oddly enough, despite "Kraven's Last Hunt" standing as one of the greatest Spider-Man stories of all time, the tale did not originally start out as something built around Spidey and Kraven the Hunter.

"Kraven Last Hunt's" writer J.M. DeMatteis's original pitch involved the Avenger Wonder Man, who similarly would have been buried alive by a villain and resurrected. But since Wonder Man dying and coming back was already an essential part of his biography, the story was rejected by Marvel's editors. Undeterred, a few years later, DeMatteis brought his storyline to DC, pitching it as a Batman/Joker comic depicting the Joker "killing" Batman and then going sane as a result. However, DC already had its big Batman graphic novel lined up for that time and it decided to take a pass (JMD would get to do his Batman/Joker story "Going Sane" in 2008).

Finally, DeMatteis was invited to write a few issues of *Spectacular Spider-Man* with Mike Zeck when he realized that what didn't exactly work for Wonder Man and Batman was actually the perfect Spider-Man story: "Peter Parker had just married Mary Jane, so you had all that emotional resonance, it was perfect. You know I really randomly came across Kraven in a Marvel Universe Handbook and I was reading it and went, 'Oh my god! He's the perfect character!'"[213]

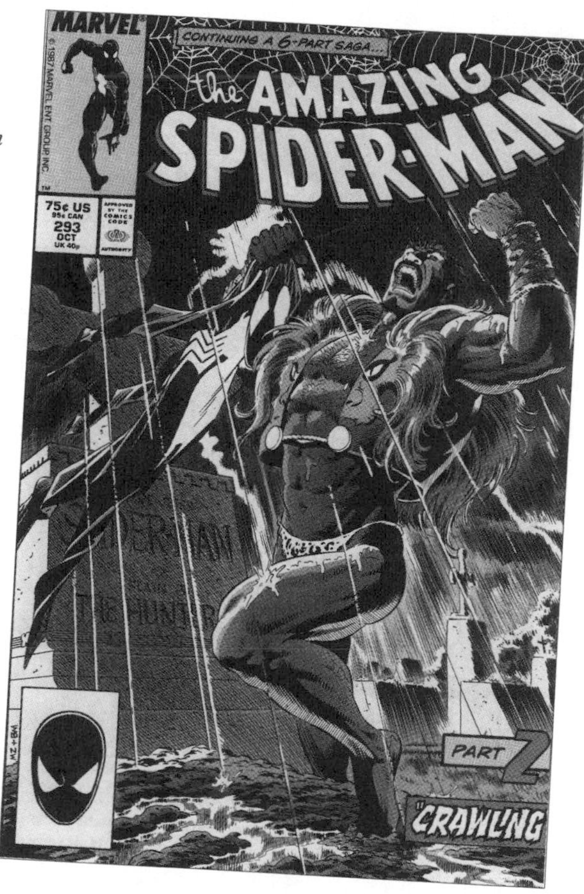

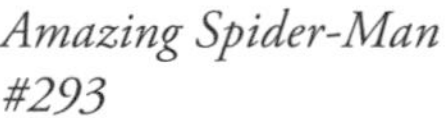
Amazing Spider-Man #293

The story is not for the faint of heart, but "Kraven" is undoubtedly a "must read" for any Spider-Man fan for the way it hones in on various essential themes that are critical to understanding Spidey, not to mention DeMatteis's writing and word play, along with Zeck's powerful visuals. It's one of the few Spider-Man stories to truly zero in on the fragile, fraught nature of Peter's marriage to MJ. While other creators would periodically use Mary Jane as a device by having her get kidnapped or abused by supervillains, "Kraven" takes a much more subtle approach in demonstrating how Peter being Spider-Man could adversely impact MJ. When Kraven captures and buries Peter, the couple is just weeks removed from being married. So when Peter disappears one night while out on the job and stays missing for two weeks (with someone else running around in his costume killing criminals), it is essentially the first trial Peter and Mary Jane's marriage faces.

Still, out of its unusual darkness, "Kraven" also plays to many of the themes and ideas that make Spider-Man famous. One of the story's most memorable scenes comes in its penultimate chapter in *Amazing Spider-Man #294*, when Spider-Man finally has his opportunity to confront Kraven and make him feel pain and suffering for what he's done. But all of that goes out the window once Kraven tells Spider-Man that he has released the sympathetically insane Vermin, a half-man, half-cannibalistic monster/experiment gone horribly wrong, into New York City's streets. Spider-Man has two choices: vengeance against Kraven, or using his great powers responsibly to save innocent people from Vermin's claws and teeth. Naturally, Spider-Man chooses responsibility for the greater good.

For those reasons, and others, fans have long propped this story up on a pedestal. In 2012, as part of Spider-Man's 50th anniversary celebration, readers of the popular comic book blog, *Comics Should Be Good*, named "Kraven" the greatest Spider-Man story to ever be published.[212]

40 Spider-Man Beats the Comics Code

Stan Lee has long been known as a pioneer in the comic book industry, pushing the boundaries of what was traditionally accepted from a superhero series. So it should come as no surprise that when faced with publishing an anti-drug Spider-Man story in 1971 that would have defied the stodgy Comics Code Authority (CCA) and

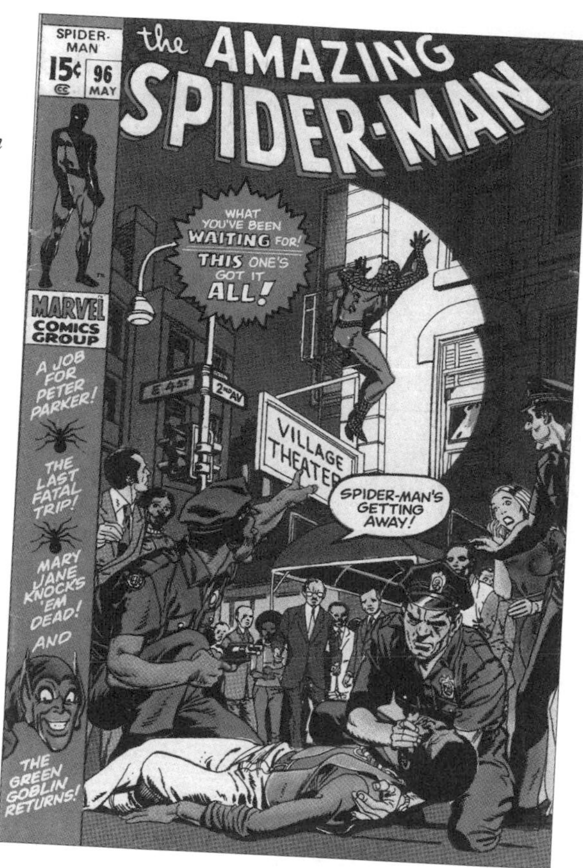

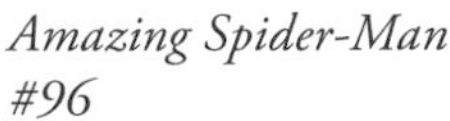
Amazing Spider-Man #96

risked being banned by retailers, Lee opted once again to push boundaries, despite the potential backlash.

The Comics Magazine Association of America first established its code in 1954 after the industry came under attack from a variety of psychologists and public officials who claimed comics had a bad influence on children.[214] The code, which was marked by a seal insignia on the cover of an approved comic book, limited any references to sex, drugs, gore, violence, or the occult. Comics that didn't receive approval from the authority risked being blacklisted by retailers, and publishers could have potentially been expelled from the association.[215]

Introducing Morbius

After the Comics Magazine Association of America loosened its restrictions on the publication of monster characters in the wake of the anti-drug *Amazing Spider-Man* storyline in 1971, Marvel got to work on making a slew of spooky new characters like Man-Thing, Werewolf by Night, Ghost Rider, and one pasty-faced blood sucker that was introduced as an adversary for Spider-Man, Morbius the Living Vampire.

Created by Roy Thomas and Gil Kane, Morbius, also known as Dr. Michael Morbius, first appeared in *Amazing Spider-Man #101*. As explained by his origin story, he's not technically a vampire because he acquires his vampiric abilities from a biochemical experiment, rather than supernatural means.

In the years that followed his first appearance, Morbius has been presented as more of a tragic antihero than just a straight-up villain. He has even teamed up with Spider-Man on a few occasions, including the popular "Maximum Carnage" arc from the 1990s. However, Morbius's uncontrollable addiction to blood has always made Spider-Man keep him at an arm's length (or more) at all times. He's even gone on to star in his own solo series on multiple occasions, most recently in 2013.

While Marvel and Lee followed the code's stringent rules without any pushback throughout the first half of the '60s, the rise of psychedelic drug culture in the United States as the nation entered the '70s necessitated a closer look at the authority's "nonsensical" draconian restrictions. A few months before the three-part story in *Amazing Spider-Man #96–98* was published, Lee received a letter from the U.S. government asking Marvel to leverage its influence on teenagers by publishing an anti-drug story.[216] Lee and artist John Romita Sr. weighed the risks of pushing forward with their story and decided to go for it. "This was a story that we knew needed to be told, but we weren't real sure how it would be received," Romita said.[217]

While the drug references sound tame by today's standards, for 1971, the comics were quite daring and edgy. The storyline depicts

Harry Osborn, Peter's college buddy, abusing some kind of anonymous pills after he is rejected for a date by Mary Jane Watson. In one panel, illustrated by Gil Kane, that feeling of losing one's mind is captured when Harry is shown saying:

"I'm drowning—falling—dying inside! Nothing seems real...."[218]

Rather than skirt the CCA altogether, Marvel did submit the issue for approval. But as legend has it, the usual code administrator had fallen ill, leaving the job of okaying the issue to a replacement. The replacement said "no" and for the first time in industry history, a mainstream comic book was published without the code's seal of approval on the cover.

Marvel's rebellion made the company come across as conquering heroes in the public's eye. The Marvel offices were flooded with positive fan mail, and the CCA and its code were perceived as being old-fashioned and out of touch. And at a time when comics were still considered funny books for kids by the "legitimate" media, the *New York Times* actually reported on the comics code controversy.

As a result of Marvel's stand, the CCA relaxed its restrictions on publishers, allowing them to tackle some of these more complex topics. The CCA's reversal also opened the door for the major publishers to once again publish comics about long-banned occult creatures like werewolves, vampires, and other monsters.[219] Additionally, Marvel's defiance opened the doors for other publishers to create their own stories that seemed ripped from the daily headlines, most notably the Denny O'Neil and Neal Adams *Green Lantern/Green Arrow* story, "Snowbirds Don't Fly," which shows Green Arrow's ward, Roy "Speedy" Harper, becoming hooked on heroin.

41 Take the Spider-Man Tour of New York City

What has long made Marvel Comics unique is that its fictitious superhero stories are primarily set in real-life cities and communities like New York, San Francisco, and Westchester County (as opposed to fictitious super-cities like Gotham, Central City, and Metropolis). And while many of Marvel's first wave of heroes used New York as a home base, none embraced the city and all its diverse neighborhoods and venues more than Spider-Man—a character whose comics over the years have been "a love letter to New York," according to Marvel's editor-in-chief Axel Alonso.[220]

So now it's time to grab a stack of Spidey comics, slip on your "I ♥ NY" shirt, make like a tourist, and check out all of these landmark buildings, parks, and cultural institutions that have been featured in Spider-Man comics and films over the years:

The Statue of Liberty (*Strange Tales Annual #2*, *Amazing Spider-Man #18*, *Spider-Man/Human Torch* miniseries, and others)**:** "Lady Liberty," France's gift to the U.S., which can be found on Liberty Island in New York Harbor, is also the designated meeting spot for Spider-Man and the *Fantastic Four's* Human Torch. Dating all the way back to the duo's first team-up in 1963, whenever these two teen heroes needed to get together, Torch would "flame on" in the sky and write, "Meet at our place" and Spidey would know where to find him.

The Empire State Building (*Amazing Annual #21*, *Sensational Spider-Man Annual #1*, *Amazing #673* and others)**:** A beacon of the New York City skyline, the Empire State Building is another "spot" for Spider-Man and one of his key supporting characters. On the eve of their nuptials, Spidey took his wife-to-be Mary Jane Watson up to the top of the building for a one-of-a-kind view and the couple kept returning to the ESB for many of their major moments together (and even a few moments after their marriage was wiped away by Marvel in 2007).

Coney Island (*Amazing #12*)**:** This classic amusement park/beach neighborhood in South Brooklyn was the site for an early battle between Spider-Man and Doctor Octopus. The issue even captures many of the neighborhood's iconic attractions like the Wonder Wheel ferris wheel and the Cyclone roller coaster.

Museum of Natural History (*Amazing #166*)**:** Home to one of the most famous dinosaur skeleton exhibits in the world, this institution naturally served as the backdrop for a battle between Spider-Man and a villain named Stegron the Dinosaur Man.

Studio 8H at 30 Rockefeller Plaza (*Marvel Team-Up #74*)**:** *Saturday Night Live* is still one of the toughest tickets to get in

Where Did Gwen Stacy Die?

It's a simple question: where did the Green Goblin murder Peter Parker's girlfriend, Gwen Stacy? And yet, the answer isn't as cut and dry as you'd think. When developing the epic *Amazing Spider-Man #121*, aka "The Night Gwen Stacy Died," writer Gerry Conway scripted the George Washington Bridge in Upper Manhattan as the spot where the Green Goblin kidnaps and murders Gwen. However, when Gil Kane penciled the scene, he illustrated the far more visually iconic Brooklyn Bridge in Lower Manhattan. Conway, who was "caught up with the emotions of the scene" when reviewing the issue, never noticed that Kane had illustrated the wrong bridge, so the GW stayed in the published story.[221]

As future stories continued to reference the events of Gwen's death, the Brooklyn Bridge and the GW Bridge were used interchangeably. Only adding to the confusion is the fact that some creators are insistent that a debate no longer exists, even though that's not technically true: "In the original comic, it's the George Washington Bridge, because of a story point, but the art was clearly the Brooklyn Bridge, and over the years, that's what it's become," said Dan Slott, who is currently scripting *Amazing Spider-Man* for Marvel.[222]

New York City, but that didn't keep Spider-Man away from this landmark television studio for a wacky story that saw him team up with John Belushi, Dan Akroyd, and the rest of the "Not-Ready-For-Primetime-Players" against the Silver Samurai.

Metropolitan Museum of Art (*Marvel Team-Up #79*)**:** Visitors can access this premier collection of art for as little as a $1, though who knows how Red Sonja found her way inside for this 1973 story. This comic marks the one and only Spider-Man/Red Sonja team-up since the "She-Devil with a Sword" is no longer licensed by Marvel Comics.

Columbus Circle (*Amazing #700*)**:** Named after the explorer Christopher Columbus, this busy traffic circle marks the spot where Doctor Octopus finally defeats (and kills) Spider-Man, setting the stage for 2013–14's *Superior Spider-Man* series starring Doc Ock masquerading in Spidey's body.

Flatiron Building: This triangular, 22-story building on Manhattan's Fifth Avenue also doubles as the home base of the *Daily Bugle* newspaper in Sam Raimi's *Spider-Man* movie trilogy released between 2002 and 2007.

Columbia University: What's with weird, wacky science experiments taking place on the campus of this Ivy League university (see also: *Ghostbusters*)? The infamous "spider-bite" scene in 2002's *Spider-Man* was filmed at Columbia.

New York Public Library: In Raimi's *Spider-Man*, poor Uncle Ben was murdered in front of this world famous library while waiting to pick his nephew, Peter, up from a study session (of course, Peter wasn't actually studying, he was too busy dressing up as Spider-Man for the first time and wrestling Bonesaw).

Roosevelt Island Tramway/Queensboro Bridge: Spanning the East River between Manhattan and Queens, the tramway and bridge were the setting for one of Peter's ultimate choices in the first *Spider-Man*: save a vehicle filled with innocents or the love of his life, Mary Jane, from the Green Goblin.

The National Museum of the American Indian: This Lower Manhattan museum doubled as the exterior for the New York Police Department's headquarters in 2012's *The Amazing Spider-Man* film.

Brooklyn Bridge Park: This beautiful waterfront park offers breathtaking views of Lower Manhattan from Brooklyn and was used as a set piece in 2014's *The Amazing Spider-Man 2* for a scene involving Peter and his old friend Harry Osborn.

Times Square: Not just a spot to find fake Spider-Men who shake tourists down for money in exchange for pictures. The "Crossroads of the World" were also the backdrop for Spidey's first battle with Electro in *The Amazing Spider-Man 2*.

42 The September 11th Issue

Marvel has long prided itself on setting its universe of fantastical superheroes in real-world cities. So after September 11, 2001, one of the darkest days in American (and most notably, New York City) history, Marvel felt it was only appropriate to respond the best way it knew how—by making comics.

Producing *Amazing Spider-Man (vol. 2) #36*, known throughout the industry as the "September 11th issue," was not a decision that was made lightly. Many of Marvel's top executives and editors witnessed the World Trade Center attacks from their Manhattan homes and offices. After returning to work a few days later, many employees struggled with the idea of continuing on with business as usual. Axel Alonso, Marvel's current editor-in-chief and editor of the Spider-books during the 9/11 attacks, felt that the comics, specifically the *Amazing Spider-Man*, needed to respond to the tragedy somehow. He called up the book's writer, J. Michael Straczynski, and asked if he had any ideas.

Like most Americans, Straczynski initially struggled to find a way to draw creative inspiration from the worst terrorist attack in American history. But then inspiration did eventually take hold, and after just a few days, Straczynski turned in a script that Alonso said "blew me out of my seat."[223] From there, the book was on its way to making history.

The comic, which featured an all-black cover, followed Spider-Man as he assisted New York City rescue workers picking through the wreckage at the site of the World Trade Center. Straczynski's script addresses the tremendous loss of life on September 11th, as well as some of the complex dialogue that was being had about the attacks in the immediate aftermath of 9/11. The emotionally raw script climaxes with a scene where Spider-Man watches a stoic Captain America at the site. Spider-Man thinks this is not the first time Cap, a soldier during World War II, has seen such horror, before concluding about September 11th, "I wish I had not lived to see this once."[224]

As tremendous as Straczynski's script was, it took a herculean effort from the book's art team—penciler, John Romita Jr., and inker, Scott Hanna—to create the visual landscape for the issue in such a short amount of time (the comic was released in mid-October, barely a month after the attacks happened). A Queens native, Romita was featured prominently in a *New York Times* article that promoted the comic's release, and was clearly struggling with having to provide artwork about such a raw, emotional event. "I have done this before—why is this so hard?" Romita said in the interview. "The answer is obvious.... There are thousands and thousands of people beneath that rubble."[225]

Years later, the 9/11 issue is still one of Marvel's finest hours—a demonstration of perseverance in the face of unimaginable sorrow. Straczynski referred to the comic as his "peak experience," as a comic book writer.[226] Alonso called it "the single most significant moment I've been attached to in comics' history. It narrowed the gap between our superheroes and the people who read us, particularly our readers in New York."

43 Ultimate Spider-Man

By the year 2000, the "amazing" Spider-Man was anything but. Comic book sales were sagging across the board. Marvel had published both a brand-new reimagining of Spider-Man's origin story called *Chapter One* (by superstar artist/writer John Byrne) and also rebooted its legacy *Amazing Spider-Man* series with a new No. 1 issue, and both events failed to inspire much response from fans and critics. And that was the least of Marvel's problems with Spider-Man. It still had to contend with the fact that one of its flagship characters was a late-twenty-something who had endured so many dark storylines—from discovering he was a clone, to separating from his supermodel wife, Mary Jane—that younger readers had seemingly tuned out the character.

To break Spider-Man's slump, Marvel's then-president, Bill Jemas, proposed a return to the character's more youthful, energetic days. But rather than hitting some kind of heavy-handed hard reset button on the *Amazing Spider-Man* series again, Jemas mandated a brand-new alternative universe where Spidey (and the mutant team the X-Men) could be returned to their points of origin and go on entirely new adventures—without being hamstrung by the rigidness of established storyline continuity. And thus, Marvel's *Ultimate* imprint was born.[227]

Ultimate Spider-Man may very well be Marvel's most successful new comic book venture of the past 20 years. Fans instantly responded to this refreshing new take on Spider-Man/Peter Parker, which set the character back in high school, but with a more contemporary origin story. There was a ring of familiarity to a lot of *Ultimate Spider-Man's* narrative elements—Peter still receives his powers from a spider-bite, and the death of his Uncle Ben is still the critical turning point that forces the character to accept that "with great power, must also come great responsibility." And there were still plenty of fantastical villains like the Green Goblin, Doctor Octopus, and Electro. But there were a lot of subtle and not-so-subtle changes to some of Spider-Man's most classic elements. And the driving force behind those tweaks and alterations was *Ultimate's* writer, Brian Michael Bendis, who ushered the series from its very first issue in 2000 to its finale in 2015.

After initially struggling to find a writer who would bring the right voice to *Ultimate*, Jemas turned to Bendis, a critical darling who had developed a following for his work on a variety of indie books in the late '90s. Bendis immediately realized that past attempts to "redo" Spider-Man were far too reverent and faithful to the original Stan Lee/Steve Ditko stories from 1962. Bendis took a far more decompressed approach to Spidey's origin. He scripted the first issue of what was only supposed to be a six-part miniseries over the course of a weekend, and in the story he turned in, Peter hadn't even made it into his iconic costume yet. But Jemas loved Bendis's approach, and the book was full steam ahead.[228]

As a counter to Bendis's indie sensibilities, Marvel tapped veteran artist Mark Bagley to provide pencils for the series. Bagley, who had enjoyed a sustained stint illustrating *Amazing Spider-Man* in the '90s, was initially resistant to the idea of once again illustrating the "Web-Slinger." He quietly kicked and screamed his way through the assignment, contemplating quitting, before an acquaintance took him aside and told him he'd be crazy to quit what was destined to be a career-defining gig.[229] Bagley listened to reason and, before it was all said and done, he and Bendis went on to set an industry record for the most consecutive issues (111) produced by the same writer/artist combo.

In addition to its more youthful mindset, *Ultimate* also took a far more pragmatic approach to Spider-Man than Lee/Ditko did. Rather than have Peter make money taking photos for the *Daily Bugle*, Bendis made him a web intern (since no major metropolitan newspaper would realistically hire a kid off the streets to take pictures). Bendis also changed Peter's dynamic with a number of characters: Aunt May, who Bendis based on his mother, was no longer a sickly frail old woman, but was a tough-as-nails maternal figure. Mary Jane Watson, the girl next door, was Peter's best friend, and later the girl he tells everything to, including his secret identity.[230]

There were *Ultimate* versions of many classic Spidey rogues like Doctor Octopus, Venom, and the Sinister Six. There was even an *Ultimate* version of the "Clone Saga," which Bendis called "the best crafted story of the whole run."[231] But they also featured subtle twists and changes from the original "mainstream" Spider-Man universe. Then, after 160 issues, Bendis had one more trick up his sleeve: the death of *Ultimate* Peter Parker, and in his place, an all-new web-slinging superhero: the half-back, half-Hispanic teenager, Miles Morales.

The creation of Miles was undoubtedly a passion project for Bendis, who long believed that a key part of Spider-Man's allure was the fact that "anyone" could be under that mask. For Bendis, Miles better represented what a young teenager in New York City would look like in today's world. "We made Miles because we wanted to make Miles, but once you make Miles, you realize it was kind of an obligation to make Miles," Bendis said. "It was the right thing to do."[232]

Despite Miles's popularity and cultural significance, falling sales finally forced Marvel to end its *Ultimate* universe in 2015 as part of the miniseries, *Ultimate End.* However, the legacy of Bill

Jemas's initial idea lives on with Miles, who is now a figure in Marvel's mainstream universe, starring in his own book, *Spider-Man* where, as Bendis said, he allows the company to "state our case for what a modern Spider-Man would be like that isn't Peter Parker."[233]

44 Brian Michael Bendis: The Ultimate Spider-Fan

When he was six years old, Brian Michael Bendis made a promise to his mother than he would one day become a Spider-Man artist.[234] It was a dream Bendis would sadly never fulfill. But before anyone sheds any tears for this unfortunate six-year-old whose dreams were shattered by the blunt force of cold, hard reality, keep in mind that this is *the* Brian Michael Bendis, one of the most prolific comic book writers in the medium's history and a guy who has scripted (but not illustrated) hundreds of Spider-Man stories over the past two decades.

Bendis is one of the masterminds behind Marvel's alternative version of Spider-Man, *Ultimate Spider-Man*. In the "mainstream" Marvel Universe, he also had the foresight to utilize Spider-Man for "Earth's Mightiest Heroes," the Avengers, leading to one of the most commercially successful creative runs in the superteam's history. And then there are all of those big-budget Marvel events Bendis has written, like *House of M*, *Secret Invasion*, *Siege*, *Age of Ultron,* and *Civil War II*. Plus, away from comics, Bendis has scripted episodes for *Spider-Man: The New Animated Series* and the more recent *Ultimate Spider-Man* cartoon. So what if he never got a chance to draw the "Web-Slinger"?

Bendis's love for Spider-Man began early for the Cleveland-born creator when, as a kid, he would carry around "pocket books" versions of the first six issues of Stan Lee/Steve Ditko's *Amazing Spider-Man* "like some would carry the Bible."[235] He was absolutely driven to one day break into comics and he wouldn't take "no" for an answer. In college, he created his own graphic novels and sold some of his work to independent publishers like Caliber and Fantagraphics. He started to gain recognition for creating the graphic novels *Goldfish* and *Jinx* before eventually being hired by Image Comics to write *Sam and Twitch*, a spinoff of Todd McFarlane's *Spawn* series.[236]

By the late 1990s, Bendis was a certifiable "name" in the industry, having won a prestigious Eisner Award for co-creating the superhero police/detective series *Powers* with artist Michael Avon Oeming. Still, everything was not exactly coming up roses for Bendis. He still found himself drawing caricatures at bar mitzvahs to make ends meet and his chance to finally break into Marvel by writing a Nick Fury series with artist Bill Sienkiewicz never advanced beyond the conceptual phase.[237] But Bendis quickly recovered when he was assigned to script *Daredevil*, which had been experiencing production delays with Hollywood director Kevin Smith at the helm.[238] And immediately after he signed on for *Daredevil*, he got a call from Marvel's president, Bill Jemas, about an opportunity to completely reinvent Spider-Man for a new generation: *Ultimate Spider-Man*.

The *Ultimate* line was Marvel's attempt to reconnect with younger audiences who might have become disinterested in the aging Spider-Man character found in *Amazing Spider-Man*. The series would be completely unburdened by previously published continuity, providing Bendis with a blank slate for Peter Parker and his world of friends and foes. Bendis knew "Spider-Man [wasn't] broken," but he also realized if the new Spidey story was going to work, he had to think a little bit out of the box. For an origin story,

AKA Spider-Man's Classmate

Fans of Marvel's offerings on Netflix may not be aware that one of the streaming service's most popular comic book shows has roots in the world of Spider-Man. Super-sleuth Jessica Jones, who debuted in *Alias #1* by Brian Michael Bendis and Michael Gaydos in 2001 and was adapted for television for the *Jessica Jones* series in 2015, has a history with Peter Parker, going back to when they were teenagers and classmates at the fictional Midtown High School.

Jessica immediately recognizes Peter when he unmasks for his Avengers teammates for the first time in *New Avengers #51*. That's when Peter remembers Jessica as "Coma Girl" from high school (Jones's coma when she was younger is a major plot point on the show).[244] Jessica and Peter's shared history is further fleshed out in an issue of *Amazing Spider-Man* when the reader learns that Jessica was actually in attendance when Spider-Man first fought Sandman in *Amazing Spider-Man #4* (moving her first appearance back from 2001 to 1963).[245]

rather than painlessly adapting 1962's *Amazing Fantasy #15*, he took a more decompressed, character-centric approach. Jemas loved Bendis's take, and *Ultimate Spider-Man* was born.[239]

Working on *Ultimate* also allowed Bendis to forge an inseparable connection to longtime Spidey artist Mark Bagley. Bendis has long joked that he envied the way Bagley broke into Marvel—by winning the Marvel Try-Out contest for artists (a contest Bendis also entered).[240] But that one-sided rivalry quickly evolved into a beautiful working relationship, and the tandem lasted 111 consecutive issues, the longest uninterrupted creative run in mainstream comic book history.

With *Ultimate Spider-Man* officially a success, Bendis soon found himself reinvigorating another major Marvel franchise in the Avengers. The team was ripe for a reboot following the events of the "Avengers: Disassembled" arc in 2003, so Bendis and writer Mark Millar pitched to Marvel's hierarchy a brand-new lineup that included only the very best heroes Marvel could find, including

Spider-Man and Wolverine. For years, Spidey was considered a major no-no for the Avengers—he was a "loner" who logically didn't fit in a team scenario (while Wolverine was just a jerk that nobody liked). But Bendis persisted, and eventually his argument won out and Spider-Man was included in the inaugural lineup of the *New Avengers* in 2004.[241]

As the lead wrier for *New Avengers*, Bendis started to incorporate other characters who have long been a part of Spider-Man's orbit. He integrated one of his personal favorites, Jessica Drew, aka Spider-Woman, and made her a focal point in a number of storylines, including *Secret Invasion*. He also cast longtime Spider-Man villain Norman Osborn (aka the Green Goblin) as a major threat to all of Marvel's heroes, including the Avengers. Suddenly, with Bendis in charge, even Captain America and Iron Man got a taste of what it's like to be Spider-Man: flailing hopelessly against a politically powerful and manipulative villain like Osborn.[242]

While writing all of these other stories, Bendis still wasn't done shaking up the world of Spider-Man and comics as a whole. In 2011, Bendis and Bagley created "The Death of Spider-Man" arc in *Ultimate*, which marked the end of Peter Parker. However, in his place, Bendis introduced a 13-year-old, half-black, half-Latino kid named Miles Morales. Despite Bendis's good intentions in showing how "anyone"—regardless of race, religion, or creed—could be Spider-Man under that mask, the ushering in of Miles was met with resistance in some unusual places, most notably some political pundits on television and radio. However, Bendis and Marvel held firm in their investment in Miles: "If Spider-Man was created today, he would be Miles," Bendis said. "It wouldn't be Peter. That's what we believe."[243]

45 Spider-Man's Big-Screen Debut: The Sam Raimi *Spider-Man* Trilogy

This might sound like pure fiction today, but there was once a time where getting Spider-Man on the big screen was no sure thing. In fact, it took nearly two decades and multiple lawsuits involving nearly half of Hollywood for a Spider-Man film adaptation to finally get the green light and go into production in the late 1990s. But miracles do happen in Tinseltown, and on May 3, 2002, Sony Pictures released the first of three *Spider-Man* films directed by Sam Raimi, kicking off what would go on to become one of Hollywood's most successful franchises.

Spider-Man's story actually begins in the mid-80s (the less said about the low-budget *Spider-Man* live-action show-turned-TV-movie in the late '70s, the better). That was when Marvel Comics first started shopping the film rights for its flagship superhero. But there were no takers. Hollywood had soured on superhero movies after *Superman 4* was deemed a flop. Independent studio Cannon Films took a shot for a paltry bid of $225,000 but after a couple years and little progress to report, Cannon was purchased by another studio, which filed for bankruptcy a short time later.

Meanwhile, at some point, Spidey's film rights, theatrical rights, and home video rights were all bid out to different studios, making a tangled mess for the studio that did eventually move forward with a Spider-Man flick. Carolco, which had produced big-budget movies such as *Rambo II* and *Terminator,* emerged as that studio, but they were soon facing lawsuits from other production companies who thought they owned a piece of Spider-Man.[246]

Superstar director James Cameron had signed on to script the new movie, but it didn't matter. By 1995, both Carolco and Marvel found themselves embroiled in bankruptcy proceedings.[247] Things looked bleak, but the legal entanglements were eventually resolved in 1998 when Spidey's film rights were sold to Sony. Cameron had moved on, but *Jurassic Park's* David Koepp was brought on to write the script. And *Spider-Man* was finally—*finally*—getting the green light. [248]

The plans for the film included a basic Peter/Spider-Man origin story, i.e., the famed spider-bite that gives him his great powers and, of course, Uncle Ben's death, which would teach Peter the lesson: "with great power must also come great responsibility." After some debate about featuring multiple villains in the movie, it was ultimately decided just to focus on one: Spider-Man's comic book nemesis, Norman Osborn, aka the Green Goblin. The film was also going to focus on the budding romance between Peter and the girl next door, Mary Jane Watson.[249]

Sony raised eyebrows when it brought in Sam Raimi to direct. Raimi was best known for the cult horror film franchise *Evil Dead,* while his only comic book movie experience was the 1990 flop *Darkman.* However, Sony was sold on Raimi's unquestioned love for Spider-Man as a character. The studio would soon be validated for its controversial choice.[250]

Leonard DiCaprio and Freddie Prinze Jr. were initially rumored to play Peter/Spider-Man, but Raimi and Sony decided on 26-year-old Tobey Maguire, a well-respected actor who starred in critically acclaimed films *Pleasantville* and *The Cider House Rules.*[251] Like Raimi, Maguire was not a "name," but he had a natural, quiet charisma to him that made him an ideal fit to play the everyman hero. For its leading lady, Sony cast another critical darling, Kirsten Dunst. Rounding out the film's trio of stars was Academy Award–nominee Willem Dafoe as Osborn.[252] Other key cast members included Rosemary Harris as the Parker-family matriarch, Aunt May; Cliff Robertson as Uncle Ben; James Franco as Peter's best friend and Norman's son, Harry Osborn; and J.K.

Simmons as the loudmouth editor/publisher of the *Daily Bugle,* J. Jonah Jameson.

After yet a few more delays—including having to edit out a sequence featuring the World Trade Center in the wake of the September 11, 2001, terrorist attacks—the film was released in May 2002.[253] The finished product was something that was very faithful to the spirit of the comics, with a notable exception being Spider-Man's "organic" web shooters (rather than developing the web-shooter wristlets like he does in the comics, the spider-bite allowed Peter to just "shoot" webbing from his wrists). It was also an undeniable hit, grossing nearly $115 million in its opening weekend and more than $400 million domestically over the duration of its theatrical release. Critics generally praised the film and it earned a score of 73 out of 100 from the review aggregator site Metacritic. And it featured plenty of talked-about and iconic scenes, such as the "upside-down" kiss shared by a masked Spider-Man and Mary Jane.

So after all that trouble, not only was Spider-Man a success, there was a sequel in the works for 2004. For *Spider-Man 2,* Sony hired Alfred Molina as Spider-Man's other nemesis, Otto Octavius, aka Doctor Octopus. Creating Doc Ock for the big screen involved a herculean effort of computer-generated imagery, as well as advanced animatronics and puppetry to bring his four mechanical arms to life. As a starting point, the crew had one of the production assistants model the Doc Ock attire with four dryer hoses attached to a girdle to get a sense for how the character would move and interact with others on the screen. CGI was used for most distance/long shots of the character, while a team of about 16 puppeteers helped to create all of Doc Ock's close-up interactions with his mechanical arms.[254]

Spider-Man 2 would also mark a leap forward in how the film captured Spider-Man's aerial acrobatics and web-swinging. For the first film, the crew utilized a "spydercam" for the movie's final

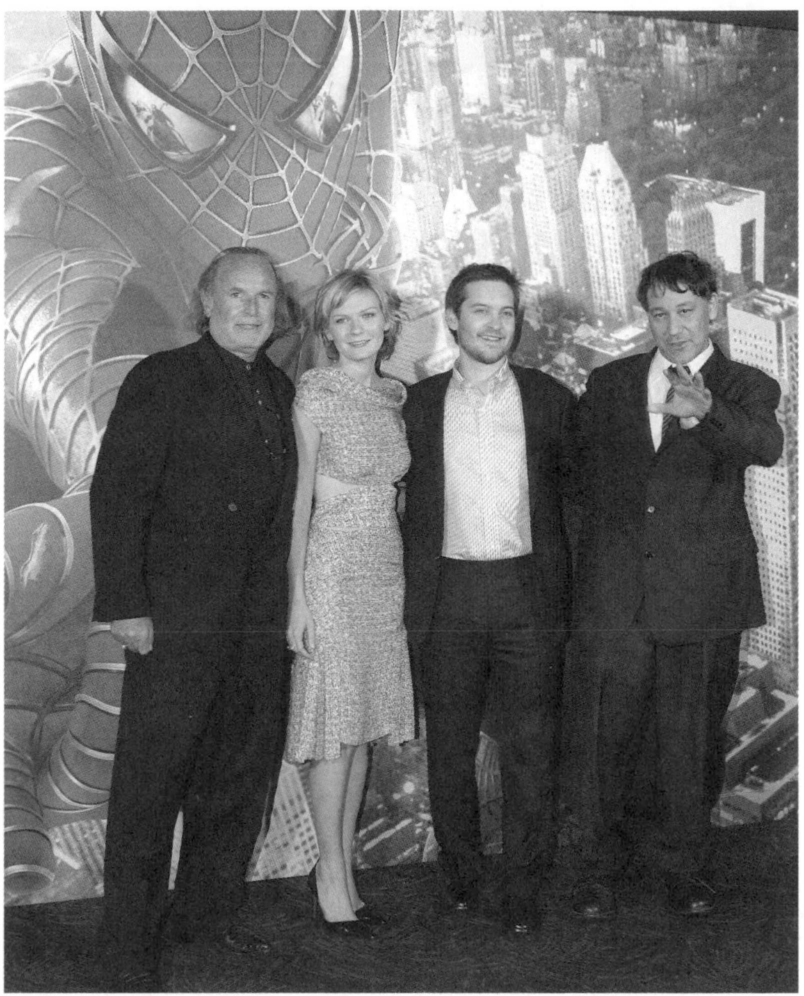

Producer Avi Arad, Kirsten Dunst, Tobey Maguire, and director Sam Raimi at the *Spider-Man 2* premiere in Paris. (Steph/Visual/Zumapress/Newscom)

shot, which consisted of a camera being rigged on a wire, depicting Spider-Man's point of view as he swung from building to building. The spydercam returned for the sequel and was used more frequently and in far more creative fashion, like rigging it 300–500 feet in the air and dropping it 50 stories to capture Spidey's aerial flight.[255]

For its story, the bulk of the script was built around the iconic Stan Lee/John Romita Sr. story "Spider-Man No More," (from 1967's *Amazing Spider-Man #50*). In it, Peter becomes so fed up with the responsibilities of being Spider-Man, he quits the gig altogether. In *Spider-Man 2*, Peter's frustration with being a masked hero manifests itself in how he forbids himself from dating the love of his life, Mary Jane, out of fear of putting her life in danger as Spider-Man. All told, *Spider-Man 2* was the most positively reviewed Spidey film to date, with a Metacritic aggregate score of 83 out of 100. The late, great Roger Ebert called it, "the best superhero movie since the modern genre was launched with *Superman* in 1978."[256]

By this point, a third film was academic. *Spider-Man 3,* which was released in May 2007, was jam-packed with new characters, like Thomas Haden Church as the granular villain Sandman, and Topher Grace as the super-popular adversary Venom. The use of Venom meant the film would also focus on the story behind Spider-Man's alien symbiote black costume, which first debuted in the comics in the mid-80s. If that wasn't enough, Bryce Dallas Howard was brought in to play Spidey's other girlfriend from the comics, Gwen Stacy, and the film still had to resolve a tangling plot thread from the first two movies involving Harry Osborn learning that his buddy was actually Spider-Man, and vowing revenge for the "Web-Slinger's" role in the death of his father.

If all of these characters and plotlines sounded untenable, that's because they were. *Spider-Man 3* had a huge opening weekend, grossing more than $150 million, a then-record, but for the first time since the franchise debuted, the studio and Raimi had to deal with some adversity in the form of tepid reviews from critics, as well as poor word-of-mouth from viewers. The overwhelming sentiment was that *Spider-Man 3* just had too much going on to cohesively work, plus there was that truly awful scene where Maguire performs a goofy disco dance in an effort to attract some ladies.

Still, despite the negativity, Raimi, Maguire, and Dunst were all on board for a fourth film. And rumor had it that theatrical heavyweight John Malkovich would play the winged villain the Vulture, with Anne Hathaway cast as Felicia Hardy (better known as the Black Cat in the comics, but reportedly a character called the Vultress in *Spider-Man 4*). However, before a script could be finalized, Raimi decided to quit the production, with Maguire and Dunst following suit, leaving Sony to find a new cast and crew for either a fourth *Spider-Man* film, or an entire new Spider-Man movie franchise. Raimi called the breakup undramatic and a result of his "own failings," but the damage was done.[257] Sony was moving on and going in a new direction. The first two Raimi movies are still considered the high watermark for Spidey on the big screen. As for the two movies that followed Raimi's trilogy? That's waiting for you in a later chapter.

46 Sam Raimi: The Movie Magic Maker

Sam Raimi would be the first to admit that putting him—a guy best known for low-budget cult horror flicks like *Evil Dead*—in charge of a billion-dollar cinematic franchise like *Spider-Man* was a risky proposition for Sony. In fact, when Raimi found out that Sony was serious about hiring him to direct its new *Spider-Man* franchise, which endured countless lawsuits, bankruptcies, and other legal challenges before finally moving forward in the late 1990s, he described his reaction as being "terrified" by the whole thing.[258]

Born in 1958 just outside of Detroit, Michigan, Raimi was an aspiring filmmaker from an early age. He attended Michigan

State University only to drop out so he could start making movies with his buddy Bruce Campbell (who would star in the *Evil Dead* movies and had a number of cameos in the *Spider-Man* films). Despite *Evil Dead's* popularity with horror buffs, Raimi never had a real box-office smash before *Spider-Man*. His two most commercially successful films were 1998's *A Simple Plan* and 2000's *The Gift*. Meanwhile, his two biggest-budget films, *The Quick and the Dead* (1995) and *For the Love of the Game* (1999), were both considered flops.[259]

But Sony's producers saw something in Raimi that made him the ideal choice over someone with a more established track record. Prior to hiring him, producer Avi Arad was enamored with just how much Raimi respected Spider-Man's rich history. Raimi was an unapologetic "Webhead" who even owned a huge commissioned poster of Spider-Man on his bedroom wall growing up.[260] He also spoke at great lengths about honoring the source material (the comics) and wanting to remain true to Spider-Man's main ethos, "with great power comes great responsibility."[261]

Raimi's infectious personality immediately sold Tobey Maguire and Kirsten Dunst, who were cast as Peter Parker and Mary Jane Watson, respectively. Dunst described Raimi as having a "twinkle in his eye" whenever he spoke about Spider-Man. Meanwhile, Maguire and Raimi instantly bonded, especially when the director reportedly went to bat for the young actor in getting the studio to hire him for the role rather than a more "bankable" name like a Leonard DiCaprio or Freddie Prinze Jr.[262] Some of the franchise's heavier hitters like Willem Dafoe (Norman Osborn/Green Goblin) and Alfred Molina (Doctor Octopus, *Spider-Man 2)* vouched for the director, with Dafoe going as far as to claim that he only accepted his role in *Spider-Man* because of Raimi. Molina, with dramatic flair, said, "the crew would have walked across hot coals for" Raimi.[263]

Raimi shockingly got very little interference from the studio while overseeing the first two *Spider-Man* films, even if he joked that he didn't necessarily "earn that freedom."[264] Unfortunately, Raimi's freedom didn't last through the third movie, which naturally is the most poorly received of the three. While Raimi has never specified exactly which character was forced upon him in *Spider-Man 3* (your guess is as good as mine **cough*Venom*cough**), he has taken full blame and responsibility for his trilogy ending on a sour note. Claiming he "didn't really believe in all the characters," Raimi said he tried to make *Spider-Man 3* work the best he could, but "if the director doesn't love something, it's wrong of them to make it when so many other people love it."[265]

Still, Raimi was game for a fourth movie until he walked away from the project due to being unhappy with the direction the studio wanted to take the franchise in. Sony opted to reboot its big-screen Spidey, sending Peter back to high school and hiring Marc Webb to direct. Raimi has admittedly not watched any of the Webb movies, joking that it would be the equivalent of going "to my girlfriend's wedding."[266]

47 Tobey Maguire: Spider-Man Comes to Life

If you squinted hard enough at Tobey Maguire's acting resume prior to being cast in one of Hollywood's most lucrative film franchises ever, you would have definitely seen some Peter Parker in there. To that point, his career consisted mostly of roles in quiet, pensive films like 1997's *The Ice Storm*, 1998's *Pleasantville*, and 1999's *Cider House Rules*. So it wasn't totally outlandish. And yet when Sony announced that Maguire would play its wise-cracking, web-slinging superhero in its first *Spider-Man* film, the general consensus was that it was more outrageous and fantastical than a teenager getting bitten by a radioactive spider and gaining the ability to climb the side of buildings and jump 50 feet into the air.

To the shock of no one, Maguire wasn't Sony Pictures' first choice to be Spider-Man. Big name actors Leonardo DiCaprio (a close friend of Maguire's) and Freddie Prinze Jr. were both rumored to be in the mix for the part when the film got the green light in the late '90s. However, *Spider-Man's* director, Sam Raimi, saw Maguire in *Cider House Rules* and was mesmerized by the authenticity of his performance. Raimi immediately went to bat for Maguire and, after initially resisting, Sony brought him in for an audition and was all in from there.[267]

Years before he was Spider-Man, Maguire was actually resistant to the idea of being an actor. He only enrolled in a theater class in school when his mother offered him $100 to do so.[268] After some commercial work and some small guest spots on television, Maguire landed his first starring role in 1992 in the short-lived Fox sitcom *Great Scott*.[269] After its cancellation, Maguire continued getting cast in various bit parts on television and in movies before getting his breakthrough role as a teenage boarding school student in the Ang Lee–directed film *The Ice Storm*.

Being Spider-Man presented some new challenges for Maguire, both emotionally and physically. To "bulk up" for the part, he kicked off a rigorous five-month physical training program that included martial arts, gymnastics, cardio, and working with a nutritionist.[270] He then needed to find a way to portray a complex character despite never having read a Spider-Man comic. Fortunately, Maguire, with Raimi's help, got the essence of Peter/Spider-Man pretty quickly: "He's someone kids can relate to.... He's a relatable, everyday kid," Maguire said in an interview with CNN in 2002. "He's not an alien or a multimillionaire. We can imagine ourselves in his position."[271]

Following the huge success of *Spider-Man*, Maguire was flying on cloud nine. He was set to earn $26 million for two sequels and was offered the role of horse jockey Red Pollard in the Oscar-baity *Seabiscuit.* However, while filming *Seabiscuit,* Maguire severely hurt his back and his participation in *Spider-Man 2* was cast in doubt. The studio went as far as to have a definitive "plan B" lined up in Jake Gyllenhaal.[272] Maguire managed to power through, and in *Spider-Man 2's* final cut, one scene even threw in a little wink and nod to Maguire's real-life struggle when Peter crash lands onto the top of a car and cries out "My back!"

Spider-Man 3 was expected to be Maguire's last run as the "Web-Slinger." Though, in a surprise twist, even after the film received negative reviews, Maguire said he was still on board for a fourth film as long as Raimi was still attached. However, once it became clear that project was plagued with issues, chiefly a number of irreconcilable differences between Raimi and the studio, Maguire (and Raimi and co-star Kirsten Dunst) quit. In a statement, the actor said: "I am so proud of what we accomplished with the *Spider-Man* franchise over the last decade. Beyond the films themselves, I have formed some deep and lasting friendships. I am excited to see the next chapter unfold in this incredible story."[273]

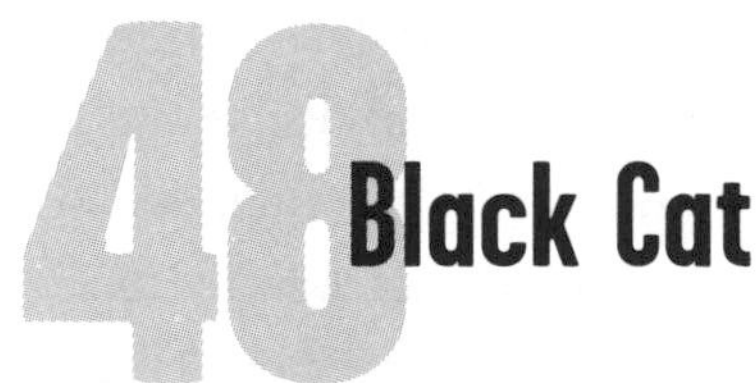

48 Black Cat

Dating back to her first appearance in *Amazing Spider-Man #194*, Felicia Hardy has always been the purr-fect femme fatale for Spider-Man. That's because Hardy, who is better known as the frisky and flirty burglar Black Cat, has come to emblemize Marvel's ultimate "bad girl" you want to love. And while elements of the character may resemble DC's Catwoman/Selina Kyle, Hardy has undoubtedly distinguished herself as her own unique breed of villainess while playing a central role in many popular Spider-Man stories.

Created by Marv Wolfman and Keith Pollard in 1979, Hardy was initially pegged as an antagonist to Jessica Drew in Marvel's recently launched *Spider-Woman* series, which was also being written by Wolfman. In fact, as initially explained in the "Letters" section of *Amazing #194*, Wolfman's original concept for Hardy was quite different from what Spider-Man fans know today: a 1940s-styled villainess, with a long dress, wide-brimmed hat, and, most importantly, not "action-orientated."[274] Soon after she was created, Wolfman left *Spider-Woman* to focus exclusively on *Amazing Spider-Man*. Rather than leave the character for *Spider-Woman's* succeeding writer, Wolfman took Hardy with him, but he also determined that her dark, "noir-ish" sensibilities wouldn't translate to Spidey's world. So artist Dave Cockrum revamped Hardy as a kittenish, action-orientated dynamo, complete with her signature black cat suit and white gloves/boots combo.[275]

Spider-Man is certainly intrigued by the Black Cat when they first cross paths, despite the fact that she callously robs and steals from others. However, the idea of ever making her and Spider-Man a couple—as Marvel eventually did—never crossed Wolfman's mind, who saw Hardy more as a distraction for Peter when her flirty ways would inevitably "make him nervous and lose control of the situation."[276] Fans loved the character all the same, and the seeds for them eventually hooking up were finally planted a few years after her introduction by Roger Stern and John Romita Jr. in *Amazing #226–227*.

In that story, Felicia promises "Spider" that she'll turn over a new leaf, only to once again break his heart by returning to her criminal ways and disappearing from his life. Still, the heart wants what the heart wants, and once Hardy returned to Spidey's life, the two finally started to date, but with a twist: Black Cat was only

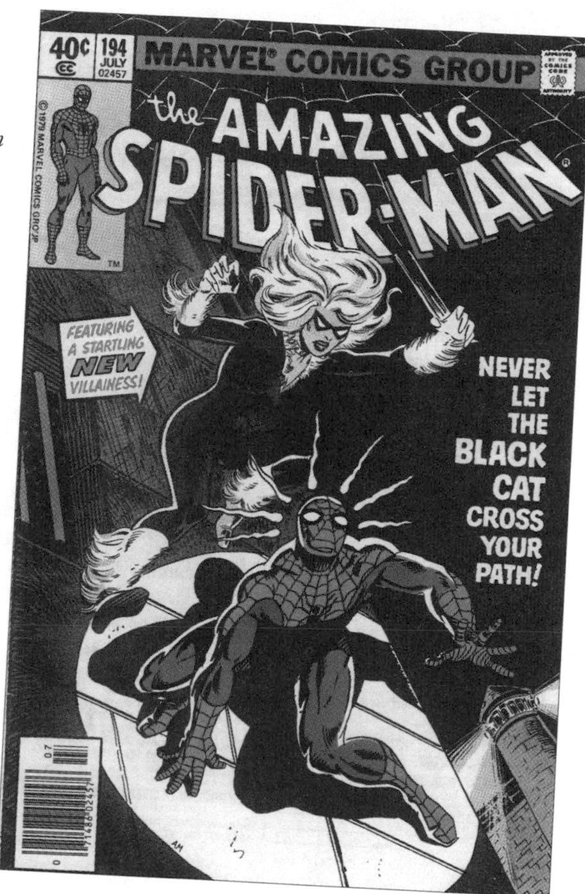

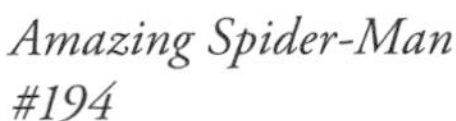
Amazing Spider-Man #194

interested in romancing Spider-Man, and even wanted to serve as his partner/sidekick in the field. But once Spidey tried to get her to love the man under the mask, the relationship went kaput. "She was the bad girl that we've all had a go-round with and who wasn't good for us at all," said longtime Spider-Man artist Ron Frenz. "She was also the girl that Pete needed to recover from, especially given her whole 'I love you as Spider-Man but not as Peter Parker' thing."[277]

By the mid-80s, Black Cat had been pushed aside to make way for a returning Mary Jane Watson, who Peter would eventually marry in 1987. But after 2007's "One More Day" storyline erased the Peter/MJ union from existence, a number of creators were once again anxious to get Spider-Cat back together. "I always thought of her as a fun, sexy character…but she's always going to want something more…even when Spidey is alone again," said Joe Kelly, who scripted a few Spider-Man/Black Cat trysts in the post-"One More Day" universe.[278]

In a surprise swerve, in today's comic book landscape, Black Cat has gone totally rogue and has emerged as a leader/boss in the criminal underworld. She also harbors a wicked vengeance for Spider-Man when her one-time boyfriend captures her and leaves her for the authorities during the *Superior Spider-Man* era (when Spider-Man was actually Doctor Octopus going around masquerading as Spidey after stealing his body). While some fans look at the current status quo and wistfully recall the days where Felicia flirtatiously called Spider-Man "Spider" before lifting the costumed hero's mask and locking lips with him, evil Black Cat only reinforces the idea that many creators have long held about Hardy from the beginning—she's the wrong girl for Spidey.

49 Gerry Conway: Prodigy Turned Villain

Gerry Conway is still really sorry about that whole throwing Gwen Stacy off a bridge thing. Sure, he's one of the most accomplished writers in Spider-Man comics' history, responsible for creating a slew of iconic characters including the Punisher, Jackal, Hammerhead, Tombstone, the wacky Spider-Mobile, and Spider-Man's clone. He was tasked with scripting the first-ever intra-company promotion involving Spider-Man and DC's Superman. And he's still writing critically and commercially successful comics today, more than 40 years after he first broke into the industry as a teenager. But Conway is also the first to admit that he will be forever known, for better or worse, as the guy who killed the love of Peter Parker's life, Gwen Stacy.

Today, Conway wears his role as the breaker of hearts, destroyer of fictitious romance, as a badge of honor, promoting himself as "the man who killed Gwen Stacy" during public appearances. But that doesn't change how at one time he was undisputedly the most hated man in comics, so much so that he even stopped attending conventions due to all the verbal abuse and threats he received.

Putting aside the vitriol, Conway is one of the comic book industry's great prodigies, a guy who started getting published when he was 15 and was named the great Stan Lee's successor as writer of the *Amazing Spider-Man* when he was barely 20.[279]

His affinity for Spider-Man was without peer: "I felt simpatico to Peter Parker," Conway said. "We were both young adult men trying to figure out how to combine relationships with careers in New York City. I felt like I knew that guy and I passionately wanted to write him."[280]

Conway got his chance with *Amazing #111*. Within his first few issues, he created Hammerhead—a hard-headed, flat-topped gangster straight out of a *Dick Tracy* comic. It was shortly after that he started to conspire with Marvel's art director, John Romita Sr., and editor-in-chief Roy Thomas to "shake up" *Amazing*. The trio discussed killing off a major character, even suggesting Aunt May before settling on Gwen. Poor, sweet Gwen.[281]

What could Conway had been thinking? Well, he was admittedly always more of a Mary Jane Watson guy, meaning he preferred the redheaded vixen to the more demure Gwen. But he also found Gwen a bit bland and boring. He determined that removing her from the equation would allow him to be more creative with the kind of stories he wanted to tell.[282] Conway, Romita, and Thomas ran the storyline by Lee, who had taken over as Marvel's publisher. Then, depending on whose account you want to believe, Lee either agreed to the story, or he agreed to the story without realizing that Conway was absolutely serious about killing off his precious Gwen. Either way, after "The Night Gwen Stacy Died" was published, Lee started complaining about it, so much so that Thomas felt compelled to publish a letter in *The Comics Journal*, where he claims that Lee not only approved of the story, but was enthusiastic about it.[283]

Regardless of what Lee actually thought, the deed was done. Not only was Gwen dead, but the way Conway and artist Gil Kane framed the scene, they insinuated that her demise was Spider-Man's fault. After the Green Goblin tossed her off a bridge, Spider-Man shoots a line of webbing and snares her by her boot. Next to that image, Conway inserted the sound effect "snap." Yes, it means what you think it means. Spider-Man's webbing snapped Gwen's neck thanks to the whiplash effect.[284] Then, for as an encore to Gwen's death, Conway and Kane killed Spider-Man's archnemesis, Norman Osborn, aka the Goblin, the very next issue.

And that's how you become the most hated man in comics.

Following the Gwen story, Conway and Romita co-created the most famous antihero in comics, Frank Castle, aka the Punisher. Inspired by the Charles Bronson film *Death Wish*, Conway originally conceived of Castle as a one-and-done character. But once he realized how cool he was—especially with his iconic skull-on-chest costume, designed by Romita—Conway decided that the Punisher would be around for the long haul.[285]

Conway's final *Amazing Spider-Man* story of the '70s would pave the road for one of the most controversial arcs in comic book history: the dreaded "Clone Saga." As fans continued to abuse Marvel about Gwen's death, Lee suggested to Conway that he should bring her back. Preferring to leave her dead, Conway instead opted to create a clone of Gwen. And with Gwen's doppelganger running around, why not create a clone of Spider-Man too? Done! And while the clone was seemingly killed in *Amazing #149*, Conway's final issue, about 20 years later a group of creators had other ideas and...well, we'll save that for a later chapter.

Following his run on *Amazing*, Conway jumped between Marvel and DC a few times, even serving as Marvel's editor-in-chief for a short stint in the '70s. Then, a decade later, he was invited back to the world of Spider-Man when he was offered a gig scripting Spidey's two "B" books: *Spectacular Spider-Man* and *Web of Spider-Man*. Conway used the assignment as an opportunity to develop many of Spider-Man's supporting castmates, like Aunt May, J. Jonah Jameson, and most famously Joe "Robbie" Robertson, in what has become a fan favorite story about the *Daily Bugle* city editor facing his past and serving time in jail for failing to report a murder he witnessed.[286]

Proving he's the master of reinvention, Conway has recently endured another career renaissance. After finding the spotlight again following the release of 2014's *The Amazing Spider-Man 2* (which adapted elements of "The Night Gwen Stacy Died"), Conway was invited to script a street-level-focused Spider-Man miniseries in 2015 called "Spiral." After "Spiral," Conway started work on *Carnage,* his first monthly ongoing book for Marvel in more than a decade. Then, in what may be an appropriate capper to Conway's career (should he ever look to call it quits one day), in late 2016, he and artist Ryan Stegman unveiled the newest Spider-Man ongoing series, *Renew Your Vows*, which is set in an alternative universe where Peter and Mary Jane are married with a child.

Just stay away from any bridges, Parker family.

50 Richard and Mary Parker

In Peter Parker's first appearance in *Amazing Fantasy #15*, the reader immediately learned that he was an orphan living with his aunt and uncle. However, what remained a mystery, and unexplained by Marvel for years to follow, was the story behind the death of his parents, Richard and Mary.

The topic was finally broached for the first time in 1968's *Amazing Spider-Man Annual #5* by Stan Lee and his brother, Larry Lieber. The somewhat controversial comic depicted Peter as being the son of two government spies who were murdered in a plane crash/explosion as part of a larger conspiracy by the nefarious Red Skull. It was certainly an unexpected plot twist, considering how Peter had been forever portrayed as being the average, everyman character who, through sheer luck and circumstance, received strange powers via a radioactive spider-bite. Having his parents be super spies for an agency that was the precursor to Marvel's ultimate espionage group, S.H.I.E.L.D., seemingly flew in the face of the randomness of Peter's transformation into Spider-Man.

Regardless, the annual issue remained canon, as well as Richard and Mary's only significant storyline of note, until nearly 25 years later when the characters shockingly "returned," only to later be revealed as androids in a scheme orchestrated by Peter's longtime adversary, Harry Osborn, aka the second Green Goblin. Following this otherwise convoluted saga, which was released in the heart of the big event-orientated '90s, Peter's parents went back to being a non-entity again in the mainstream comic book universe. Still, that hasn't stopped other creators from trying to explore Richard and Mary's origins some more. In the alternative universe-based *Ultimate Spider-Man* series, Richard was a biologist who, while working on a cure for cancer, inadvertently creates the *Ultimate* version of the supervillain Venom.

The characters were further elevated by Marc Webb's two *The Amazing Spider-Man* films in 2012 and 2014. Perhaps in an effort to distinguish themselves from Sam Raimi's trilogy of *Spider-Man* movies released a decade earlier, Webb's Spider-verse leaned heavily on building its narrative around the mystery of Richard and Mary's deaths. Both movies opened with sequences involving Richard and Mary (played by Campbell Scott and Embeth Davidtz, respectively), with the second one depicting the fateful plane crash from the comics. The films also suggest that Richard's scientific research, conducted while working for the evil corporation Oscorp, was directly linked to how Peter eventually became Spider-Man.

Unfortunately, the Webb movies' emphasis on Richard and Mary has also been cited as one of the main reasons *The Amazing Spider-Man* series was so unpopular with fans, who believed the studio dedicated too much screen time to characters who weren't all that important to Spider-Man's larger mythology. And that's only when you take the final production into account. According to reports about an earlier draft of the *The Amazing Spider-Man 2,* Sony planned to have Richard appear at the end of the film and become the first character in the Webb-verse to state the famous Spider-Man ethos: "with great power comes great responsibility" (a line of dialogue that was outrageously absent from the first *The Amazing Spider-Man*).[287]

51 Marvel Team-Up

Spider-Man's the first person to describe himself as a loner. But his quirky personality (not to mention his popularity with readers) were the catalysts behind the "Web-Slinger" headlining Marvel's first foray into a team-up series, i.e., a comic that features two heroes joining forces, in *Marvel Team-Up*.

Originally intended as a vehicle for Spider-Man and Human Torch, *MTU* launched in 1972 and ran for 150 issues before its cancellation in 1985. While the title isn't considered a proper Spider-Man book per se, he starred in all but 11 installments (and one of those was actually a far-out *What If...?* story involving Peter Parker's Aunt May becoming the herald of the cosmic, planet-eating Galactus...seriously, don't ask) and is considered by most to be Spidey's first "B" title—that is, an ancillary book published in addition to the "main" comic, *Amazing Spider-Man*.

The formula for *MTU* was repetitive but effective. In nearly every issue, Spider-Man would cross paths with a random superhero du jour, and after some witty banter and/or bickering, the pair would eventually come together to face off against a common threat. Stories would often be resolved in one issue, but occasionally, an arc would extend to two, three, or four issues, in which case, typically additional heroes (or threats) would be introduced. Spidey's monthly partners ran the gamut from your A-list studs like Captain America, Thor, or Iron Man, to the more obscure/absurd "heroes" like Killraven, the Frankenstein monster, or Howard the Duck. Sometimes, there would be strategic reasons behind a pairing; such as providing more exposure for a hero on the cusp of getting his or her own book or trying to save a book that was on the verge of cancellation. For example, Werewolf by Night's appearance in *MTU #12* preceded the debut of his own ongoing series by a month, while the Cat was inserted into *MTU #8* only to see her series canceled a short time later.

But the book also managed to introduce some popular characters and ideas on its own. *MTU #65* marked the first American appearance of Marvel UK hero Captain Britain (as well as the X-Men villain, Arcade), while police Captain Jean DeWolff (who is probably better known for her death) first appeared in *MTU #48.*

Some Other Spidey Team-Ups

Comic creators just loving pairing Spider-Man with other heroes. While proper team-up books are often the venue for these shenanigans, Spider-Man has also been the co-star of various other miniseries and ongoing books that relied strongly on him needing to get along with another Marvel superstar. Here are some of the very best:

Astonishing Spider-Man & Wolverine: Jason Aaron and Adam Kubert put Spider-Man and the grouchy Canadian Wolverine on a time-traveling adventure for this six-issue 2011 miniseries.

Spider-Man/Human Torch: Current Spider-Man writer Dan Slott's love letter to both Spidey and his best frenemy, Johnny Storm/Human Torch. Ty Templeton provided the art for the mini, which ran for five issues in 2005.

Ultimate Six: Brian Michael Bendis and Trevor Hairsine team the *Ultimate Spider-Man* with the *Ultimate* universe's version of the Avengers, the Ultimates in this seven-issue miniseries from 2003 to 2004. Could this mini serve as a template for a future Spider-Man/Avengers cinematic story?

Spider-Man/Deadpool: Since artist Rob Liefeld's original concept for the foul-mouthed Deadpool was basically a rip-off of Spider-Man, it only made sense to team these two up eventually. Joe Kelley, who had a sustained run writing *Deadpool* in the '90s before jumping to *Amazing Spider-Man* in the late 2000s, teams with artist Ed McGuinness, in this ongoing series that launched in 2016.

And fans of S.H.I.E.L.D./*West Coast Avengers* comics should note that Bobbi Morse debuted her more popular Mockingbird persona in *MTU #95*.

The series also served as a breeding ground for up-and-coming writers and artists who would go on to do bigger and better things in the industry. Years before he wrote the all-time great Spider-Man tale "Kraven's Last Hunt," J.M. DeMatteis enjoyed a sustained run scripting *MTU* in the early '80s. And shortly before Chris Claremont and John Byrne changed comics forever with their work on *Uncanny X-Men*, they cut their teeth pairing Spider-Man off with the likes of Iron Fist, Luke Cage, and Red Sonja (a character Marvel was licensing at the time). Claremont would actually credit his time on *MTU* for helping him hone his craft as a writer since he was faced with the challenge of having to work with a new cast of characters every issue.[288]

The series is also known for some of Marvel's sillier moments, like that one issue that saw Spidey team up with the cast of late-night variety show, *Saturday Night Live*. John Belushi, one of the "Not Ready for Primetime Players," was reportedly such a huge fan of Marvel that Claremont and a few other creators received an invitation to the after-party for the premiere of *National Lampoon's Animal House* in 1978.[289]

But the party had to end eventually. In 1985, Marvel's editor-in-chief, Jim Shooter, decided the era of force fed team-ups needed to end and he pulled the plug on *MTU* in favor of a new Spider-Man book, *Web of Spider-Man*. Of course it's hard to deny a good formula, which led to the creation of other team-up books co-starring Spider-Man in the years that followed (including two additional volumes of *MTU*), such as *Avenging Spider-Man* and *Superior Spider-Man Team-Up* between 2012 and 2014.

52 The Punisher

Demonstrating that you can never truly know what the next big thing in comics might be, Frank Castle, aka that enduring anti-hero, the Punisher, was originally created to be a one-time stooge in a 1974 issue of *Amazing Spider-Man*. The fact that the character has gone on to star in various comic book series, movies, television shows, cartoons, videos games, etc. remains a happy, unintended accident.

Created by Gerry Conway and artist John Romita Sr., the Punisher's comic book debut in *Amazing Spider-Man #129* features the character, wearing his now-iconic death's head skull shirt, working for another new villain, the mysteriously masked Jackal. Per the Jackal's orders, Castle hunts Spider-Man, who has been accused by the *Daily Bugle* newspaper of murdering Norman Osborn. It would be a few years before readers received the full context of Punisher's famous origin story—former U.S. Marine who turns into a vengeance-filled psychopath after his family is murdered by drug dealers. But a lot of Castle's patented paranoia-filled self-righteousness is on display in that first appearance.

And yet that was almost Punisher's only appearance. The real villain Conway was pushing at the time was Jackal. But once it became clear that "the Punisher was a much cooler character than the Jackal!" it became a matter of when not if to "welcome back Frank."[290]

Conway's concept for the character came on the heels of the successful 1974 Charles Bronson film *Death Wish*, which depicts a man becoming a vigilante after his wife is murdered and his daughter is sexually assaulted by criminals. Some other inspirations included Clint Eastwood's iconic rogue cop, Dirty Harry, and an

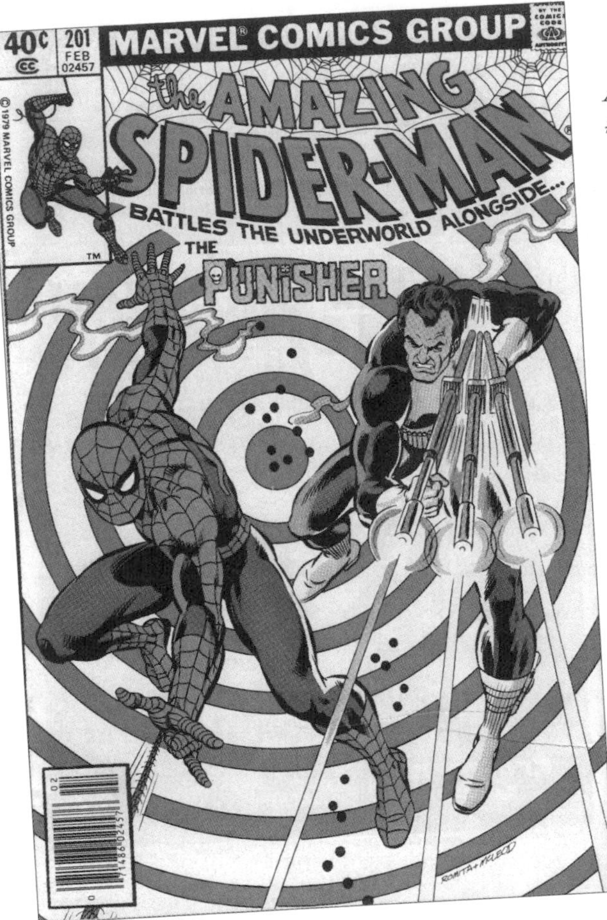

Amazing Spider-Man #201

old paperback pulp character, the Executioner.[291] After Conway developed a rough sketch of the character, Romita, Marvel's art director and a frequent collaborator with Conway during the writer's run on *Amazing Spider-Man*, tweaked the design—most notably by adding the now-iconic skull insignia that stretches across Castle's entire chest. Stan Lee provided the finishing touch by suggesting the name "Punisher."[292]

Punisher would periodically appear in other Spider-Man stories over the course of the '70s, but Conway recalls that Marvel was still somewhat hamstrung by the Comics Code Authority (which policed comic book content for extreme violence and other questionable material) in terms of how far they could push Castle's deranged brand of vigilante justice.[293] It wasn't until Frank Miller/ Klaus Janson's critically acclaimed run on *Daredevil* in the late '70s/ early '80s that Punisher became more of a mainstream character. Miller cast the street justice–swearing Castle as the Daredevil's ideological opposite.

In 1986, Marvel finally featured Castle in his own book, publishing the five-part *The Punisher* miniseries by Steven Grant and Mike Zeck. The success of that mini led to the character getting his own monthly ongoing series in 1987, which ran for more than 100 issues. Then in 1989, Dolph Lundgren portrayed the character in the live-action *The Punisher*. Granted, the film is considered a flop in almost every sense of the word, but the message was still loud and clear: Punisher was a sensation.

When sales started to plummet throughout the comic book industry in the mid-90s, most Punisher books were either canceled or discontinued. Still the character has endured in the comics and other media, including two major films (2004's *The Punisher*, starring Thomas Jane, and 2008's *Punisher: War Zone*, starring Ray Stevenson). And the character is currently in the midst of another major renaissance thanks to Jon Bernthal's transcendent performance as Castle in the second season of *Daredevil* on Netflix. Fans responded so well to Bernthal that Castle is set to star in his very own Netflix series in the near future.

And in a fun twist, this latest iteration of the Punisher is actually linked to Spider-Man: Bernthal created his Marvel Studios audition tape for the role while filming *Pilgrimage* in Ireland with a young actor named Tom Holland—who also sent Marvel an audition tape for the role of Spider-Man (a role Holland ultimately was offered and accepted).[294]

53 Tom DeFalco: All in the Spider-Family

As the calendar was flipping from 1983 to 1984, Tom DeFalco was dealing with a serious problem as it related to Spider-Man. DeFalco, who had edited the Spider-books (i.e., *Amazing Spider-Man*, *Spectacular Spider-Man,* and *Marvel Team-Up*) for a number of years, had just handed the editorial baton over to Danny Fingeroth. Shortly thereafter, writer Roger Stern, who was in the midst of one of the greatest creative runs in *Amazing Spider-Man* history, decided to resign from the title so he could focus on scripting *Avengers* full-time. Artist John Romita Jr. also left *Amazing*. DeFalco met with Fingeroth to discuss potential options to replace Stern and JRJR—if it was even possible to replace such universally beloved creators.

"I made some suggestions for replacements…and Danny just had this goofy look on his face," DeFalco said. "'Why aren't you writing this stuff down?' I said to him. 'Because I already know who I want to write the book,' he said."[295]

Fingeroth had pegged DeFalco as the new writer of *Amazing*, an idea that absolutely shocked and dismayed DeFalco. "No way could I follow Roger," he said. "Whoever followed him would look like a bum."[296] Bum indeed. DeFalco went on to be one of the most beloved Spider-Man writers of all time, enjoying multiple stints on various Spider-books, and even serving as Marvel's 10th editor-in-chief between 1987 and 1994.

During his initial run on *Amazing*, DeFalco and artist (and close friend) Ron Frenz brought an old-school tone and aesthetic back to the book, reminiscent of the Stan Lee/Steve Ditko years. But DeFalco wasn't only about nostalgia. In the '80s alone he co-created a number of new characters, like the Rose, Puma, and

Silver Sable, and helped develop the black alien suit saga that, in turn, led to the creation of fan-favorite Venom. He would later work on such landmark stories as the "Clone Saga" and "Maximum Carnage." And just when it seemed like maybe he was out of new ideas, in 1998, he co-created Spider-Girl, aka, Mayday Parker—a hypothetical *What If...?* story that became an ongoing series set in an alternative universe starring Peter Parker and Mary Jane's child.

Perhaps Spider-Man was just in DeFalco's blood. Born in Queens, New York (like Peter), in 1950, DeFalco was a big comic book fan starting at an early age, reading strips like *Dick Tracy, Pogo,* and *On Stage*. When he was a little older, DeFalco discovered *Fantastic Four* on the spinner rack, opening his eyes to the wonders of Marvel Comics. From that point on, DeFalco set out to devour all the Marvel Comics he could find.[297]

DeFalco was an avid writer in high school and college, freelancing for newspapers and selling short stories. But he wanted to create comics. He got his first chance at Archie Comics, handling random tasks including opening mail for the "Dear Betty and Veronica" letters section. After seven years, he left Archie for DC, only to get invited into the Marvel family after attending a poker game with writers/editors Len Wein and Marv Wolfman and the company's editor-in-chief, Jim Shooter. After a short stint freelancing, DeFalco was soon offered an exclusive contract to work for Marvel.[298]

DeFalco quickly ascended Marvel's ranks under Shooter, eventually serving as the editor-in-chief's right-hand man.[299] He started editing all of the Spider-books before the aforementioned conversation with Fingeroth landed him the gig writing one of Marvel's flagship characters. But before DeFalco could dive in, he first needed to script a pair of *Amazing* issues that Stern had plotted before he left the title. One of them was *Amazing #252*, the first appearance of Spider-Man's black suit. DeFalco had earlier worked with a fan who pitched the story to Shooter as part of a Marvel tryout contest. When DeFalco failed to churn a tangible story out of the fan, he, Stern, and others took over, introducing some twists, including the fact that the suit was actually an alien symbiote seeking a "host."[300]

Ron Frenz provided pencils on *Amazing #252* before becoming the books' regular artist at *#255*. The DeFalco/Frenz partnership is considered by many to be one of the most magical in Spider-Man history. DeFalco himself has called it a "defining moment" for his career.[301] Both had an undeniable passion for Spidey/Peter, often having long phone conversations where they discussed nuanced things like who the characters were and what their motivations should be. When it came time to create some new rogues, Frenz and DeFalco referred to a deck of "animal cards" as an inspiration for the likes of Puma, Silver Sable, and Black Fox.[302]

Unfortunately, the DeFalco/Frenz run was not without some controversy. Fingeroth had left his perch as Spider-book editor, and a young man named Jim Owsley (now known as Christopher Priest) took over. DeFalco and Frenz frequently butted heads with Priest, who accused the duo of missing deadlines and forcing him to hire fill-in writers/artists (DeFalco and Frenz both dispute these claims). Additionally, Priest clashed with DeFalco/Frenz over various storylines. In early 1987, Priest, claiming he was being encouraged by Shooter, fired DeFalco and Frenz from the book, effectively ending their run. Shortly thereafter, Priest was then relieved of his duties by Shooter. And then, by April 1987, Shooter was forced out as editor-in-chief and DeFalco was in charge.[303]

DeFalco has called his eight years as editor-in-chief a "forgotten realm."[304] However, the first few years of DeFalco's reign marked some of the most financially successfully times in Marvel's history. Thanks to a comic book collector's bubble fueling speculators, sales were at an all-time high. In 1991, Marvel became a publicly traded company. During this time, DeFalco continued to keep his writing chops sharp, scripting *Fantastic Four* and *Thor*. However, by the mid-90s, things started to fall apart for Marvel and the industry as a whole. The speculator bubble burst and sales collapsed. After some clashes with upper management, DeFalco resigned as editor-in-chief in 1994.

However, before his resignation, DeFalco oversaw the beginnings of one of the most controversial Spider-Man stories ever. A couple of his writers, Terry Kavanagh and Howard Mackie, had pitched an idea to the Spider-office about bringing back Peter Parker's clone, who last appeared in a Bronze Age storyline in *Amazing Spider-Man #150*. The story was originally designed to last about three or four months and would involve the clone returning and staking a claim as being the "real" Spider-Man. It would then be revealed that the clone was legitimately Peter, giving the Peter readers had been seeing for the past 15 years the opportunity to ride off into the sunset with his wife, Mary Jane. DeFalco initially thought the pitch was absurd, but was eventually turned by Kavanagh and Mackie's enthusiasm. He even pitched his own ideas for the story, like how Mary Jane should be pregnant, to add some extra stakes to Peter's inevitable departure from the book.[305]

Even after leaving his post as editor-in-chief, DeFalco stayed on to script the "Clone Saga" on *Spectacular Spider-Man*. But once the storyline resolved (if you can call it that), Marvel moved DeFalco back to *Amazing Spider-Man*, where he wrote a number of stories including the resurrection of Doctor Octopus and an origin story for longtime Spidey rogue Electro. Around this time, DeFalco was also assigned to do an issue of *What If...?*. He called up his old friend Frenz and kicked around an idea of bringing back the unborn child of Peter and Mary Jane with spider-powers of her own. The *What If...?* issue starring Mayday Parker was successful enough to become the flagship title of a new universe of Marvel books called MC2. While it was never a sales juggernaut, *Spider-Girl* developed enough of a cult following to be published for more than 12 years. And when Marvel launched its "Spider-Verse" event in 2014, featuring every Spider-Man from every alternative universe, Mayday played a key role, and DeFalco was brought back to script a few short *Spider-Girl* stories.

"We made characters people care about and gave them real stories," DeFalco said. Then, in a sentence that could serve as an analogy for his own career at Marvel, added, "*Spider-Girl* didn't sell and yet Marvel published it for 13 years."

54 John Romita Jr: Junior

The letters "J" and "R" are an important part of John Romita Jr.'s legacy in the comic book industry. Not only because fans and other creators affectionately refer to him as "J.R." or "JRJR," but also because of who the senior is to his junior: his father, the legendary Marvel artist and the company's former art director, John Romita.

With a father as talented and influential as Romita Sr., one would think a career in comics would have been a cinch for JRJR. Unfortunately, that hasn't always been the case. That's of no fault of Romita Sr., who J.R. describes as "my hero" and "one of my biggest fans."[306] Instead, Romita Jr.'s family tree has seemingly inspired some petty jealousy, and in some cases, some flat-out vindictiveness from select members of the powers that be. But rather than quit, JRJR doubled down and emerged both a better person and artist—arguably one of the greatest Spidey illustrators ever.[307]

Romita Jr. has the unique distinction of penciling two sustained runs of *Amazing Spider-Man*—in the early 1980s and later on in the early 2000s. And then there's all of the Spider-Man "B" books and miniseries he's illustrated, plus the scores of other iconic

Marvel creations he's worked on like Iron Man, Daredevil, the X-Men, Punisher, Hulk, Wolverine, and Thor.

"It was so much fun seeing the pages [from Romita Jr.] every month, because every month he would get better," said Roger Stern, who scripted *Amazing* during JRJR's first stint on the book in the '80s. "J.R. had the genes. He had the magic."[308]

Born in Queens in 1956, Romita Jr.'s unofficial start as a comic book artist came as a 13-year-old in 1969, when his father was penciling *Amazing*. JRJR had doodled a villain he named "the Prowler." Stan Lee, Spider-Man's co-creator and the main writer of the book, was nonplussed by J.R.'s costume and character design, but he loved the name the Prowler and ran with it after some alterations by artists John Buscema and Jim Mooney.[309]

JRJR officially got his start in the late '70s, when he was hired to illustrate reprint covers as part of Marvel's United Kingdom (UK) imprint. He eventually got the opportunity to illustrate a six-page back-up in *Amazing Spider-Man Annual #11* titled "Chaos at the Coffee Bean." Romita Jr. has since derided the piece as "terrible." Regardless of his own personal opinion, the story ultimately led to his first ongoing gig at Marvel, providing pencils on the landmark *Iron Man* run that was co-plotted by David Michelinie and Bob Layton. But despite the success/legacy of that *Iron Man* run, which included such notable stories as "Demon in a Bottle" (the arc that depicted Tony Stark's battle with alcoholism), JRJR struggled in his working relationship with Michelinie and Layton. He was rarely involved in the storytelling process and Layton, who also provided inks over Romita Jr.'s pencils, changed the entire visual dynamic of JRJR's output.[310]

After a few years on *Iron Man*, Romita Jr. began his first run penciling the book that made his father a star, *Amazing Spider-Man*. Initially working with writer Dennis O'Neil, Romita Jr. again found a lot of his early work on the title to be unrecognizable because of the way the inker changed the finished stylings of his pencils.[311] Still, over the course of his run with O'Neil, he co-created such characters as Madame Web and the villain Hydro-Man, before Stern joined the book and kicked off one of the most popular creative pairings in Spider-Man history.

Stern/JRJR co-created a number of all-time great characters and storylines, like the supervillain the Hobgoblin and the "Nothing Can Stop the Juggernaut" two-parter. *Amazing's* success earned Romita Jr. an assignment on one of Marvel's hottest books, the *Uncanny X-Men.* Drawing the X-Men was considered one of the toughest gigs in the business, with so many characters and storylines running concurrently. So it was no surprise that, when Stern left *Amazing,* JRJR used that as an opportunity to leave the "Wall Crawler" as well and focus all of his energy on *X-Men.*[312]

Romita Jr.'s work on *X-Men* was critically well-received and financially successful, but as he was warned by other artists, illustrating the book was an overwhelming job. JRJR started having difficulties meeting deadlines, so he left the book and eventually found his way to *Daredevil,* alongside writer Ann Nocenti. JRJR has often credited this stint on *Daredevil* for allowing him to grow as an artist and storyteller. For the first time in his career, he had the opportunity to provide finished pencils on his pages and Nocenti even sought his creative input on a number of plots.

JRJR's experience on *Daredevil* would later benefit him in the mid-90s, when he provided pencils for what he has called his favorite work ever in comics—the *Daredevil: Man Without Fear* miniseries, which was scripted by the iconic Frank Miller and was the source material for a large chunk of the first season of Marvel's *Daredevil* on Netflix.[313]

But beyond *Man Without Fear*, the '90s were a weird time for Romita Jr. When the industry was going good, JRJR rode the gravy train with everyone else. But after it crashed, Romita Jr. found himself getting passed over for a number of plum assignments in favor of younger, "hotter" artists. That's when the behind-the-back whispers about his familial connections started circulating again. He was eventually assigned to *Web of Spider-Man* and *Peter Parker: Spider-Man*, two "B" books in the Spider-Man line, so he used this as an opportunity to "redefine" himself in the eyes of the industry.[314]

Romita Jr.'s luck started to change in the early '00s, after Marvel pulled itself out of the financial muck. In an effort to revitalize Spider-Man, JRJR was paired with *Babylon 5* creator J. Michael Straczynski on *Amazing Spider-Man*. The book's editor, Axel Alonso, recruited the longtime television writer to bring a new attitude to Spider-Man. The duo's first story together, "Coming Home," is considered a modern-day classic. Spider-Man was back. And JRJR was back on top again.

Immediately following the conclusion of "Coming Home," Straczynski/JRJR found themselves producing one of the most famous single issues in comic book history: *Amazing Spider-Man vol. 2 #36*, dubbed the "September 11th issue." In the aftermath of one of the worst attacks on American soil, executives at Marvel wanted to respond to the tragedy in some fashion. They agreed to create an issue of Spider-Man that discussed the nature of the attacks and how it might have impacted the superhero community. It was a deeply personal experience for JRJR, a New York City native. He was featured prominently in a *New York Times* article the day the comic published in October 2001. In the years since the comic was published, he has called it both the project he's most proud of and one of the hardest things he ever had to draw, not because of the imagery itself, but because of the real-world context.[315]

He once again hit a Spider-Man saturation point in 2004 and left *Amazing* to pursue other projects. When Marvel moved to a thrice-monthly printing schedule for *Amazing* in the late '00s, Romita Jr., a notoriously fast artist, was recruited to illustrate "New Ways to Die" with writer Dan Slott. The six-part arc featured Spider-Man fighting Norman Osborn/the Green Goblin for the first time since earlier in the decade. Concurrently, JRJR also continued to work on his first-ever creator-owned project, *Kick-Ass*, with writer Mark Millar (which was adapted into a film in 2010).

To the shock of many, Romita Jr. left the cozy confines of Marvel in 2014 for the first time in his career to pencil *Superman* with Geoff Johns for the "distinguished competition," DC. He later provided illustrations for *All-Star Batman* with Scott Snyder in 2016. Even with all of his success, JRJR remains his own biggest critic, often downplaying his skill and legacy by joking about how the best way to describe his style is "deadline style."[316]

However, he has one advocate who will never undersell him: "I had terrible misgivings when John Jr. first started in the business," said Romita Sr. in one interview. "It's hard for a son to become a success in the same industry as his father. I would have been happy back then just to know that John Jr. was going to make a living in comics. The fact that he's excelling is beyond my wildest dreams."[317]

55 George Stacy

New York City police captain George Stacy has the dubious honor of being more famous in death than life. Created by Stan Lee and John Romita Sr. in 1968's *Amazing Spider-Man #56*, Stacy, usually dubbed "Captain Stacy," was the father of Peter Parker's girlfriend, Gwen. His death, in *Amazing #90*, is considered one of the true watershed Spider-Man moments during the Silver Age of comics because he was the first major supporting character in Spidey's orbit to bite the dust since Uncle Ben in *Amazing Fantasy #15*.

During the bulk of his appearances, Stacy was depicted as being both a father figure to the orphaned Peter (whose only living adult role model was his Aunt May) and a defender of Spider-Man's crime fighting (despite the fact that the rest of the police force saw Spidey as a vigilante operating above/outside the law). As such, Stacy had a particular fascination with Peter's "relationship" with Spider-Man, considering all of those photographs he always managed to take of the "Web-Slinger" for the *Daily Bugle* newspaper. The reasoning behind Stacy's almost-borderline infatuation with all things Spider-Man would be later revealed with truly tragic ramifications.

In *Amazing #90*, Spider-Man is doing battle with Doctor Octopus on top of a building when one of Ock's tentacles crashes into the exterior of the building, knocking bricks and rubble down to the street below. Captain Stacy, who is watching the fight from the street, sees the falling bricks headed right toward a young boy in the area. Pushing the child out of the way, Captain Stacy is hit by the debris and lays on the ground lifelessly. As Spider-Man approaches, the man utters these chilling last words: "Be good to her, son! Be good to her. She loves you so very much."[318]

In that moment, Peter realizes that Stacy knew all along that he was secretly Spider-Man. Unfortunately, in the aftermath of his death, Gwen blames Spider-Man's involvement as much as Doc Ock's. Peter's shame for what happened to Captain Stacy leads to him breaking things off with Gwen for a brief stint, but the two eventually reunite (only for Gwen to be killed by the Green Goblin in *Amazing #121*—in other words, Stacy is a pretty cursed surname in the Spider-verse).

Captain Stacy's death became one of those seminal moments in Peter's life that's often referenced again and again in storylines where Spider-Man is dealing with some kind of failure or loss. Years later, Stacy's death becomes a critical plot point in 2012's *The Amazing Spider-Man* film by director Marc Webb. Stacy, played by Denis Leary, is killed in the movie's climatic battle between Spider-Man and the Lizard. However, running counter to what happened in the comics, as he lies dying, the cinematic version of

Stacy tells Peter to protect Gwen by staying away from her. Stacy's words continue to haunt Peter headed into 2014's *The Amazing Spider-Man 2*, causing him to break things off with Gwen for a good chunk of the film.

56 Betty Brant

Betty Brant may not have been Peter Parker's greatest love, but she was his first girlfriend, which counts for something. Created by Stan Lee and Steve Ditko in *Amazing Spider-Man #4*, Betty was initially J. Jonah Jameson's shy secretary at the *Daily Bugle* newspaper, but has since grown into one of Peter's closest friends and a staple of Spider-Man's supporting cast.

Betty and Peter's romance was on unsteady footing almost from the very beginning. While the two shared a mutual attraction, Betty was looking for a nice "normal" relationship with a man, while Peter was constantly coming up with excuses to hide his secret superhero identity from his girlfriend. Additionally, Betty was a few years older than Peter, which added some storyline tension. In numerous Lee/Ditko stories, Betty would inevitably become jealous when she caught Peter chatting/flirting with one of his female high school classmates, like Liz Allan, the sometimes-mean girl who quietly had a crush on Peter.

The death knell for Peter/Betty came after Betty's brother Bennett was accidentally killed in the crossfire from a battle between Spider-Man and Doctor Octopus. Betty blamed Spider-Man, and Peter felt ostracized. In *Amazing #18*, Ned Leeds was introduced by Lee and Ditko as the *Bugle's* new ace reporter, and a rival for Betty's affections. While Peter didn't totally abandon the idea of being with Betty, by the time Ditko left *Amazing Spider-Man* in 1966 Peter had moved on to a pair of women who were "glamoured up" by new artist John Romita Sr: Gwen Stacy and Mary Jane Watson.

Betty still managed to hang around in the comics, even when she was completely out of the picture for Peter. She married Ned in *Amazing #156* (and in typical comic book tradition, the wedding was nearly foiled by the appearance of a supervillain, the D-list baddie, Mirage). But after a while, that relationship went south too. Betty grew tired of Ned's world traveling as a foreign correspondent, and left him, attempting to win back Peter in the process. Not wanting to mess around with a married women, Peter purposefully acted like a jerk to drive her back into her husband's arms.

Still, Betty continued to have a straying eye and was suspected of cheating on Ned with Peter's high school bully-turned-buddy Flash Thompson during a long-running subplot in the '80s. In a shocking twist, Ned was revealed to be the supervillain the Hobgoblin and was murdered by a rival criminal. Betty's character took a weird turn after that, including a short stint where she joined a suicide cult. Fortunately, Betty was rescued from a descent into absurdity by Roger Stern and Ron Frenz in the 1998 miniseries, *Hobgoblin Lives*, which depicted her as a *Bugle* reporter attempting to absolve her late husband's wrongdoings as the Hobgoblin. Ned's name was later cleared in the story and wealthy businessman Roderick Kingsley was unveiled as the Hobgoblin. Betty continued her career as a reporter following *Hobgoblin Lives*, while also maintaining her tight friendship with Peter, especially during the "Brand New Day" storyline in the late 2000s, when Betty refers to him as "my best friend."[319]

Given her long-term importance to Spider-Man's cast of characters, Betty has frequently appeared in a supporting role in other media. She was Peter's main love interest in the *Spider-Man* cartoon that aired in the late '60s (also known as *Spider-Man '67*) and also played a key role in some early episodes of the *Spectacular Spider-Man* animated show from the late '00s. Elizabeth Banks portrayed Betty in all three Sam Raimi-directed *Spider-Man* films and Angourie Rice will play her in *Spider-Man: Homecoming*.

57 Joe Robertson

Joe "Robbie" Robertson is one of the more understated characters in the Spider-Man universe. However, his impact on Spider-Man comics, and the industry as a whole, should not be undersold.

First appearing in *Amazing Spider-Man #51* in 1967, Robertson was created by Stan Lee and John Romita Sr. as part of Marvel's company-wide effort to bring more diversity to its comics.[320] Over the span of a year, Marvel had introduced the Black Panther in the *Fantastic Four* and Bill Foster/Black Goliath in the *Avengers*. While Robertson was not a costumed superhero, he was one of the comic book industry's first African American supporting characters to be more than just comic relief.

As city editor, and later editor-in-chief of the *Daily Bugle*, Robbie has often been portrayed as a calm and rational counterbalance to the fiery head of the newspaper, J. Jonah Jameson. Over the course of his relationship with Jonah—which is depicted as a sincere friendship by most creators—Robertson has pushed back against some of Jameson's sensationalism, while appearing to be more of a confidant and mentor to the paper's staff, including Peter Parker.

As a black character being written during the all-too-real Civil Rights era of American history, Robertson and his son Randy (who would later become Peter's roommate) were frequently used in the late '60s as an outlet for Marvel to tell more socially aware stories. When Randy and other students are accused of desecrating a priceless artifact at Empire State University, the teenager accuses his even-keeled father of being part of the "white man's establishment" for not more readily defending him.[321] A few years later, Jameson chooses his friendship with Robbie over a golden opportunity to hang Spider-Man out to dry when a racist politician seeks the *Bugle's* endorsement running on a platform of "law and order" against costumed vigilantes.[322]

Probably Robertson's most famous storyline came in the late '80s from longtime Spider-Man scribe Gerry Conway. Conway used his late '80s run on *Spectacular Spider-Man* and *Web of Spider-Man*, two "B" books, to focus on Spider-Man's supporting cast and came up with a truly memorable tale for Robbie involving his childhood relationship with Marvel's newest underworld boss, Lonnie "Tombstone" Lincoln. It turns out that Robbie witnessed Tombstone committing murder, but since he never reported it, has to stand trial and face jail time. Readers, including many within Marvel's offices, were so compelled by Robbie's trial, they'd desperately ask the book's editor Jim Salicrup to assure them that everything was going to work out for the character.[323]

In addition to the comics, Robertson has been a key supporting character in the mid-90s *Spider-Man: The Animated Series* and the late-2000s' *Spectacular Spider-Man* animated show. He appeared in all three Sam Raimi-directed *Spider-Man* films—again, as the calm and cool Yin to Jonah's bombastic Yang—and was portrayed by Bill Nunn.

58 Spider-Man '67: The First Adaptation

Okay, let's just get the sing-a-long out of the way: "Spider-Man, Spider-Man, does whatever a spider can." I know it. You know it. Everybody knows it. It's probably one of the most famous cartoon theme songs this side of meeting *The Flintstones*.

For many hardcore fans, the 1967 animated adaptation of Spider-Man—the first media representation of Spidey outside of the comic books—was a portal into the wild world of the "Web-Slinger." For example, Dan Slott, current writer of *Amazing Spider-Man*, first fell in love with superheroes by parking himself in front of a television every day after school and watching the Adam West–led *Batman* live-action series and the *Spider-Man '67* cartoon back-to-back.[324] Ron Frenz, a longtime Spider-Man artist, had a similar experience, first becoming exposed to Spidey via the Saturday morning cartoon, which debuted in September 1967 on ABC.[325]

The series ran for 52 episodes between 1967 and 1970 and was initially produced by the relatively unknown Canadian-based Grantray-Lawrence Animation studio. The company went bankrupt shortly after *Spider-Man's* debut and was taken over by Grantray-Lawrence's distributor, Krantz Films, until the show's cancellation.

Beyond its catchy theme song, *Spider-Man* was best known for its low-budget sensibilities, which have since earned the series good-natured mockery from various fans and critics. Most notably, Spider-Man's iconic "webbing" design was only drawn on small portions of his costume as a way to save time, and various clips and backdrops for the series were recycled ad nauseam. From a plot standpoint, *Spider-Man* focused almost exclusively on the character's life at the *Daily Bugle* newspaper, alongside publisher/editor

The Spider-Man Theme Song

Time to embrace that silly little earworm one more time as we celebrate the five greatest covers on the *Spider-Man '67* theme song:

5. **Aerosmith:** One of America's greatest rock 'n' roll bands ensured an entirely new generation would know about Spidey catching thieves just like flies when it recorded a cover version for Sam Raimi's 2002 *Spider-Man* film.
4. **Big John Bates:** This 2001 cover gives the *Spider-Man* theme a surf-rock beat.
3. **Woody Shaw:** The jazz trumpeter lent a bouncy, improv vibe to the landmark theme song, which appeared on his 1984 album *Setting Standards* as "Spider-Man Blues."
2. **Michael Buble:** The best-selling Canadian crooner released his sultry version of the theme song on his 2001 independent album *BaBalu*. It was later included on the soundtrack to 2004's *Spider-Man 2*.
1. **The Ramones:** The kings of punk rock included their cover version of the *Spider-Man* theme as a hidden track on their 1995 album *Adios Amigos*. Since then, it's been included on a Ramones *Greatest Hits Live* compilation and has been featured in a number of other media, including the *Guitar Hero: Warriors of Rock* video game.

J. Jonah Jameson and Peter's girlfriend, Betty Brant. Meanwhile, other supporting cast members from the comics, like Aunt May, Gwen Stacy, and Mary Jane, were hardly referenced at all.

Those at Marvel who valued quality over quantity were ultimately disappointed by the show. But years later, Marvel's former art director John Romita Sr. came to appreciate all the good *Spider-Man* did for the "Wall Crawler" and his comics, despite the fact that the show was so visually low budget: "Down through the years, every time I've gone to conventions, I have spoken to hundreds of people who have told me they had never heard of Spider-Man before the cartoon show," Romita said.[326]

59 Spider-Man Goes "Spectacular"

For years following his departure as lead writer of *Amazing Spider-Man*, Spidey's co-creator and Marvel's then-publisher Stan Lee yearned for a second Spider-Man comic book series. After launching *Marvel Team-Up* in 1972, the series was quickly dismissed for its one-and-done stories that had very little bearing on Marvel continuity. So in 1976, Marvel tried its hand at creating yet another Spidey "B" book, *Peter Parker: The Spectacular Spider-Man*. This one managed to stick and went on to publish more than 260 issues, including some of the greatest Spider-Man stories of all-time, like "The Death of Jean DeWolff" and "The Death of Harry Osborn."

Gerry Conway, Lee's first successor scripting *Amazing Spider-Man*, was initially tapped to write *Spectacular*. However, Conway left the book (and Marvel) as quickly as he started writing it, kicking off a long-running trend that would earn *Spectacular* the moniker "red-headed stepchild" from a number of creators and editors who worked on it during its 22-year run.[327]

The red-headed stepchild comparison was not necessarily an indictment of *Spectacular's* quality. Once Conway left the book, a steady stream of top-notch creators followed him, like a young Frank Miller, who provided pencils for a Spider-Man/Daredevil team-up in *Spectacular #27*, making it the first time Miller would illustrate the "Man Without Fear" (the character who would eventually make Miller a star).

However, regardless of the talent assigned to *Spectacular*, Marvel was frequently pulling its top creators off the title to go work on special projects. All-time great Spidey-scribe Roger Stern would be told during his run on *Spectacular* that he was going to

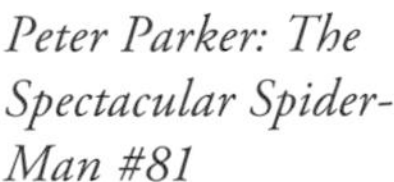

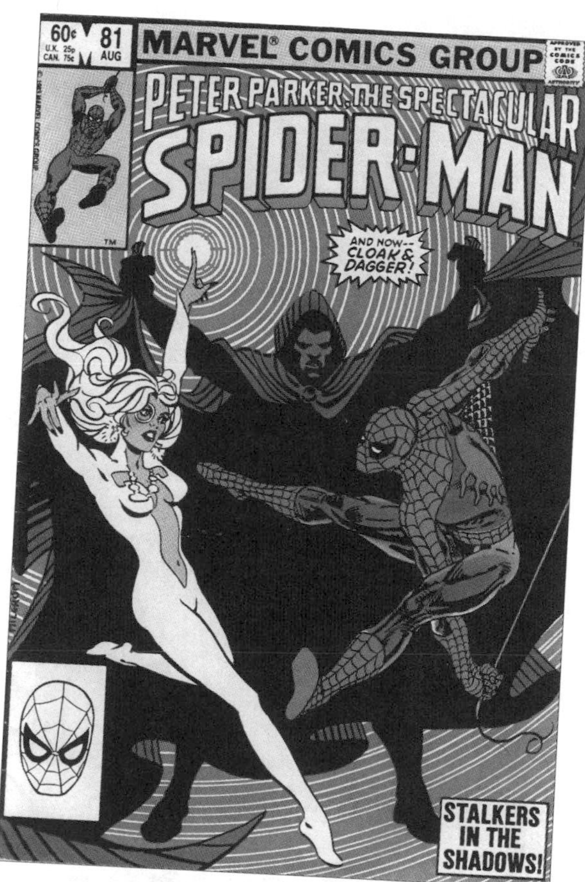

Peter Parker: The Spectacular Spider-Man #81

collaborate with such standouts as Marie Severin and John Byrne, only for both artists to leave the book after a few issues to work elsewhere. Still, Stern credits his 15-issue *Spectacular* run as a valuable experience, providing him with a low-pressure opportunity to learn how to write Spider-Man before he really needed to bring his "A" game on *Amazing Spider-Man*.[328]

Over time, various editors and creators would also look to change the tone of the book to distinguish it from the "main" series. In the mid-80s, Marvel turned to newcomer Peter David to transform the title into a dark police procedural, a la *Hill Street Blues*. The end result of this sharp change in tone was the landmark storyline "Death of Jean DeWolff," which saw the grisly murder of police captain Jean DeWolff at the hands of a ski-mask-wearing sociopath known as the Sin Eater.[329]

In the latter half of the '80s, Conway returned to the character who first made him an icon in the industry when he started scripting *Spectacular* and the other Spider-Man "B" book, *Web of Spider-Man.* His *Spectacular* run consisted mostly of stories that focused on Spidey's supporting cast, like Joe "Robbie" Robertson and Glory Grant. J.M. DeMatteis took a similar approach when he was assigned to the book in the early '90s: "Since *Spectacular* wasn't the flagship book, (editor Danny Fingeroth) let me go off and write these interesting character stories starring Aunt May and Harry Osborn," DeMatteis said.[330]

Unquestionably, DeMatteis's greatest *Spectacular* storyline involved the mental breakdown of Harry Osborn, Peter's best friend and son of his nemesis, Norman Osborn, aka the Green Goblin. "The Child Within" explored Osborn's descent into madness for failing to live up to his father's lofty expectations, culminating with his tragic death in *Spectacular #200.* DeMatteis would later return to *Spectacular* in the late '90s, where he continued to write character-centric stories involving Peter's high school bully, Flash Thompson.

Spectacular Spider-Man was eventually canceled by Marvel in 1998 as part of a larger effort to reorganize the Spider-Man books and consolidate all of the various spinoff series into just two titles. The series experienced a short-lived revival between 2003 and 2005, where it ran for 27 issues. However, the book eventually gave way to other "B" titles and is now primarily regarded as a relic of history, to be studied and, of course, read and appreciated.

60 Must Read: "The Death of Jean DeWolff" (*Spectacular Spider-Man* #107–111)

Peter David and Rich Buckler's "The Death of Jean DeWolff" is a must-read for Spider-Man fans, not for how it pays homage to great stories of the past, but for how it takes everything you think you know about the character and knocks it down like a house of cards. It is violent, dark, despairing, preachy, and void of the usual brand of superhero spectacle one expects in a Spider-Man comic. But the storyline is never boring or feckless. It is completely unapologetic about the way it haunts its readers by making them see the world of Spider-Man through a different lens.

Prior to "DeWolff's" development, some of Marvel's editors had requested a new, darker tone for *Spectacular Spider-Man* that was akin to the police drama *Hill Street Blues*. And that's what the story delivers from jump street. The opening pages of the arc provide some biographical background on DeWolff only to reveal that she had been brutally murdered in her own apartment. Before the end of the first issue, the assailant violently strikes at another member of New York's establishment: a judge and friend to attorney Matt Murdock, aka the blind superhero Daredevil. With two public officials shockingly murdered, New York City is put into a state of hysteria, and the usually fantastical world of Spider-Man is transformed into a grounded, very realistically scary world of crime and violence.

For an extra dose of cold, dark reality, the featured villain in "Death of Jean DeWolff" is a ski-mask-wearing, shotgun-toting average Joe who goes around calling himself the Sin-Eater. Sin-Eater declares war on those he believes are part of a corrupt system, namely cops, judges, and, in one scene, a priest. Any innocent people harmed during his rampages are just collateral damage. This is best evidenced in *Spectacular #108*, when the villain fires his shotgun at Spider-Man and inadvertently kills a bystander when Spidey dodges the blast.

One of the main recurring themes of the arc is the disparate approaches Spider-Man and Daredevil take toward apprehending the Sin-Eater. Daredevil wants to go "by the book" and let the legal system do the work it's supposed to do. But in a surprise twist, the usually more rational Spider-Man is riled up by the loss of his friend, DeWolff. So he sets out to scour the dregs of the criminal underworld, enacting street justice: forcibly coercing information and confessions because the ends justify the means.

Spider-Man and Daredevil both get a break in the case when the Sin-Eater, who is actually Stan Carter, a police officer himself and a former agent of the espionage group S.H.I.E.L.D., overplays his hand. He shows up at the house of *Daily Bugle* publisher J. Jonah Jameson, intending to add to his hit list. After discovering that Jameson is out of town, Carter turns his patented shotgun on Jameson's secretary, Betty Brant, who is house sitting with the publisher's wife, Marla.

Spider-Man shows up at the scene in the nick of time, but rather than web Carter up and leave him for the cops, he starts beating him into a quivering pulp. Moments before he crosses *the* line (the line Spidey has *never* crossed before), Daredevil intervenes and implores the "Web-Slinger" to stop acting like a psychotic vigilante. Cooler heads ultimately prevail, but not before the reader is left with a rather uncomfortable truth about Spider-Man that elevates "DeWolff" to iconic status today: there are moments where this otherwise moralistic hero can sometimes fail in being a beacon of rational justice and virtue. In other words, even our heroes can sometimes let us down.

61 The Jackal

If you like stories about Spider-Man clones then you probably like the Jackal. You don't like clones? Well, hopefully you still have a soft spot for a guy who is among Spidey's most antagonizing villains.

The costumed villain known as the Jackal was first introduced in 1974's *Amazing Spider-Man #129* by Gerry Conway and Ross Andru. However, the man under the mask, Miles Warren, first appeared during the Silver Age in *Amazing #31* as Peter Parker and Gwen Stacy's science professor at Empire State University. When developing the Jackal, Conway drew inspiration from Stan Lee and Steve Ditko's Crime Master/Green Goblin saga in the mid-60s, which saw both villains get introduced with secret identities that Spider-Man attempted to unveil. The Crime Master turned out to be just some random guy, while the Green Goblin was unmasked as wealthy industrialist Norman Osborn—a character with some name recognition today, but at the time, he was just another random individual who had only been introduced by name by Lee/Ditko a few issues earlier. Conway believed the resolution to the Goblin mystery was a "cheat," since the storyline's buildup insinuated that the character was a longtime cast member in the Spider-Man universe. So with the Jackal, he wanted to unmask him as someone who had a long-running connection to Peter, thereby providing some context for all of his evil machinations.[331]

Upon introducing the villain, Conway had hoped to establish the Jackal as a master planner/manipulator who employs a stable of goons and crooks to fight Spider-Man. Warren becomes the Jackal after he blames Spider-Man for Gwen's death in *Amazing #121*. The reader eventually learns that Warren was actually in love with

Gwen when she was his student, which explains his descent into madness following her tragic demise at the hands of the Green Goblin.

The Jackal's first appearance is notable for also being the issue that introduces the world to Frank Castle, aka the Punisher. Conway originally intended for Castle to be a one-off character and a hired goon of the Jackal's. But once it became clear that the Punisher was a pretty cool character in his own right, Conway kept the vigilante street fighter around while continuing to unfurl his Jackal saga.[332]

The Jackal's end game is revealed to involve the dreaded "C" word—clones. Not quite as many as would later appear in the "Clone Saga" in the '90s, but still...clones (ugh). Warren clones Gwen and then, in Conway's final issue on the series (*Amazing #149*) clones Spider-Man so Peter can have the ultimate battle against himself. Both the Spider-clone and Jackal are presumed dead by the end of the issue but...come on now. This is comics. Does Jackal look like Uncle Ben to you? Of course he didn't die.

Instead, the character is revived, along with the Spider-clone, and a score of all new clones (including Kaine, the demented first clone, who's actually a pretty nifty character) for the "Clone Saga." Jackal also received a bit of a character upgrade for the big '90s event, with many fans and critics comparing his characterization to Batman's "Clown Prince of Crime," the Joker: "There's something of the Joker in there, for sure, but I think Jackal stands as his own character, as well," said writer J.M. DeMatteis, who scripted the Jackal's return in the '90s. "I think he's a fantastic villain, one of the best in Spidey's history in that he doesn't stand in anyone else's shadow."[333]

Still, given the general unpopularity of the "Clone Saga" upon its completion in 1997, the Jackal went into hiding for a bit before finally reemerging as a major antagonist again as part of the 2011 *Amazing Spider-Man* storyline "Spider-Island." In 2016–17, Dan

Slott, as part of the "Clone Conspiracy" arc, introduced a new man under the Jackal mask—Peter's presumed-dead clone, Ben Reilly. For this story, Reilly/Jackal masterminds a plan to resurrect all of Spider-Man's deceased friends, family, and foes. "His mad scientist schemes are very much about testing the limits of what he can do," said "Dead No More" writer Dan Slott. "Now, he's kind of reaching the ultimate limit with the biggest god complex all-time."[334]

62 The Clone Saga

Sadly, you did not suddenly find yourself in the darkest timeline. This is actually a chapter in this book dedicated to Spider-Man's "Clone Saga," considered by many fans and critics to be the creative low point in the character's storied history.

A lot of that criticism is warranted. After stretching on for more than two years and almost 100 comic book issues in length, the "Clone Saga" emblemizes all of the 1990s' awful excesses and sales-driven editorial mandates. It is filled with plot holes, has a number of frustrating dead ends in terms of how its mystery elements unravel, and tramples over a ton of classic characters and past Spider-Man storylines with all of the grace and nuance of a drunken bull in a Pottery Barn. However, the story is also unfairly maligned. On paper, the initial premise behind the "Clone Saga" is a unique story about identity that could have potentially opened up a ton of new narrative directions for the Spider-Man universe. Unfortunately few, if any, of those initial ideas managed to factor into the final story.

The "Clone Saga's" roots can be traced back to a story by Gerry Conway and Ross Andru in the '70s involving a clone of

Spider-Man that was presumably killed while battling the real Spidey. Spider-Man sheepishly dumps his doppelganger's body in a smokestack and no one ever heard from the clone again….

Oh, if only that were the case. Terry Kavanagh, a longtime writer/editor for Marvel, was a huge fan of the '70s story, but thought the resolution of dumping the clone into a smokestack was a bit…tepid. Fast-forward to the mid-90s and Marvel's editors were desperate to shake things up with Spider-Man, who at that point was a brooding twenty-something married to supermodel Mary Jane Watson. Worried that Spidey was losing his charm with younger readers (and older ones too), Marvel implored its staff to come up with some kind of big event, akin to the other blockbusters which had dominated the comic book industry during the decade like "Death of Superman" and Batman's "Knightfall."

Kavanagh looked back to that smokestack from the '70s and suggested the company bring the clone back—except the clone would actually be the *real* Spider-Man. That would then allow Marvel to build its Spider-books around the original "Web-Slinger," while the grouchy, married version could ride off into the sunset with his wife and live happily ever after.[335] Also, this storyline wasn't meant to be a "saga" at all. Kavanagh and his good friend and fellow Spider-Man writer, Howard Mackie, worked up about three or four months' worth of stories. After winning over some of their other Spider-office collaborators, Kavanagh and Mackie took their dramatic pitch to the top: Marvel's editor-in-chief (and former Spider-Man scribe) Tom DeFalco.[336]

DeFalco was initially nonplussed by the premise, comparing the clone idea to the primetime soap opera *Dallas*, where Bobby Ewing is presumed dead only to show up in the shower, with the whole thing being dismissed as a dream. Still, Kavanagh and Mackie pushed back, explaining everything that happened to these characters over the past 20 years had still actually happened, as written. "It just happened to characters who were not aware of their real identities," Kavanagh added.[337]

DeFalco relented and even started contributing to the storyline, including suggesting that Mary Jane should get pregnant, adding more urgency to the idea that Peter and MJ needed to leave the books to go off and live their lives. But as an added benefit, the creative team wanted to leave things so that if Marvel ever wanted to check back in on Peter and MJ, they could potentially develop a "new adventures" of Peter and Mary Jane series (or something similar), which would only help to expand the Spider-Man line of books.[338]

Starting in 1994's *Web of Spider-Man #114*, a mysterious stranger that knew many people in Peter's life first appeared. Finally, in *Web of #117*, Peter's clone revealed himself and announced that he was going by the name Ben Reilly, a combination of Peter's Uncle Ben and his Aunt May's maiden name, Reilly. However, in an ominous twist, Ben, who believes himself to be a clone, has "memories" of his past that insinuate he might actually be the real McCoy. The story was an immediate success for Marvel, which was both a blessing and a curse for the creative team. Sales on one book nearly tripled, validating Kavanagh and Mackie's belief in their idea. However, after only two months, Marvel had already gotten sales-driven stars in its eyes. The company mandated the story be stretched out beyond its three-to-four-month timeline."[339]

That's when the trouble started. In an effort to add some length to the arc, but also keep it compelling and interesting, some major shifts in Spider-Man's status quo were introduced. His longtime villain, Doctor Octopus, was killed in the saga's "Web of Death" arc. Then, in one of the most emotionally tender Spidey stories of all time, Peter's Aunt May passed away in *Amazing Spider-Man #400*. Most of these stories were well-received and sold great numbers, but the clone arc was already starting to accelerate out of control.[340] More than a year after the story kicked off, Marvel finally got the status quo it wanted: Ben Reilly was revealed to be the one "true" Spider-Man and Peter and Mary Jane rode off into the sunset to start their family.

But by that point, the original brain trust behind the "Clone Saga" had been dismantled. Kavanagh left Marvel, DeFalco was forced out as editor-in-chief (though he remained on as a writer), and J.M. DeMatteis was no longer writing *Amazing*. Of all the creators involved from the beginning, Mackie was one of the few survivors. Plus Marvel was on the brink of collapse, as comic book sales across the industry plummeted as the collector's speculator bubble burst. "That wasn't fun," Mackie said of being the last man standing in the Spider-office.[341]

The new status quo starred Ben Reilly (dubbed "Spider-Ben") as the star of the books. But as quickly as he took over, Marvel's hierarchy seemingly wanted the "old" Peter back. Mackie tried to convince his bosses that there was a way to have their cake and eat it too: they could keep Spider-Ben in *Amazing Spider-Man* and launch some new books featuring Peter and Mary Jane. But Marvel wasn't having it. "It was driven by fear of the book failing," Mackie said.[342]

Peter's return to the webs was marked by one more shocking plot development: the return of Norman Osborn as the Green Goblin, who had been killed off decades earlier in one of Marvel's seminal stories. Mackie vehemently opposed the idea, but it didn't matter.[343] Osborn is seen emerging from the shadows in *Amazing Spider-Man #417* and then reveals himself as the mastermind behind the "Clone Saga" the entire time (not the Jackal, as had been earlier written by Kavanagh, Mackie, and others). And for icing on the cake, Osborn kidnaps (and presumably kills) Peter and Mary Jane's newborn child. And with that, the "Clone Saga" was finally over.

For many years following the storyline's conclusion, Marvel all but ignored the "Clone Saga's" existence. It had become a dirty phrase throughout the comic book industry. Many fans and critics used it as a measuring stick for the worst comic book stories of all time. But a little more than a decade after it ended, something started to shift regarding the "Clone Saga." One of the arc's key characters, Kaine, Peter's "first" clone, who was driven to insanity when he was rejected by his "father," the Jackal, was brought back for a number of stories during the "Brand New Day" era of *Amazing Spider-Man*.

Over in the *Ultimate* universe, Brian Michael Bendis and Mark Bagley did their own version of the "Clone Saga" for *Ultimate Spider-Man* which was (much) shorter and very well received. In 2011, DeFalco and Mackie were brought in to script a six-part miniseries dubbed *Spider-Man: The Real Clone Saga*, which better reflected Mackie and Kavanagh's original pitch. Kaine starred in his own monthly series, *Scarlet Spider*, which ran for nearly two years. And in 2016, Dan Slott created what many consider to be the third installment of the "Clone Saga" in his event "Dead No More," which stars a new Jackal: a back-from-the-dead Ben Reilly.

In other words, the "Clone Saga" is no longer such a joke around the industry. And for those who believed in the idea from the get-go more than 20 years earlier, they finally had their moment of vindication: "The generation that's speaking about comics right now is the generation that grew up reading those stories," Kavanagh said. "It was a good solid story where the execution was dragged out for too long. I understand the jokes because I was making them myself. But I don't think anyone ever was making fun of the idea of Spider-Man facing his own clone in an identity quest to decide who earned that life most."[344]

63 Todd McFarlane: The Phenom

The words "superstar" or "legendary" are tossed around quite a bit when fans talk about certain comic book artists and writers, but only a small number of these individuals actually live up to these platitudes. Todd McFarlane, whose career catapulted into the stratosphere in the late 1980s when he started penciling *Amazing Spider-Man,* is one of those individuals. In the years following his departure from Spider-Man, he has led a number of successful business ventures in the worlds of comics and toys that make him one of the industry's all-time greats. He's also an industry trailblazer, having left a lucrative gig on a Spider-Man book that was launched specifically to allow him to pencil *and* write, to be one of the co-founders of Image Comics, an independent umbrella company the produces numerous creator-owned titles such as *Spawn* (McFarlane's book), *The Walking Dead*, *Saga,* and *Savage Dragon.*

But years before McFarlane brought seismic changes to the industry, he started out as a rather young and shy artist looking to break into comics. Born in Calgary, Alberta, Canada, in 1961, McFarlane was your token "best artist in class" kid all throughout elementary and high school who trained himself in the comic book medium by emulating his heroes, such as George Perez, John Byrne, and Frank Miller.[345]

He broke into the industry at DC and was eventually assigned to illustrate "Batman: Year Two." But in a theme that would dominate his career arc, he wanted more for himself. Jim Salicrup, a Marvel editor who had just been assigned to oversee the Spider-office, immediately started recruiting the young artist. McFarlane performed some standout work alongside writer Peter David on the *Incredible Hulk* before quickly working his way up to one of Marvel's biggest book: *Amazing Spider-Man.*[346]

Salicrup was immediately struck by McFarlane's ambition and professionalism. He was always looking for ways to better himself while also seeking new challenges, like inking his own work (he got his first chance to do that on the double-sized *Amazing #300*).[347] He also sought to define his style by introducing numerous distinct visual features and innovations, like making Spidey's eyes bigger, bringing back the "webbing" under his armpits, and arguably his most famous invention of all, a thicker strand of webbing that coiled around itself dubbed "spaghetti webbing."[348]

Together, with writer David Michelinie, McFarlane took an already popular book to unprecedented heights. They introduced a new supervillain, Venom, in *Amazing #300* and he was an instant sensation. Salicrup would call it his "favorite time at Marvel," adding that McFarlane "knew how to excite the audience so that they were paying attention."[349]

Unfortunately, after three years, including two three-month stints where he provided pencils on a bi-monthly basis, McFarlane started to burn out. He was also champing at the bit to get an opportunity to write some of his own comics in addition to penciling. While it might have seemed like a risky proposition on the surface—allowing a relative newcomer to write, pencil, and ink his own work—Salicrup put on his thinking cap and came up with a new venue for McFarlane: a brand-new Spidey book called *Spider-Man* (no adjective) that would allow McFarlane to run the whole show: plot, art, and dialogue. Per McFarlane's urging, Marvel even agreed to print the book on a higher-quality paper stock, which upped the price a bit, but gave readers (and McFarlane) the impression that the company was producing a fancier grade of comic.[350]

Spider-Man #1 was a record breaker, selling nearly 2 million copies in 1990. Part of the sensation can be attributed to astute marketing: the book was published with multiple "variant" covers, further fueling the comic book collecting boom that was overtaking the industry. Still, the book's impact on the industry is unquestioned. As part of a 25th anniversary celebration of the comic on the website *Comics Alliance*, author Patrick Reed wrote: "It created a whole new style of creator-focused marketing that would lead to Rob Liefeld and Jim Lee being given their own X-books.… *Spider-Man #1* paved the way for the high-flash/low-substance 'extreme' era of comics that would follow."[351]

Still, McFarlane soon grew restless. He and his wife had started a family, plus he was getting fed up with dealing with Marvel's bureaucracy. Rather than stick around and grow unhappier, McFarlane left his gig on *Spider-Man* to face the unknown. He soon found his calling as one of the co-founders of Image, which emphasized creator rights and ownership. Under the Image umbrella, McFarlane's studio, Todd McFarlane Productions, created the hit occult book *Spawn* in 1992. Its first issue sold more than 1.7 million copies, an amazing feat for an indie title. The book went on to inspire an animated series and live-action feature film in the '90s.[352] McFarlane would also experience enormous success in other venues. In 1995, he founded McFarlane Toys, an action figure manufacturer that is known for its realistic figures depicting athletes, as well as characters from comics, movies, television, music, video games, and other media.

Despite his mainstream popularity, McFarlane has not completely ruled out ever returning to the character and medium that made him famous. When asked in 2014 about illustrating Spider-Man for Marvel again, he said he couldn't envision ever working on a Marvel-owned project again. However, "Is it possible that someday I'll wake up and have an itch to do a Spawn and Spider-Man crossover? Yeah. Would Marvel be interested? I don't know."[353]

64 Carnage

What do you get when you take a murdering sociopath on the level of *Nightmare on Elm Street*'s Freddy Kruger and combine him with a vengeful, super-powered alien symbiote hell-bent on killing Spider-Man? You get Carnage, one of the wildest and most sadistic villains in Spidey's rogues' gallery.

Created by David Michelinie and Mark Bagley during the peak of the comic industry's "extreme" period in the early 1990s, Carnage first appeared in *Amazing Spider-Man #361* and was an instant hit with readers, driving *Amazing's* already-high sales to even higher levels. The character marks the union of Cletus Kasady, a serial killer locked in a maximum-security prison, and the spawn of the alien symbiote possessed by another one of Spidey's arch-villains, Eddie Brock/Venom. Once he becomes powered by the symbiote, Kasady becomes the ultimate killing machine, molding his arms and legs into knives and axes so he could slice and dice as he pleases. And given Kasady's mental instability, Carnage does a lot of killing. When Michelinie created the character, his general concept was "a character who was like Venom, but without the sense of morality."[354]

Bagley's initial visual concept for Carnage was an all-black character (like Venom) with a big red splotch in the middle of his torso, resembling a gunshot wound. However, the design was rejected by Marvel's editors, who feared such a provocatively violent character could spark some pushback from the Comics Code Authority. So Bagley reimagined the character as he's best known today—a red figure covered in small black circles and lines that Bagley himself has called a "pain in the [neck] to draw."[355]

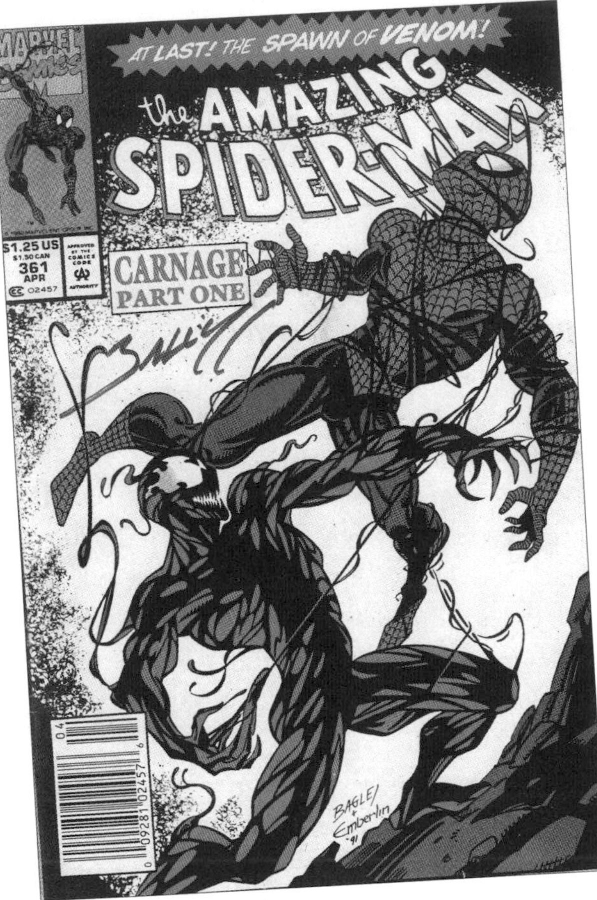

Amazing Spider-Man #361

The dawn of a threat like Carnage presented Marvel with an opportunity to create some unusual alliances. Spider-Man actually teamed with Venom in many of the villain's earliest appearances, including the mammoth-sized 1993 crossover "Maximum Carnage." The polarizing story (which has appeared on numerous "best of" and "worst of" lists) features Carnage leading a ragtag team of rogues like the sonic-screaming villainess Shriek and the Demongoblin against Spidey, Venom, and a hodgepodge of other random heroes like Captain America, Iron Fist, and Black Cat.

As time has gone on, various creators started to struggle with using Carnage in an effective way that marked both character growth, and a sensible new direction for the character. In a not-so-subtle statement, writer Brian Michael Bendis, during his run on *New Avengers*, had Carnage get ripped in two (in space) by the godlike-powered Sentry as a way to get the villain out of circulation. But Carnage eventually returned (they always come back). Zeb Wells, who has written Carnage as the lead character in multiple miniseries over the past decade, called Kasady "chaos" and a "hopeless case." Wells said, "That makes him fun on one level, but terribly hard to write for long periods of time."[356]

Longtime comic writer Gerry Conway seemed up to the challenge when he and artist Mike Perkins launched a *Carnage* monthly ongoing series in 2015. Conway approached the book as if it was a Bronze Age–era monster book starring the likes of Dracula or Man-Wolf, using his villain as "a force of nature that passes through the situation.... He's a motivating force the same way Hurricane Katrina is a force."[357]

65 Dan Slott: The Mad Genius of Modern Spider-Man

Dan Slott, who has enjoyed one of the longest tenures scripting *Amazing Spider-Man* in the book's history, is unquestionably one of the world's biggest Spider-Man fans. He even remembers the first time he met him.

As a kid in Stockton, California, Slott walked into a 7-Eleven and saw a sign announcing that Spider-Man would be singing autographs at the store. Slott immediately purchased some comics and came back a few days later to get his Spidey signatures. After wondering how Spider-Man would even arrive at the store—there were no tall buildings for him to swing on—the "Web-Slinger" himself showed up…on the back of a pickup truck. "And that's how Spider-Man showed up in Stockton, California," Slott joked.[358]

Slott's bizarre chance encounter with Spider-Man might explain why many of his most famous stories are among the most outlandish and eye-popping in the character's history. Slott has never been shy about trying to push the character in new directions, whether it's having his brain swapped with his archnemesis like in *Superior Spider-Man*, having every Spider-Man ever from across the multiverse team up like in "Spider-Verse," or making Peter Parker a billionaire CEO of his tech company a la Tony Stark in *Iron Man*. And while some fans have reacted with some misplaced anger from the writer's machinations—Slott even received death threats via social media after "killing" Peter Parker in *Amazing Spider-Man #700*[359]—the book has been enormously successful with him at the helm.

Everyone who has ever worked with Slott at Marvel refers to him as the ultimate idea man, filled with passion and exuberance. That's probably due in large part to how he scratched and clawed his way to the top, scripting one of Marvel's flagship books. He broke into the comic book industry at the lowest rung in the ladder possible, as an intern at Marvel in the early '90s. He pitched stories like a madman to whoever may be listening, which is how he ended up in the "kiddie book" division, scripting *Mighty Mouse* and *Ren and Stimpy* (though his stint on *Ren and Stimpy* allowed Slott to work with Spider-Man as part of a wacky team-up).[360]

After a few years of "kiddie books" and inventory stories, Slott grew frustrated and debated quitting comics altogether. But he received a lifeline via an assignment on the DC Batman book *Arkham Asylum: Living Hell* in 2003. That put Slott back on Marvel's radar, and he eventually landed a gig writing *She-Hulk* as a "superhuman law" book. He even wrote his first (semi-serious) Spider-Man story when She-Hulk represented Spidey in his lawsuit against *Daily Bugle* publisher J. Jonah Jameson for defamation of character.[361]

Following *She-Hulk*, Slott pitched the universally beloved *Spider-Man/Human Torch* "I'm With Stupid" miniseries, which follows the two best frenemies on untold adventures set in various eras of Marvel history. But Slott was still under the impression that a writer of his stature would never get a stint on the big book, *Amazing Spider-Man*, so he treated the mini as his "love letter to Peter Parker."[362]

Of course, that was not all she wrote for Slott and Spider-Man. Following the controversial "One More Day" story that saw the dissolution of Peter and Mary Jane's marriage, J. Michael Straczynski, *Amazing Spider-Man's* lead writer, left the book, creating an opening for Marvel to fill. Rather than hiring one new creative team, Marvel instead chose to publish *Amazing Spider-Man* three times a month with a rotating "brain-trust" of writers and artists (later dubbed the "webheads"). Slott knew he was walking into a volatile situation, given the fan backlash of "One More Day," but he didn't care. "You tell me Spider-Man is riding a unicorn and has a monkey sidekick and I'm there," he said.[363]

Slott's teammates would later credit him as the architect and driving force of *Amazing's* narrative during the "Webhead" era. Regardless of this praise, Slott was still uneasy when he heard that the rotating team experiment would end in 2010. He asked his editor, Stephen Wacker, if he could script a Spider-Man team-up "B" book only to be offered the lead (and sole) writing position on *Amazing*.[364]

Slott immediately took to being the alpha dog. His first arc, "Big Time," showed a more confident and successful Peter getting a job at a technology company where he could invent new weapons and accessories to benefit his double life as Spider-Man. From there, Slott continued to churn out over-the-top stories like "Spider-Island" and "Ends of the Earth." But those were just an appetizer for his biggest and most polarizing idea ever: *The Superior Spider-Man.*

The Superior Spider-Man, which starred Doctor Octopus, Spidey's mortal enemy, as the "Wall Crawler" after the villain engineers a mind/body swap with his adversary, made Slott a bona fide comic book superstar. It was consistently one of Marvel's top sellers and put Slott in high demand at conventions and autograph signings. In the wake of *Superior's* success, Slott continued to pump out new ideas full throttle.

After resurrecting Peter Parker (in time for *The Amazing Spider-Man 2*'s opening weekend in 2014), he crafted such provocative tales as *The Amazing Spider-Man: Learning to Crawl*, which reimagined Peter's earliest days after the death of Uncle Ben, and "Spider-Verse," a storyline that involved every Spider-Man (that Marvel had rights to) from across the multiverse in a battle for their survival. Slott even got to handle the third rail of comics, better known as the Peter/Mary Jane marriage, in his *Amazing Spider-Man: Renew Your Vows* miniseries, which looked at an alternative version of the couple that stays married and had a child.

In the most recent volume of *Amazing Spider-Man*, Slott is once again writing a successful Peter Parker—this time as the billionaire head of his own company, Parker Industries. Like most of Slott's stories, fans are either smitten by his wacky new concept or outraged by his "changes" to Peter's character. But Slott doesn't let any negativity discourage him. He has said multiple times that he has no intention of ever leaving the pages of *Amazing Spider-Man*. In the meantime, he's going to keep cooking up new ways to torture Peter...and potentially some fans.

66 Mark Bagley: Contest Winner

Mark Bagley owes his storied career as a comic book artist to a contest. After years of trying to break into the industry, Bagley was ready to give up when he turned 27. He had a steady job while living in Atlanta with his wife and child, and he figured if he didn't get his big break in comics by the time he was 30, he'd finally pull the plug on his career. That's when a friend of his pushed the *Marvel Try-Out Contest* on Bagley. The book was first created in the early 1980s as a way for Marvel to recruit up-and-coming artists by offering a deconstructed comic that entrants could complete and submit. Bagley actually thought the whole thing was a scam—a way for Marvel to rob hopeless dreamers of $20. However, his friend convinced him otherwise and, to Bagley's surprise, he won. He flew out to New York City to serve as a fill-in artist and he hasn't looked back since.[365]

Bagley has quietly emerged as one of the most influential Spider-Man artists of the past 30 years. In 1991, after only a few years at Marvel, he was handed the keys to one of the prized art jobs in the industry, *Amazing Spider-Man*. His stint on the book came on the heels of the very successful Todd McFarlane and Erik Larsen eras, after both left Marvel in the early '90s to co-found Image Comics. Over the course of his nearly 60-issue run on *Amazing*, Bagley co-created a number of iconic characters, including the supervillain Carnage and the Scarlet Spider. He also worked on several era-defining events like "Maximum Carnage," the "Return of Peter Parker's Parents," and the "Clone Saga."

After leaving the Spider-books in the mid-90s, he was lured back to the friendly neighborhood in 2000, when Marvel was looking to reimagine Peter Parker and Spider-Man for more contemporary audiences. Brian Michael Bendis was tapped as the lead writer for a six-issue miniseries dubbed *Ultimate Spider-Man.* Bagley, quite reluctantly, provided pencils. And yet, six issues eventually became 111 issues—the longest uninterrupted creative run by a writer/artist tandem in mainstream comics' history.

Bagley has been a fan of comics dating back to Stan Lee/Steve Ditko's landmark run on *Amazing* in the '60s. He was especially influenced by two artists who followed Ditko on the book, John Romita and Gil Kane. As he was honing his craft, Bagley knew he would never truly be fulfilled unless he got to work on *Amazing Spider-Man.* "It was the pinnacle," he said.[366]

His first Marvel gig was on a new book, *New Warriors.* After 25 issues, editor Danny Fingeroth gave Bagley the call he had long dreamed about: he was going to pencil *Amazing Spider-Man.* Bagley was paired with longtime writer David Michelinie, who scripted *Amazing* during its peak popularity in the late '80s and early '90s. Within his first year on the book, Bagley designed one of Marvel's biggest creations of the '90s, Carnage, someone he would later joke was a "pain" to draw.[367]

Once Michelinie left the book in 1994, J.M. DeMatteis, who had previously written Spidey's "B" book, *Spectacular Spider-Man*, joined Bagley on *Amazing.* Bagley was initially skeptical of the DeMatteis hire. He was concerned that JMD's cerebral/psychological sensibilities would be a mismatch for a mainstream book like *Amazing.* But after a "bumpy" start, the duo quickly settled in and created some magic together. *Amazing #400,* which featured the emotional death of Peter's Aunt May (she later came back, but that's neither here nor there) is considered one of the greatest Spider-Man stories of all time. The story had a huge impact on Bagley and his family, claiming that even his wife "cried" after reading it.[368]

By the time the "Clone Saga" ramped up in the mid-90s, Bagley stopped having fun on the book.[369] He quit in 1996 but didn't exactly fade into obscurity, working on the critically acclaimed *Thunderbolts* with Kurt Busiek. But like the siren's song, Spider-Man was calling. He was dragged back to Spider-Man "kicking and screaming" for *Ultimate Spider-Man*. He was worried about being typecast as a guy who could only draw Spider-Man and was also concerned that fans would find the premise of *Ultimate*—a retelling of Spidey's origins set in an alternative universe—to be a gimmick. In retrospect, Bagley is the first to admit he couldn't have been more wrong: "I thought [*Ultimate*] looked beautiful," he said. "I loved the coloring and the inking, and the fans loved it too. They thought it was great. I was stunned. I had just assumed that everybody was going to hate it."[370]

Bagley and Bendis just had that spark that few creator tandems have. It took some time, but Bagley grew to understand and embrace all of Bendis's nuanced changes and impressions on the world of Spider-Man. The duo also worked remarkably fast. Bagley churned out finished pages so quickly, *Ultimate* was able to publish issues every few weeks rather than once a month (or longer). After about 70 issues, Bagley and Bendis started to openly acknowledge that if they could stick together just a little longer, they could break the all-time consecutive issues by the same creative team record.[371]

Of course, even after leaving *Ultimate*, Bagley would be back. He returned to *Ultimate* as part of the historic "Death of Spider-Man" storyline that, aptly enough, marked the end of the *Ultimate* universe's Peter Parker. In 2015, Bagley and Bendis reunited again for *Ultimate End*, which marked the final chapter in Marvel's *Ultimate* line. While most of what Bendis and Bagley created years earlier had been wiped from existence, Bagley looks back on his work with ultimate nostalgia: "It was just this nice mix between the two of us...I fell in love with those stories."[372]

67 Spider-Man and the Avengers

Few would question that Spider-Man has long been one of Marvel's greatest heroes. But when it comes to the "Web-Slinger's" relationship with "Earth's Mightiest Heroes," the Avengers…well, that's a little complicated.

Despite the fact that the Avengers have long represented the gold standard of Marvel's superheroes—bringing together the best of the best like Captain America, Iron Man, and Thor—Spidey has not always been a welcome part of this assembly of might and virtue.

One of Spider-Man's earliest encounters with the Avengers came in 1966's *Amazing Spider-Man Annual #3*, written by Stan Lee with art from John Romita Sr. and Don Heck. In it, the Avengers reach out to Spider-Man about becoming a member of the superhero group. However, before granting him entry, he has to pass a nearly impossible test—wrangling the Hulk, who has just gone on another one of his patented rampages. Spider-Man is initially turned off by the fact that he needs to "qualify" to be an Avenger. When Spidey inevitably confronts the Hulk, he meets his human alter-ego, Bruce Banner, and feels pity for him. Spider-Man intentionally fails his audition, concluding, "Maybe it was just fate's way of saying Spider-Man was cut out to be a loner!"[373]

Spider-Man remained a "loner" for many years to follow. Even when Spider-Man was the star of his very own team-up series, *Marvel Team-Up*, all of those stories were written under the premise that he was a quirky solo act who had a difficult time getting along with others. Spidey eventually got another audition with the Avengers in a 1983 story by Roger Stern, and even looked like he might finally get a coveted spot on the team, only to get psyched out again when Captain America informs him that he can't qualify because no one from the U.S. government would endorse him. Spider-Man ends the comic by once again confirming that him as an Avenger is a "dumb idea."[374]

Spider-Man joining the Avengers continued to be Marvel's version of Charlie Brown, Lucy van Pelt, and a football for another 20 years or so until finally—*finally*—some of the company's top creative minds said enough was enough. During one of Marvel's famed retreats in the mid-2000s, writers Brian Michael Bendis and Mark Millar pitched a wholesale reboot of the Avengers with some fresh blood on the team. Similar to how DC reinvigorated its Justice League superteam a few years earlier, Bendis and Millar thought that only the very best of Marvel's superheroes should be on the team—including Spider-Man and, probably even more controversially, the mutant Wolverine.[375]

Marvel's hierarchy knew the book, dubbed *New Avengers*, would sell. But there was some definite opposition to putting Spider-Man (and Wolverine) on the team, especially from *Avengers* editor and Marvel's current executive editor, Tom Brevoort: "I didn't think it was a bad idea *per se* from an Avengers point of view for Spider-Man to be in the Avengers. I thought it was a bad idea from a Spider-Man point of view for Spider-Man to be in the Avengers."[376]

Brevoort was worried that giving Spider-Man access to all of the resources that come with being one of "Earth's Mightiest Heroes" might damage his "everyman" hero status. Like, if Peter Parker couldn't make rent one month, could he now suddenly call in a loan from his billionaire teammate, Tony Stark?

But any concerns were much ado about nothing. *New Avengers* was a smash hit and Spider-Man being an Avenger was no longer a foreign idea—so much so that, when Marvel Studios started building its cinematic universe in the late '00s, with movies about Iron Man, Thor, Hulk, and Cap, fans started clamoring for Spider-Man, whose movies were then being produced by a separate studio, Sony, to be included. So when Marvel and Sony came to an agreement in 2015 to feature Spider-Man in the shared cinematic universe with the Avengers, it was only a matter of time before Spidey popped up alongside "Earth's Mightiest Heroes," as he did in 2016's *Captain America: Civil War*.

68 Civil War

As one of Marvel's flagship characters, Spider-Man has always been a factor in some of the company's big crossover events, such as *Secret Wars* or *Infinity Gauntlet*. However, for 2006–07's *Civil War*—arguably the most popular event in Marvel history—Spider-Man was put in the unique position of being stuck between two of the company's biggest icons in Iron Man/Tony Stark and Captain America. In fact, Spider-Man's role in this storyline is considered so critical that it's widely believed that the 2015 deal consummated between Marvel Studios and Sony Pictures was driven by a desire to feature Spider-Man (a Sony cinematic property) in Marvel's 2016 blockbuster, *Captain America: Civil War* (which was loosely adapted from the comics).

The comic book version of *Civil War* was conceived by writer Mark Millar, with input from a number of other creators, during one of Marvel's retreats in the mid-00s. The story reflected some of the very real geopolitical developments in the world in the aftermath of the September 11th, 2001, terrorist attacks via the Superhuman Registration Act, which was passed after a battle between the New Warriors and the villain Nitro resulted in the deaths of hundreds of innocent people in Stamford, Connecticut.

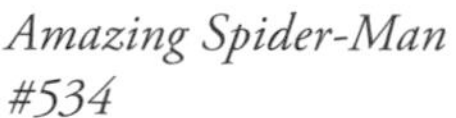
Amazing Spider-Man #534

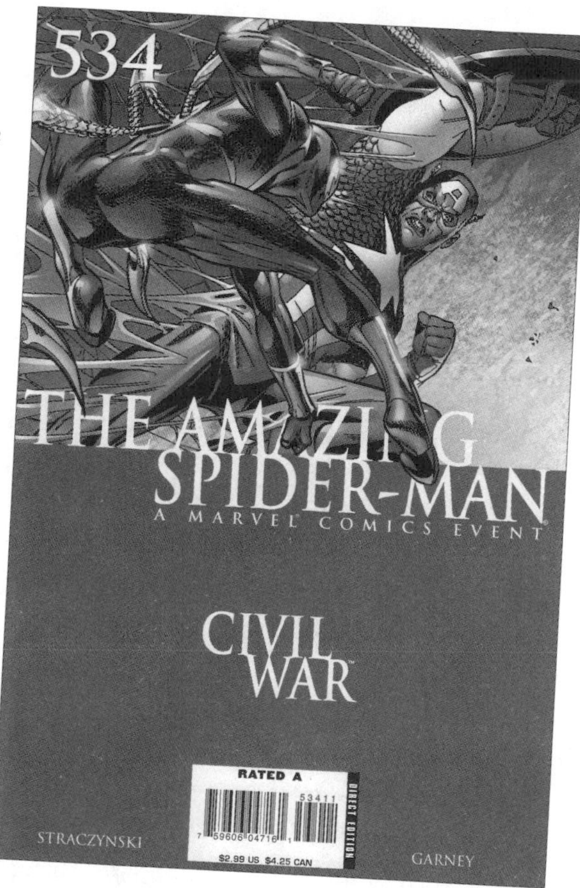

The act mandated that all individuals with extraordinary abilities had to register their identities with the government so their actions could then be monitored. The fictitious legislation was a not-so-subtle analogy to the U.S. Patriot Act, which greatly enhanced the American government's abilities to perform surveillance on individuals suspected of being terrorists.

Similar to some of the blowback the Patriot Act received in the real world, the Superhero Registration Act split Marvel's superhero community into two factions—hence the "civil war." Pro-registration forces were led by Tony Stark, who believed the legislation would provide full transparency to all citizens. Opposing the act was Captain America, who believed in an individual's right to privacy.

The middle ground was represented by Spider-Man. "Spider-Man is the everyman hero, so if you create a situation where there's a polar argument about a particular issue, you put him in the center and you can pull him between the two sides," said Marvel's executive editor Tom Brevoort.[377]

In the lead-up to *Civil War*, Peter Parker, Spidey's civilian alter-ego, had developed a strong friendship with Stark. Tony even created a brand-new costume for Spider-Man, known as the "Iron Spider" due to its Iron Man–esque technological capabilities (as well as some extra appendages that made Spider-Man resemble more of an actual spider). However, while Peter's kinship to Tony was strong, as Spider-Man, he had long sought to protect his secret identity so as not to endanger the lives of his family and loved ones. Shockingly, in *Civil War #2*, Peter comes out in favor of the registration act and publicly unmasks himself. But as the war between Iron Man and Captain America escalates, Peter finds Tony increasingly untrustworthy and switches sides, making himself a fugitive of the government and half the Marvel community.

As the main story played out in *Civil War*, a more Spidey-centric examination of events transpired in *Amazing Spider-Man #532–538*, which was being created by writer J. Michael Straczynski and artist Ron Garney. While there were some discrepancies between the *Civil War* and *Amazing* creative teams about which book should be the first to reveal major plot points related to the character (like Spidey's unmasking, which took place in *Civil War* rather than in *Amazing*), JMS and Garney still got to create some fun moments in Spider-Man's home book. In *Amazing #534*, Garney, who made a name for himself illustrating *Captain America* in the '90s, laid out an explosively dynamic fistfight between Spidey and Cap.

Spider-Man's unmasking and fugitive justice were short-lived. Following the events of 2007's "One More Day" storyline, which notably featured the dissolution of Peter and Mary Jane Watson's marriage via a spell cast by the devilish Mephisto, the same magic created a "blind spot" for anyone who witnessed Spider-Man's unmasking, allowing Peter to have his secret identity back. Just like magic!

Still, the Spider-Man legacy in *Civil War* managed to live on. Once it became known that the third *Captain America* film would be based on *Civil War*, fan speculation was rampant that Marvel Studios would somehow find a way to work Spider-Man into its story. At that point, Sony had just distributed the second *The Amazing Spider-Man* film, which financially underperformed expectations and received mediocre-to-bad reviews. According to media reports of a Sony e-mail hack in late 2014, Joe and Anthony Russo, directors of *Captain America: Civil War*, also made overtures about producing a new Spider-Man movie.[378]

When Marvel and Sony announced in early 2015 that Spider-Man would be allowed to appear in Marvel's *Avengers* films, the news was quickly followed up with reports that Spidey would play a role in 2016's *Civil War* as a precursor to his own solo flick in 2017. Ultimately, Spider-Man, as played by Tom Holland, appeared in about 20 minutes of the film, including the dramatic airport fight sequence between all the heroes. Similar to the *Civil War* comics, in the film, Spider-Man starts out on team Iron Man. Whether Spidey betrays the older Tony Stark remains to be seen, though it should be noted that Chris Evans, the actor who plays Captain America, jokingly lobbied for a role in *Spider-Man: Homecoming*, so perhaps a recruitment pitch is in the cards.[379]

69 Miles Morales

The one thing that is always a constant in the comic book industry is change. And when it came to Marvel's *Ultimate Spider-Man*—a character set in an alternative universe—the company made the very daring choice to have a new Spider-Man that more accurately reflected how the world has changed since the character was first introduced in 1962.

Miles Morales, a half-black, half-Hispanic teenager, was unveiled as the new *Ultimate Spider-Man* in 2011's *Ultimate Fallout #4,* following the death of that world's Peter Parker. Miles's introduction garnered national attention from the mainstream media, eliciting a broad cross-section of opinions, ranging from ardent support, to those who felt Marvel was being too "politically correct" in creating a non-white Spider-Man.

But for Miles's co-creator, writer Brian Michael Bendis, the decision to cast his star character as a minority was one rooted in logic and responsibility. Bendis had long believed that one of the keys to Spider-Man being so relatable to readers for the past 50-plus years was the fact that "anyone" could be Spider-Man. With that in mind, "we made the determination that, if Spider-Man were created today, there's a very large percentage chance that, based on where he's living and who he is, that he would be a person of color," Bendis said.[380]

Within a few months of being brought to life by Bendis and artist Sara Pichelli, Marvel launched its own Miles-centric series, *Ultimate Comics: Spider-Man*. In it, we get the full origin of this new character. Like his web-slinging predecessor, Miles is smart and somewhat nerdy. He gains his powers when he's bitten by a genetically modified spider that was stolen by his ne'er-do-well

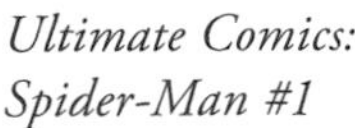

Ultimate Comics: Spider-Man #1

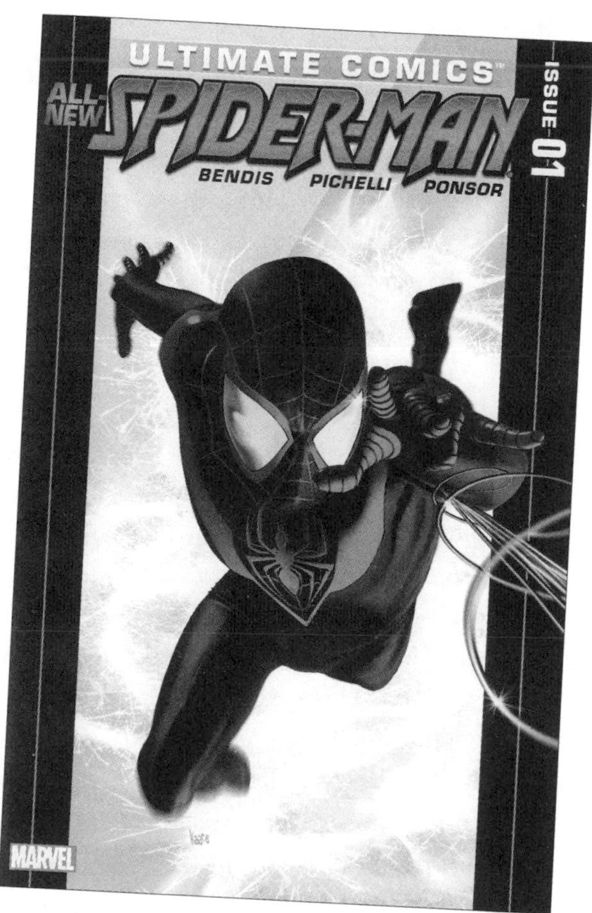

uncle, Aaron. Miles's discovery that both his father and his Uncle Aaron have criminal backgrounds dovetails with one of book's central conflicts: with his newfound powers, Miles questions if he is inherently a "good" person since two of his biggest role models are morally questionable. As a result, Miles initially resists becoming a costumed superhero, but after witnessing Peter's death at the hands of the Green Goblin, the boy decides (like his predecessor) that he has a responsibility to do good in the world.

Miles's power-set is similar to Peter's but with some distinct differences. In addition to having the proportionate speed, agility, and strength of a spider, Miles can camouflage himself with his surroundings and has a "venom sting" that can temporarily paralyze an opponent. In the comics, Miles receives his new black and red costume (conceived by Pichelli) from the espionage group S.H.I.E.L.D. and is given his web-shooters from Peter's Aunt May, who also lends the boy her blessing to be the new Spider-Man.

In addition to Miles's parents, Jefferson and Rio, and his Uncle Aaron (who is later inadvertently killed while fighting his nephew), the new *Ultimate* introduces a few other characters, most notably Miles's hopelessly adorable best friend Ganke, as well as *Ultimate* versions of Katie Bishop and the super-powered duo Cloak and Dagger.

Despite the amount of attention Miles received following his debut, sales across the entire *Ultimate* line continued to sag before Marvel pulled the plug on the imprint in 2015. The *Ultimate* universe was destroyed as part of an "incursion" within Marvel's multiverse in the *Ultimate End* miniseries. However, Marvel still wanted to continue to tell Miles's story, so during the *Secret Wars* event, Miles and his family were granted amnesty by the powers that ended the *Ultimate* universe and were allowed to migrate over to the mainstream Marvel Universe.

This chain of events led to Marvel announcing a new adjectiveless *Spider-Man* series in early 2016 starring Miles as the one "true" Spider-Man—i.e., a teenage Spidey with teenage problems. Meanwhile, Miles would coexist with the mainstream Peter Parker, who was busy being a grown-up running his own company. While Bendis assumed that Marvel would ask him to move on from the character following *Secret Wars*, he was surprisingly tapped to script *Spider-Man*. "My goal in life now is that Miles isn't the diversity Spider-Man, he's just Spider-Man," Bendis said. "The conversation completely goes away because it's so normalized that no one even notices."[381]

70 Must Read: "Coming Home" (*Amazing Spider-Man vol. 2 #30-35*)

Marvel's decision to bring in veteran television writer J. Michael Straczynski (creator of *Babylon 5*) and pair him with longtime comic artist John Romita Jr. on *Amazing Spider-Man* in the early 2000s was the shot in the arm the series desperately needed. Marvel was going through its own rebirth during this period, having staved off bankruptcy and regained its prominence in the comic book industry thanks to a slew of hit titles and outside-the-box creative hires. For Spider-Man, JMS's fresh approach brought out the best in his artist, JRJR, bringing a wave of energy and excitement that was best on display in the very first arc the two created, 2001's "Coming Home."

Despite the not-so-subtle insinuations of its title, "Coming Home" (which was awarded the prestigious Eisner Award in 2002) is more than just another "back to basics" story that waxes nostalgic about the good old days of Spider-Man. Rather, the arc is chock full of new ideas, attitude, swagger, and intrigue. Even the opening page of the arc's first issue feels radically different from anything that preceded it. Peter's Aunt May is a caring but assertive matriarch who sounds more comfortable offering her nephew sound advice rather than stacks of syrup-rich wheatcakes. Further into the story, Peter changes the course of his life when he decides to more intimately make a difference in kids' lives when he agrees to be a high school science teacher at his old stomping grounds, Midtown High.

But the heart and soul of "Coming Home" is the mystically existential battle that is waged among Spider-Man and two newly created characters, the vampiric villain Morlun and the enigmatic old man with spider-powers, Ezekiel. Ezekiel raises one of the most profound questions in Spider-Man history: did Peter receive his amazing powers from a radioactive spider bite or did the spider awaken his inherent abilities? This query might sound like some college dorm room-style philosophical ramblings, but the distinction is important because Morlun is on the hunt for Spider-Man because he believes the "Wall Crawler" is the purest form of a spider "totem," a sacred object or being that is emblematic of familial or tribal lineage. And since Morlun feeds on the life-force of those with totemic powers, Spider-Man is quite the catch for the villain.

Spider-Man's eventual confrontation with Morlun is simply one of the greatest struggles in the character's history. Spider-Man has certainly faced dire circumstances and overwhelming odds in the past (some of those stories are even discussed prominently in previous chapters of this book), but Morlun presents an otherworldly threat to his life, unlike anything he's ever encountered before. Additionally, since Morlun's "hunting" of Spider-Man is the equivalent of him getting a cheeseburger on the corner, his cavalier "nothing personal" attitude toward wanting to kill the hero supercharges their battle with raw emotion and anger.

Spider-Man's attempts to fight the god-like Morlun are met with bemusement and indifference. When Spidey attempts to flee and collect himself, Morlun baits him back out of the shadows by threatening to harm innocent people. Finally, with his back against the wall, Spider-Man thinks back to all of the new information he's been getting about the source of his powers and how his adversary needs to feed on him. He develops a path to victory that is typical Spider-Man: risky, selfless, and brilliant. He injects himself with a dose of radiation and allows Morlun to "feed" on him. When the radiation instead starts to poison and weaken the villain, Spider-Man is able to beat Morlun into submission (until an associate of Morlun's delivers the killing shot with a gun).

In that turning point moment when he finally gains the upper hand on Morlun, Spidey shouts the words "I'm not pure!"[382] that speak volumes for the character and the intriguing things JMS and JRJR had in store for him over the next few years. On the most basic level, Spider-Man/Peter's purity was being adversely affected by the dose of radiation he had just injected himself with. But more broadly, "I'm not pure" refers to Peter as a heroic, but flawed, character. Spider-Man makes mistakes. He's impulsive. He has moments of selfishness (including his most famous when he let a criminal run by him who went on to murder his Uncle Ben). These "impurities" make Peter all the more realistic and relatable to the reader.

71 Webb of Spider-Man: *The Amazing Spider-Man 1 & 2*

Despite the fact that 2007's *Spider-Man 3* received some middling reviews, Sony Pictures was defiant in pushing onward with its multi-billion-dollar franchise, planning a fourth *Spider-Man* movie with director Sam Raimi at the helm, with returning co-stars Tobey Maguire and Kirsten Dunst as Peter Parker and Mary Jane Watson. But things hit a serious snag. Raimi reportedly had some disagreements with the studio over the direction of the film, causing him to leave the production. Maguire and Dunst followed suit. Suddenly, Sony was left without a director or a star for one of Hollywood's most successful superhero film properties.

Sony's response was a fresh cinematic start for Spider-Man. Marc Webb, fresh off of directing the indie romcom *500 Days of Summer,* replaced Raimi, and British actor Andrew Garfield, who earned rave reviews for his role in *The Social Network*, was cast as the new Peter/Spider-Man. In lieu of Mary Jane, Sony shifted its focus to Peter's other great comic book love, Gwen Stacy, casting the hot up-and-coming actress Emma Stone. With this trifecta, Sony had the main ingredients it needed for a new Spider-Man franchise, dubbed *The Amazing Spider-Man*.

The rest of the cast was rounded out with a number of theatrical heavy hitters. Academy Award–winner Sally Field was cast as Aunt May. Golden Globe Award–winner Martin Sheen was Uncle Ben. For a new villain, Rhys Ifans got to play the double part of Curt Connors and the Lizard. Lastly, for a unique casting choice, comedian and television actor Denis Leary would play New York police captain George Stacy, Gwen's father.

Sounds like a pretty cool reboot, right? Well, in a sign of things to come, despite the fact that it looked like a reboot and smelled like a reboot, Sony's producers, most notably Avi Arad, insisted they were not rebooting the cinematic Spider-Verse. Instead, Peter was going back to high school and moviegoers were going to endure yet another story about how he gets spider-powers, but the reported goal of the new film was to just fill in some storyline gaps from the Raimi trilogy. All righty then….

In its defense, *The Amazing Spider-Man* unquestionably sought a different tone and aesthetic style than its three predecessors. Rather than get overly steeped in Peter's guilt over the death of his Uncle Ben, the films instead focused on a rather minor subplot from the comics involving Peter's deceased parents, Richard and Mary Parker. In the comics, Peter's parents leave their child with his aunt and uncle to go on a secret spy mission for the U.S. government when they are killed in a plane crash. Webb believed focusing on this storyline would shine new light on Peter's origins and provide more context as to who he was as a character.[383]

The Parker parent subplot certainly added a layer of darkness that was absent from the Raimi films, though Garfield's banter and delivery as Spider-Man was noticeably snappier and funnier than Maguire's. The series also did away with the unpopular "organic" web shooters in favor of the truer-to-the-comic mechanical shooters that Peter—a science nerd at heart—invented himself. In fact, nearly every facet of *The Amazing Spider-Man* embraced science and technology more than its predecessors. Everyone in the film was noticeably "plugged in," using cell phones, computers, exotic-looking software, etc.

Despite the fact that the film's summer 2012 release coincided with Spider-Man's 50th anniversary in the comics, *The Amazing Spider-Man* was overshadowed by the much-more-ballyhooed *The Avengers* and *The Dark Knight Rises*. The film received a cumulative critic score of 66 on Metacritic.com. In probably the most succinct description of everything that worked and didn't work about the movie, Steven Rea wrote in the *Philadelphia Inquirer*: "Don't come to *The Amazing Spider-Man* looking for originality."[384] The movie brought in $62 million during its opening weekend and grossed $262 million domestically overall, both lows for the franchise.

Still Sony was undeterred by the mediocre press and immediately got to work on its sequel with Webb, Garfield, and Stone all back in tow. After having a rather straightforward hero vs. villain dynamic between Spider-Man and the Lizard in the first film, *The Amazing Spider-Man 2* tripled down on the bad guys, casting Academy Award–winner Jaime Foxx as the classic rogue Electro; Dane DeHaan as Peter's best friend-turned-enemy, Harry Osborn/Green Goblin; and Paul Giamatti as Aleksei Sytsevich, the Russian gangster who becomes the armor-suited Rhino. Additionally, prior to *The Amazing Spider-Man 2*'s release, Sony made it clear that it was all-in on its franchise by announcing there would be third and fourth films in the series. And following the model set by Marvel Studios' cinematic universe, Sony wanted to create its own interconnected film-scape by developing two Spidey spinoff flicks starring the supervillain group the Sinister Six and Venom.

It was a lot to process, and many critics believed *The Amazing Spider-Man 2* suffered as a result. In addition to having three villains to fit into the narrative, the sequel continued to develop the arc involving the mystery of Peter's deceased parents. Recognizing that the very real on-screen chemistry between Garfield and Stone (who had started dating while filming the first movie) was one of the best parts of the first film, *The Amazing Spider-Man 2* also focused a great deal of its story on the Peter/Gwen relationship. Oh, and then there were all of the teasers and Easter Eggs that laid the groundwork for two more Spidey sequels and the Sinister Six and Venom movies.

Critically and financially, *The Amazing Spider-Man 2* marked a low point for Sony's once-proud franchise. It grossed only $202 million domestically and earned an aggregate score of 53 on Metacritic. Sony knew it was in trouble, and a hack of the studio's e-mail in late 2014 revealed that some of its executives had been in communications with Marvel Studios about trying to restore the franchise to its former glory. A resolution to these concerns materialized in 2015 when Marvel and Sony agreed to co-produce the next Spider-Man film, while the Spidey character would be allowed to interact on screen with Marvel's Avengers heroes (including the "Web-Slinger" having a small role in 2016's *Captain America: Civil War*). And with that, the Webb-verse came to a resounding thud of an end, only to provide fans with new hope about better days ahead now that Spider-Man is a part of the Marvel Cinematic Universe.

72 Andrew Garfield: Dream Role

Much like Peter Parker, Andrew Garfield was a reluctant hero. While auditioning to play the titular role in Sony's "reimagined" (don't call it a reboot) film franchise, *The Amazing Spider-Man*, the young British actor considered the enormity of what he was possibly getting himself into. Garfield had long considered himself an actor with a capital "A"—namely the kind of guy who would never be a megastar, but would also garner respect from the theatrical community for his dedication to the craft. Playing a superhero in a big-budget blockbuster movie would potentially fly in the face of all that. And yet, during the arduous audition process, Garfield was reminded of his three-year-old self: a child who loved and adored the costumed superhero: "He was just like, 'You're doing this for me.' You get one life and who am I to turn down playing one of my greatest heroes?" Garfield said.[385]

The then-27-year-old actor landed on Sony's radar after his star-turning role as Eduardo Saverin, the co-founder of Facebook, in 2010's Academy Award–winning film *The Social Network*. When Garfield was auditioning for Spider-Man, he was initially skeptical about the idea of redoing the Spider-Man mythology on the big screen. He was a huge fan of the Sam Raimi–directed trilogy of films that were released between 2002 and 2007 and, from both a physical and personality standpoint, was dissimilar from his Peter Parker predecessor, Tobey Maguire. However, the studio saw these qualities as a positive for Garfield. His skepticism was interpreted as thoughtfulness for the role. And casting someone who was a totally different kind of actor from Maguire aided Sony's efforts to definitively turn the page on the Raimi movies.

Still, what cinched the part for Garfield was director Marc Webb's opinion of the actor: Webb's take on the character was distinctively different than Raimi's. Outside of the costume, his Peter was less of a nerd/geek and more of an awkward social outcast (which is actually truer to how the character was portrayed in the early 1960s run of *Amazing Spider-Man* comics by Stan Lee and Steve Ditko). Webb also wanted the film, and his main character, to be more "plugged in" to technology, utilizing cell phones, advanced computer software, etc. Even the new Spider-Man costume was crafted as if a teenager who was good with computers input his ideas for superhero attire into a graphic design software program.[386] Garfield met all of these benchmarks for Webb. "He embodied the spirit of an adolescent," the director said. "He had that nervous quality I was looking for."[387]

The final piece needed to help Sony fulfill its latest Spider-Man mission was finding the perfect co-star to play opposite of Garfield as Peter's girlfriend, Gwen Stacy. Emma Stone's star had been on the rise after a number of well-received roles in movies like 2009's *Zombieland* and 2010's *Easy A*. When Sony brought the actress in to meet Garfield, the two had instant chemistry. Garfield would go on to describe the actress, who he started dating while filming *The Amazing Spider-Man*, as a "shot of espresso" for the production.[388] The two continued their off-screen romance through the filming and release of *The Amazing Spider-Man 2* in 2014 before reportedly calling things off in 2015.

In the aftermath of 2015's Marvel/Sony deal that allowed Marvel Studios to use Spider-Man as part of its cinematic universe with Avengers, Garfield was relieved of his duties as Peter/Spidey. British teen actor Tom Holland was cast as his replacement, and Spidey was once again going back to high school. Considering some of the mixed reviews *The Amazing Spider-Man 2* received after its release, Garfield has since sounded more relieved than upset about these developments: "I started to feel the separation of myself from the world and from my community and it really hit me in a very sad and scary way," Garfield said in a 2015 interview. "I was really scared to be on some kind of forced pedestal."[389]

73 Must Read: *Spider-Man: Blue*

Power and responsibility will always be one of the overarching themes for Spider-Man, but other critical elements to Peter Parker's story include love and loss. The 2002–03 six-part miniseries *Spider-Man: Blue,* which was written by Jeph Loeb with art from Tim Sale, is probably the best example of how exploring the quieter, more sentimental aspects of Peter's life can result in a truly heart-warming, if not tragic, story.

Blue is one part recap, another part re-imagination of a critical point in Peter/Spider-Man's biography—the months following the departure of Spidey's original artist and co-creator Steve Ditko and the arrival of the great John Romita Sr., who collaborated with Stan Lee for many years on *Amazing Spider-Man.* Romita is best known for how he "softened" some of the harsh edges that Ditko had initially installed into Spider-Man's world.

With the arrival of the redheaded bombshell Mary Jane Watson, and the increased exposure of the beautiful but demure Gwen Stacy, many readers and critics have compared this period of *Amazing* to something out of an *Archie* comic (complete with Betty and Veronica vying for the male lead's affections). But because *Blue* was published nearly 40 years after the Lee/Romita issues, Loeb and Sale are able to tone down some of the run's dated hokeyness and instead create a nostalgia-fueled, wistfully composed walk down Lover's Lane depicting how Peter and Gwen first got together and fell in love.

Like the best kind of retrospectives, *Blue* dances around the edges of established continuity. It captures a number of events that originally transpired in *Amazing #40–48* and *Amazing #63,* but uses these happenings as little grace notes that complement the larger symphony of Peter and Gwen's budding romance. So the reader gets to experience abbreviated versions of Spider-Man's battles against the likes of the Vulture and Kraven the Hunter, but with the understanding that the superheroics are not actually driving the narrative's drama. Instead, this story gently depicts two young kids struggling to come to terms with, and ultimately connecting over, their feelings of affection for each other.

The rest of the drama is supplied by the fact that the reader knows the ultimate outcome of this romance: Gwen is tragically killed by the Green Goblin and Peter never forgives himself for it. This is best emblemized in how the story sets up its flashback: while rummaging through some things in the house he shares with his wife, Mary Jane, Peter finds a box of mementos that includes an old Valentine's Day card from Gwen. While MJ is elsewhere, Peter starts to pontificate into a tape recorder about his old love. Before the story ends, we learn that the Valentine's Day card was actually given to Peter on the night of his first kiss with Gwen.

In that context, it might seem a bit weird that Peter appears to still be pining for his college girlfriend while his supermodel of a wife is right downstairs. But that's probably too cynical of a way to look at the situation given *Blue's* gentle, sympathetic tone toward its cast. Loeb and Sale even address this idea in how *Blue* ends: MJ eventually walks in on Peter and his tape recorder and, rather than being upset or jealous about what he's doing, she tells him to say hi to Gwen for her, and that she misses her old friend too.

Her reaction is obviously meant to be a stark contrast to the flimsy, party-girl MJ that was depicted in the flashback sections of this story. Additionally, the scene expertly depicts how MJ is fully cognizant of the influence this other woman has had on her husband's life. How, without the sincere affection and care Gwen showed Peter when they first kissed on that Valentine's Day, Peter might have never developed the capacity to truly love someone romantically. And without Gwen's death, MJ might have never been able to look at her own life in a meaningful way that would have allowed her to embrace Peter and teach him how to love again (or love herself enough to settle down with Peter).

Ultimately, *Blue* is an essential read for Spider-Man fans because it shows how Spidey comics transcend the standard superheroics the medium is best known for. At its core, Spider-Man is a very human story, filled with tangible, real emotions of love, loss, regret, doubt, joy, and sorrow. *Blue's* six issues hit upon almost every one of these emotions, and do it in a fashion that is highly self-contained and reader-friendly to casual fans looking for a Spidey comic that's just a little bit different than the usual punching and kicking fare.

74 Spider-Man Joins the Marvel Cinematic Universe

Once upon a time, there were three distinct movie universes starring Marvel characters: the X-Men (including Wolverine) and the Fantastic Four's cinematic rights belonged to 20th Century Fox; Spider-Man belonged to Sony Pictures; and the Avengers, including solo films for Iron Man, Hulk, Captain America, and Thor (among others) were distributed by Marvel directly as Marvel Studios. So, despite the fact that all of these characters had frequently interacted with each other in the comics—teaming up or, in some cases, fighting against one another—having them appear together on the big screen was a nearly impossible task embroiled in legal issues and other red tape. The only hope for a different outcome would be if any of these studios believed the benefits of having these characters play together in movies outweighed the likely costly entanglements that prohibited that from happening.

But just because something seems improbable doesn't mean it's impossible. By 2014, Sony's Spider-Man franchise had lost its sparkle. After releasing three highly successful *Spider-Man* movies directed by Sam Raimi between 2002 and 2007, Sony went in a new direction, bringing in a whole new cast and director, Marc Webb. The first film, 2012's *The Amazing Spider-Man*, performed well at the box office and had some decent reviews, but also received criticism for rehashing Spidey's origin story again.

Two years later, Sony produced a sequel that received mostly negative reviews while financially underperforming its predecessor. Despite the feedback, Sony still wanted to pursue some additional sequels, along with some potential Spider-Man spinoff films built around the Sinister Six and Venom, but these ideas were never able to gain traction. Instead, as a 2014 hack of Sony's e-mail server revealed, the studio had engaged Marvel over the possibility of making Spider-Man a "shared" property.[390] If that wasn't enough to get fans speculating, Marvel had also announced that its next Captain America film would be loosely adapted from *Civil War*—a comic book story that prominently features Spider-Man.

The long-rumored deal was finally announced in February 2015. Marvel and Sony had agreed to allow Spider-Man to "cross over" into the Marvel Cinematic Universe. Financial terms of the deal weren't entirely clear, but what was important to fans was the fact that Sony would still be distributing Spider-Man films as it had been for the past 15 years, but Marvel Studios could now use the "Web-Slinger" in its Avengers movies. Additionally, Marvel, which, with a few exceptions, had produced a full slate of movies that were both financially successful and critically well-received, would be serving as a creative consultant to Sony as well as a co-producer.[391]

The next stop for Marvel and Sony was finding a new star and a director. Andrew Garfield, who had played Peter Parker in the past two Spider-Man films, was relieved of his duties. Ditto for Webb. Reports out of Hollywood were that Marvel wanted some younger, newer blood. However, the studio also wanted to avoid exploring Spider-Man's origin story again. After an arduous audition process, in June 2015, Marvel/Sony announced that Tom Holland, a teenage actor who had been featured in *The Impossible* and *Wolf Hall*, would play Peter Parker/Spider-Man. And for its director, the studio picked the relatively unknown Jon Watts, whose claim to fame was directing the independent thriller *Cop Car*.[392]

Shortly after the Holland/Watts announcement, an even more interesting bit of casting news had leaked out. To play the critical role of Peter's Aunt May, the only parental figure in Spider-Man's life after the death of his Uncle Ben, Marvel and Sony selected Academy Award–winning actress Marisa Tomei. While nobody had any concerns about Tomei's acting chops for the role, some heads were turned over the fact that in the comics Aunt May had long been depicted as being frail and elderly. Tomei, often the object of someone's affections in many of the films she starred in, was unquestionably not your traditional Aunt May.

However, as casting news trickled in, the Hollywood rumor mill confirmed something else that got fans buzzing: Spider-Man was being written into a new draft of *Captain America: Civil War*.

Other casting and crew announcements were made in steady succession over the next year. The movie's screenplay was going to be written by John Francis Daley and Jonathan Goldstein, who had scripted 2015's *Vacation*. Robert Downey Jr. was going to reprise his role as Tony Stark/Iron Man and be the first Marvel Cinematic Universe actor to cross over to a Spider-Man film. Disney teen-queen Zendaya was cast as a female lead, "Michelle." In April 2016, an official title for the movie was made public: *Spider-Man: Homecoming*, along with a release date of July 7, 2017. And a few months later, after much speculation, Michael Keaton, a critical part of the superhero movie resurgence in the late 1980s when he portrayed Bruce Wayne/Batman in 1989's *Batman*, was cast as a major character in *Homecoming*. At 2016's San Diego Comic Con, fans learned the Vulture was the film's featured villain, with appearances from other rogues, including Shocker and the Tinkerer.

Meanwhile, Holland's debut in *Civil War* was a rousing success, with numerous critics calling Spider-Man a highlight of the film despite the fact that he only accounted for about 20 minutes of screen time. "In just two scenes...Spidey's new guardians achieve more with the character than Sony managed in the past three or four movies," said a review in the British publication *Independent*.[393]

75 Tom Holland (Third Spidey's a Charm)

As part of the landmark agreement between Marvel Studios and Sony Pictures that now allows Spider-Man to stand shoulder-to-shoulder with the Avengers in the Marvel Cinematic Universe, both studios agreed that the time was right to find a new (and younger) Peter Parker/Spider-Man to follow in the footsteps of his theatrically web-slinging predecessors, Tobey Maguire and Andrew Garfield. More than 1,500 actors were seen by the studios, who were specifically looking for someone who could more realistically pass as a high school student. After months and months of whittling their list down, British-born Tom Holland, 18, emerged as THE choice as the new Spider-Man.[394]

Holland had been on Marvel and Sony's radars from the beginning. Holland, meanwhile, assumed the studios were looking to build their new Spider-Man movie around Miles Morales, the half-black/half-Latino character from the *Ultimate Spider-Man* comic series, rather than Peter. Still, he reached out to his agent anyway only to discover that the studios had initiated contact with him. So

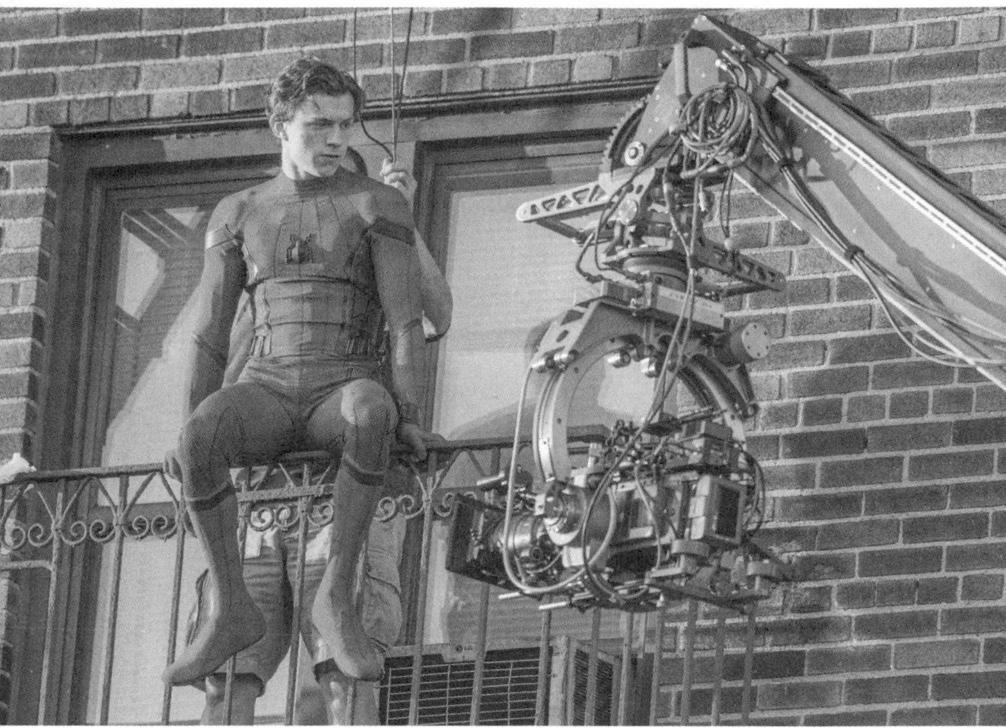

Tom Holland on set filming *Spider-Man: Homecoming* in 2016. (Rex Features/ AP Images)

Holland sent something along to Marvel's casting director, Sarah Finn, and the process began.[395]

In retrospect, Marvel/Sony's interest in Holland was not surprising. Even as a young actor, he had a reputation for his physicality. As part of the filming for the Ron Howard film *The Impossible*, which stars Chris Hemsworth, aka Marvel's Thor, Holland was tossed around like a ragdoll in a 35,000-gallon tank as a part of a disaster sequence. He is also an expert at dance and movement, having taken lessons since he was seven, and having been cast in the titular role in the West End production of *Billy Elliot the Musical* at age 12.[396]

Meanwhile, playing the role of Spider-Man had long been a bit of a dream for Holland. He recalls frequently dressing up as the character as a child and loves the fact that Spidey is so easy for people to relate to.[397] During the audition process, Holland received a helping hand from the Thunder God himself, Hemsworth, who spoke highly of the teenager during conversations with Marvel and Sony executives.[398] Holland also received a boost from Jon Bernthal, who plays the Punisher (introduced in an issue of *Amazing Spider-Man*) in Netflix's *Daredevil* series. Bernthal and Holland filmed the period drama *Pilgrimage* together in Ireland and ended up filming some tapes together to send along to Marvel for their respective auditions.[399]

For one of the last parts of the audition, Holland performed screen tests with Iron Man and Captain America themselves, Robert Downey Jr. and Chris Evans, respectively.[400] The story behind how Holland found out he got the part sounds like something ripped straight out of the comics: While scrolling through his Instagram feed, he saw that Marvel had announced their choice. When he clicked on the link and saw that he was Spider-Man, Holland thought he had just been punked by a friend, so he called his agent and confirmed the news. Then Marvel Studios president Kevin Feige called to officially make Holland's dream a reality.[401]

Holland would make his big-screen debut as the "Web-Slinger" in 2016's *Captain America: Civil War*. His last-minute inclusion in the film actually impacted the amount of screen time dedicated to another superhero making his Marvel Cinematic Universe debut, the Black Panther (played by Chadwick Boseman). Rather than provide more of Black Panther's backstory, the script was altered so as to show Tony Stark meeting Peter and Aunt May at their home in Queens and recruiting the young hero to fight for his side in his confrontation with Captain America.[402]

Despite some critics claiming Spider-Man's role in *Civil War* was unnecessary to the film's larger story involving Iron Man and Captain America, Holland's 20 minutes or so of screen time provided a tantalizing peek as to what moviegoers should expect from Holland in his solo film debut. As one reviewer for *The Verge* wrote, "Any die-hard fan worried about this being the third take on Spidey in 15 years should know that Tom Holland is arguably the best onscreen Spider-Man to date. It's as if the movie took the twitchy charm of Andrew Garfield and the do-gooder attitude of Tobey Maguire and molded it around Holland's palpable energy. It's a magnetic performance."[403]

76 Jon Watts: From *Cop Car* to *Homecoming*

When Marvel Studios and Sony Pictures announced Jon Watts as the director of their latest Spider-Man reboot, *Spider-Man: Homecoming*, a number a people likely said, "Who?" But Watts is just the latest relatively unknown/inexperienced director to be handed the keys to one of Marvel's blockbuster franchises. Certainly, even the biggest *Buffy the Vampire Slayer* fan had to be surprised when Marvel entrusted Joss Whedon to guide the Avengers through their first two movies. And while many of us have laughed uproariously at television comedies *Community* and *Arrested Development*, the Russo Brothers probably weren't on any casual fan's short-list of directors for the past two *Captain America* films. But that's exactly how things have trended for Marvel and its cinematic universe over the past decade. So welcome to the club, Jon Watts.

Watts is best known for directing 2015's *Cop Car*, an independent thriller starring Kevin Bacon (thereby bringing everyone in the Marvel Cinematic Universe one degree closer). His other claim to fame has been the countless short vignettes he's directed as part of the satirical *Onion News Network* web series. Then there's that whole *Clown* movie about a clown monster who eats children....

Regardless of what may seem like an offbeat portfolio, Watts made an immediate impression on the person who matters most: Marvel Studios head Kevin Feige, who said he found himself liking the director the more and more he got to meet with him. "It always comes down to ultimately, 'We can make a movie with this person for two years, we could spend almost every day with this person for two years. Let's go,'" Feige added.[404]

Though even Watts said he was surprised when his name showed up in Marvel/Sony's announcement alongside their choice for a new Spider-Man, Tom Holland ("Have they seen *Clown*?" he's joked in some interviews). However, he does share some kinship with the last two directors who worked on Spider-Man, Sam Raimi and Marc Webb—especially Raimi, whose claim to fame in Hollywood prior to Spidey was the cult *Evil Dead* horror series.

Now that he's in the director's chair, Watts appears to have a very definitive sense of what he's trying to achieve in *Spider-Man: Homecoming*. In numerous interviews, Watts has alluded to *Homecoming* having a John Hughes vibe, referring to the legendary director of such angsty-teen dramedies as *The Breakfast Club*, *Pretty in Pink,* and *Sixteen Candles*. And when you hear Watts talk about some of his comic book inspirations for the film—Brian Michael Bendis's *Ultimate Spider-Man*, which took Spider-Man back to high school, and the *Spider-Man Loves Mary Jane* all-ages series, which focused almost exclusively on the soap opera elements of Peter's classmates at Midtown High School—the premise behind combining the character-centric sensibilities of a John Hughes film with a hormone-fueled superhero romp makes a lot of sense. A promotional image for *Homecoming* released in September 2016 even pays homage to the iconic movie poster for *The Breakfast Club*.

The other vibe Watts is clearly going for is authenticity. *Homecoming* will have what is arguably Marvel's most diverse cast yet, with actors like teen-queen Zendaya and Donald Glover (who years ago openly lobbied to play an African American Spider-Man) portraying key roles in the ensemble. "It's been really fun to just look for things that none of the other Spider-Man movies have really explored before," Watts told *The Daily Beast* in June 2016. "And really making it a high school movie, and committing to that, and not having that just be the beginning of the movie.... When you're looking at it through that prism, it really opens up the door to a lot of possibilities."[405]

77 "One More Day"

Spider-Man has certainly been featured in his fair share of controversial stories during his 50-plus years of history: "The Night Gwen Stacy Died," "The Clone Saga," and "The Death of Jean DeWolff" have all earned some degree of ire from fans for one reason or another. However, when it comes to fan venom, 2007's "One More Day" stands in a class by itself. It's a story that implemented what is arguably the most significant retcon—the act of retroactively changing previously established storyline continuity—in Spider-Man's history by wiping away Peter Parker/Spider-Man's long-term marriage to Mary Jane Watson.

Now don't get it twisted. Marvel's editors and executives had been gunning for Peter and MJ's marriage for years before "One More Day" finally came to fruition. In fact, there was a ton of opposition from creators just to the idea of Spider-Man getting married back when that story became a reality in 1987. Critics argued that Peter's marriage to Mary Jane robbed the character of his usefulness and everyman qualities (what average Joe ends up with a *supermodel*?). But once the marriage was in place, it became a Sisyphean task to end it (especially since everyone agreed that Peter becoming a divorcee or widower would age him even more). And all that hand-wringing ended with "One More Day."

Joe Quesada, Marvel's dynamic editor-in-chief during the 2000s, has said from the very beginning of his editorial tenure at Marvel that he believed a married Peter Parker "wasn't the best thing for an ongoing Spider-Man universe."[406] The seeds for "One More Day" were first planted during one of Marvel's creative retreats about two years before the story was actually published. A number of Marvel's editors and creators started tossing around ideas for the marriage before *Amazing Spider-Man's* then-writer, J. Michael Straczynski, suggested a premise similar to the central idea of the 1998 romantic comedy *Sliding Doors*—where the audience watches two potential outcomes for a character unfold based on whether or not she's able to catch a train. Those at the retreat agreed that a "path or door not taken" approach to the marriage might be easier to implement than finding a single point in Spider-Man's history and erasing it from history, thereby risking a "domino effect" that could have created a continuity nightmare in other segments of the character's timeline.[407]

For Peter/Mary Jane, that door not taken was a retcon where Peter missed his wedding ceremony after being distracted by some Spider-Man business. That marriage would have never happened, but everything else in Spider-Man's history would remain intact. After this retcon, Peter and MJ were still romantically involved and had even lived with each other for 20 years. But nothing they had experienced was as husband and wife.

It wasn't a perfect solution, but Marvel was rearing to go. They even had Spider-Man reveal his secret identity during its *Civil War* event because they knew with "One More Day" coming later

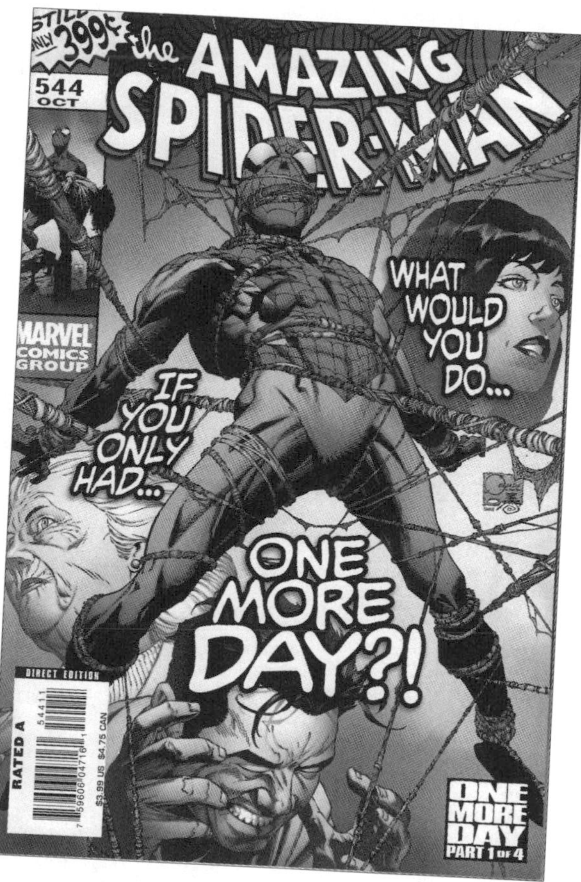

Amazing Spider-Man #544

that year, they could just wipe that moment from existence.[408] But leading up to the story's publication, there were still some disagreements about "One More Day's" ultimate execution. Quesada and Straczynski were interested in using the storyline as a way to resurrect Peter's first love, Gwen Stacy, who had been killed years earlier by the Green Goblin in one of the most famous comic book stories ever. There was some pushback from other creators, and the "keep Gwen dead" crowd seemed to win out, but when JMS turned in his last scripts for "One More Day," there were a couple of surprises in there that Marvel had to contend with.[409]

But before that, all the pieces were in place for "One More Day" to begin in *Amazing Spider-Man #544*. After revealing his secret identity, Peter's Aunt May is inadvertently shot by a sniper bullet meant for Spider-Man. Peter naturally blames himself, but has no one to run to because he has turned his back on many of his superhero allies during the *Civil War* conflict over the Superhero Registration Act. And that's when the drama behind the drama started to take hold.

Despite months and months of advanced press and publicity, the last two installments of "One More Day" in *Sensational #41* and *Amazing #545* were delayed because, very suddenly and to the surprise of nearly everyone involved, major rewrites were required. Straczynski had apparently started to object to the story's direction and rather than hand in a script he considered to be subpar, he instead wrote a story that was dramatically different from what Quesada and Marvel had agreed upon.

In the new script, the mechanism that undid Peter and Mary Jane's marriage would have undone all of Spider-Man's previously established continuity all the way back to 1971's *Amazing Spider-Man #98*. That meant there was a way for Gwen to return. It also meant, under JMS's machinations, that every story that Spider-Man had been featured in since 1971 never actually happened. Nobody at Marvel, outside of Straczynski, wanted "One More Day" to end on that note, especially since there were a number of storylines in place following its publication that would have been rendered totally moot by this curveball of a script.[410]

While Quesada and JMS put on an air of cordiality when asked about the stand-off publicly, Straczynski was not going to get his way, so he asked to have his name removed from the credits page for the final two issues. In an effort to save face, Marvel chose to credit both JMS and Quesada for the plots.[411] Still, nearly 10 years after the story was published, JMS has said multiple times over that he was unhappy with "One More Day" and that he felt editorial got too involved in the storytelling process. Marvel, in its defense, has never denied these claims and has continued to sing high praises about Straczynski's work on Spider-Man.

So what was it about this storyline that caused such a major breakdown behind the scenes? In the penultimate chapter of "One More Day," Mephisto, essentially Marvel's version of the devil, approaches Peter and Mary Jane with a deal that could save his aunt's life. Peter initially rebuffs Mephisto but MJ asks to hear him out. Then, in *Amazing #545*, Mephisto lays it all out there: he would save Aunt May's life, but in exchange, he wanted to erase Peter and Mary Jane's marriage from existence. When pressed about making Peter's identity as Spider-Man a secret again, Mephisto agreed to that as well. Peter, with MJ urging him to "be a hero," agrees to the deal.

And as a final gut-punch, before he enacts his "spell," Mephisto reveals to the couple that if they had stayed together, they would have had a child together, a little girl. And with that, and one final reference to Mary Jane's iconic line from her first appearance, "Face it, Tiger…you just hit the jackpot!" the marriage is over.[412]

Peter then wakes up, grabs a wheatcake from Aunt May's kitchen and heads out to a party where the guest of honor is… *Harry Osborn*?! Harry had been killed off years earlier in *Spectacular Spider-Man #200*. And on that note, "One More Day" concludes and the "Brand New Day" era of *Amazing Spider-Man* commences with a whole host of questions and intrigue.

Unfortunately, the fan backlash to "One More Day" was real and hostile. Fans raged that a hero who espouses "with great power must also come great responsibility," would ever make a deal with the devil. "Without a doubt, this issue is going to be the most universally reviled, controversial issue of *Amazing Spider-Man* ever published," wrote a review on the longtime fan site SpiderFan.org.[413] Spoiler alert. It was.

Marvel still finds itself defending the outcome of "One More Day" to this day, while also trying to find new ways to address the segment of fans who "swore off" Spider-Man comics after it was published. In 2015, as part of its *Secret Wars* event, Marvel released a miniseries, *The Amazing Spider-Man: Renew Your Vows*, which was set in an alternative universe and depicts the married life of Peter and Mary Jane *and* their daughter, Annie. *Renew Your Vows* ended up being one of Marvel's best-selling *Secret Wars* books, so the premise was revived in 2016 as its own ongoing series (still set in a different universe/continuity) with Gerry Conway on scripts and Ryan Stegman providing pencils.

78 Superior Spider-Man

After reading about all of the drama behind "One More Day," I bet you're all looking forward to a chapter about something that is far less controversial, right? Okay, well how about a couple of words about 2012–14's *Superior Spider-Man* era? Oh...that's right, you said *less* controversy....

So if you thought a certain segment of Spider-Man's fan base was ticked off by Marvel mystically annulling Peter Parker's marriage to Mary Jane Watson via a deal with the devil, you should have seen the response to Dan Slott's epic story about Spidey's longtime nemesis, Doctor Octopus, swapping brains with Peter and leaving the hero to rot and die inside of Doc Ock's decaying body. To call some people's response to the story "rational" all depends on whether or not you consider issuing death threats to a comic book creator over social media to be "rational."

And yet, one of the big differences between "One More Day" and the *Superior Spider-Man* was that the former was critically panned as a cheap stunt, while the latter is actually considered one of the better Spider-Man stories to be published over the past 20 years. It is because of that distinction that, despite some of the insanity *Superior* inadvertently inspired—and let's be clear, death threats are pretty insane, regardless of how they're issued—the entire saga needs to be looked back upon as a period of bold creativity. Plus, it wasn't like *Superior's* premise just randomly popped up one day after an editorial mandate. Slott first started planting the seeds for the story nearly 100 issues earlier in *Amazing Spider-Man #600*, when he reintroduced Doctor Octopus as being broken down and cancer-ridden. Doc Ock is also carrying this helmet, which allows him to transfer his brainwaves to otherwise inanimate objects like these small robots called Octobots. Please pay attention to that helmet....

Spider-Man uses the helmet in *Amazing #600* (ugh). He then uses it again about 70 issues later during Slott's "Spider-Island" arc (OMG). If you're not yet convinced of Peter's impending doom, it's worth noting that during Slott's "Ends of the Earth" arc, Spidey defeats Doc Ock after he designs a suit that's able to tap into the supervillain's brainwaves. Yeah, sharing brainwaves with your deadliest enemy is probably not a good idea.

So along comes *Amazing #698*, which was promoted by Marvel as the first part of the storyline "Dying Wish"—an arc that was going to end with a "bang" in *Amazing #700*—wherein we got a rather curiously written Spidey tale that follows our hero on a standard day in the life. Nothing seems that out of the ordinary until Spider-Man goes to visit Doc Ock in prison as the supervillain clings to his life. In that scene, Doctor Octopus utters the words "I'm Peter Parker..."[414] causing Spidey to take off his mask and admit that he is actually Doctor Octopus. Yep. You better believe all that brainwave swapping left Peter in an awful, awful predicament.

After one last valiant effort by Peter, he is defeated and killed by Spider-Man/Doc Ock in *Amazing #700*. However, before he dies, Peter manages to impress all of his memories upon Spider-Ock, including his guilt, sense of honor, and moral code. The scene leads to Spider-Ock vowing to carry on in his old enemy's name as a hero. But this being the arrogant Doctor Octopus, he vowed he was going to be a "superior" hero in every way, making him the *Superior Spider-Man*.

Cue the fan outrage. After *Amazing #700's* publication, fans took to Twitter or to Internet message forums/blogs to let their complaints be heard. They photoshopped images of Spider-Man's co-creator, Stan Lee, shredding an issue of *Amazing #700* (it was actually a picture taken in the '90s that showed Lee jokingly destroying a copy of DC's "The Death of Superman" comic). And yet, when the sales figures came in for *Amazing #700*, it had moved more than 200,000 copies (despite a $7.99 sales tag). A few weeks later, *Superior Spider-Man #1* became the best-selling comic of January 2013, moving more than 188,000 copies. If people hated Slott's new take on Spider-Man, they certainly had a funny way of showing it.

Superior Spider-Man ran for 31 issues and featured a dark, but at times quite funny, spin on the standard Spider-Man story. In it, Spider-Ock tries (really, really tries), to be a somewhat decent hero, even leveraging his technological and scientific know-how to reduce crime throughout New York City and become a more efficient superhero. But because this was still Doctor Octopus, a guy who has tried to destroy the planet on numerous occasions, all of his tactics were shrouded in some kind of twisted logic and immorality, making *Superior* read more like a referendum on what it means to be Peter Parker, Spider-Man, rather than some kind of celebration of an amoral, pretend hero. There were some occasional missteps, and many fans thought the book stumbled to the finish line with an overly rushed finale. However, it was a series that kept people talking, and kept the heat squarely on Slott's shoulders, which he loved and encouraged: "One of the fun things for me about doing *Superior* is...I got to do my best shot at being an evil, cackling villain myself," Slott said in one 2014 interview. "Telling Spider-Man fans over and over again that Peter Parker was dead, and cackling the whole time."[415]

Indeed, as is almost always the case in comics (unless you're Peter's Uncle Ben), the real Spider-Man returned from the dead and succeeded where Doc Ock had failed by defeating the Green Goblin. As a twist, when Peter comes back from the dead, he finds that his life is completely different: he lost his job at Horizons Lab, has a new girlfriend in Ann Marie Marconi, earned his doctorate, and was running his own tech company, Parker Industries. Naturally, Slott being Slott, all of these elements are still being paid off in some way in the current issues of *Amazing Spider-Man*. And he takes all of the criticism and platitudes in stride. When asked about his legacy on Spider-Man comics during a 2016 interview, Slott jokingly responded: "They'll go, 'Why did you *do* that? Why'd you kill Spider-Man?'"[416]

79 The Spider or the Man?

We've come far enough into this endeavor to know that Spider-Man isn't actually a spider. Under the mask and costume, he's a living, breathing man named Peter Parker. However, over the years, that hasn't stopped a number of creators from playing around with the "spider or the man" motif—i.e., stories that explore Spidey's more animalistic, arachnid side.

Probably the most famous instance of this theme came in 1971's *Amazing Spider-Man #100*, which also happened to be one of the last issue of the series written by Spidey's co-creator, Stan Lee (with art by Gil Kane). The comic kicks off what is more commonly known as the "Six Arms Saga." In it, Peter (once again) is fed up with all of the lousy responsibilities that come with being a masked superhero. He goes to see Doctor Curt Connors, who offers Spidey a serum that promises to eliminate his powers so Peter can finally live a normal life. Instead, in one of the great cliffhangers in Spider-Man history, the magic potion transforms poor Peter into a six-armed freak. Roy Thomas, who succeeded Lee as *Amazing's* lead writer, was nonplussed by having to deal with Lee's outrageous plot twist, so much so that he admittedly ignored it when finishing out the arc in *Amazing #101–102*, a storyline that's famous for introducing the tragic villain Morbius the Living Vampire.[417]

"The spider or the man" motif got a more postmodern take in the early 2000s, when *Babylon 5* creator J. Michael Straczynski took over writing duties on *Amazing Spider-Man*. During his run, JMS saw to it to incorporate more mythology and mysticism into Spider-Man's world. In his very first arc, "Coming Home," Straczynski introduced the idea that Spider-Man had "totemic powers," meaning powers that were mystical in nature rather than science-based. Straczynski's philosophy was espoused via one of his new creations, the enigmatic Ezekiel.

Ezekiel asks Peter why he fights so many villains who are animalistic in nature (like Doctor Octopus, Rhino, or Scorpion). The old man believes these "totemistic pretenders" are attracted to Spider-Man's spiritual purity. Ezekiel then proceeds to really drop a philosophical bomb on Peter when asks if he thinks he got his powers from the radiation from a spider-bite, or did the radioactive spider-bite awaken some latent form of power in his body.[418] It's definitely a chicken-or-the-egg-type quandary, but it's also one that fueled a lot of the drama in Straczynski's multi-year run with Spider-Man.

The spider-totem subplot led to the creation of one of Spider-Man's most fearsome villains, Morlun, a near-immortal who feeds, like a vampire, on the spiritual essence of totems. Over the course of "Coming Home," Ezekiel warns Peter that Morlun would hunt him relentlessly because he represents a "pure" form of totem. However, in order to defeat Morlun, Peter injects himself with a dose of radiation, thereby making himself impure.

Straczynski, and a cadre of other writers and artists, would dial up more Spider-Man mysticism in 2005–06's 12-part crossover, "The Other." The story suggests that Peter has an entire set of untapped powers that require an "awakening." When Morlun returns and appears to have killed Peter, he "molts" his skin like a spider and is reborn as "the Other." All of his wounds and scars are healed, and he has acquired even more fantastic powers in addition to his existing ones, including organic webbing (like what is featured in the Sam Raimi–directed *Spider-Man* movie trilogy), night vision, feeling vibrations through his webbing, and being able to adhere objects directly to his skin.

"The Other" certainly marked an evolution for the character, but it also presented a whole set of questions and potential plot holes that made the storyline far too cumbersome to keep in continuity. When the Spider-Man universe experienced a semi-reset following the publication of "One More Day" in 2007, all of Peter's newly acquired "spider" powers are removed from the equation and barely referenced again. "The Other" is teased again during 2011's "Spider-Island" arc, but this time it's Spidey's failed clone, Kaine, who taps into the hidden mystical power-set, while Peter glibly jokes, "been there, done that."[419]

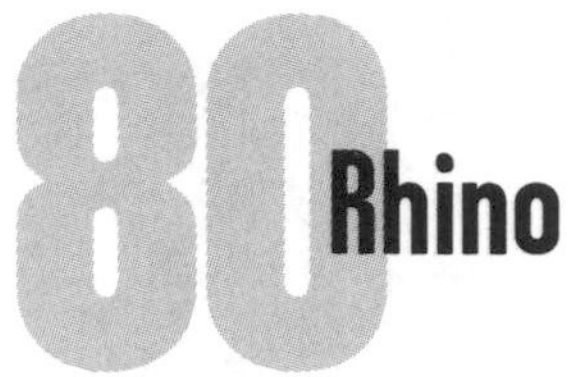

80 Rhino

Who would have thought that a big, beefy guy dressed in a rhinoceros costume would be depicted as such a dim-witted meathead since his creation more than 50 years ago? But that's exactly the case when it comes to Aleksei Sytsevich, the supervillain known across the Marvel Universe as the Rhino.

Debuting in *Amazing Spider-Man #41*, Rhino was the first new Spidey adversary co-created by the legendary artist John Romita Sr. after he took over penciling *Amazing* from the book's original illustrator, Steve Ditko. As explained in his origin story in *Amazing #43*, Sytsevich was your standard dime-a-dozen criminal enforcer until he volunteered to subject himself to an experiment that bonded a molecular adhesive to his body, giving him nearly impenetrable armor, as well as enhanced speed and strength. To defeat the villain, Spider-Man has to concoct a special web fluid that dissolves his armor-like skin.[420]

Perhaps out of recognition that a villain as powerful as the Rhino is a bad fit in the more "street level" world of Spider-Man, the character was actually shuffled over to the Hulk's orbit for a number of years before circling back to where he started and joining the Sinister Syndicate supervillain team (outfitted with a number of C- and D-list baddies like Shocker, Boomerang, and Speed Demon) in *Amazing #280*. Still, the Rhino remained fixed on the lower rungs of Spider-Man's rogues gallery before finally being elevated in the 2000s, thanks to the brilliance of a pair of stories that added needed nuance and depth to Sytsevich's character.

The first was 2001's "Flowers for Rhino," by Peter Milligan and Duncan Fefredo, which was published in *Spider-Man's Tangled Web #5–6*. Modeled after the classic science fiction novel *Flowers*

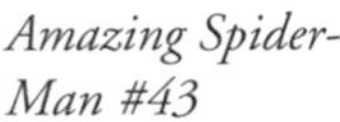

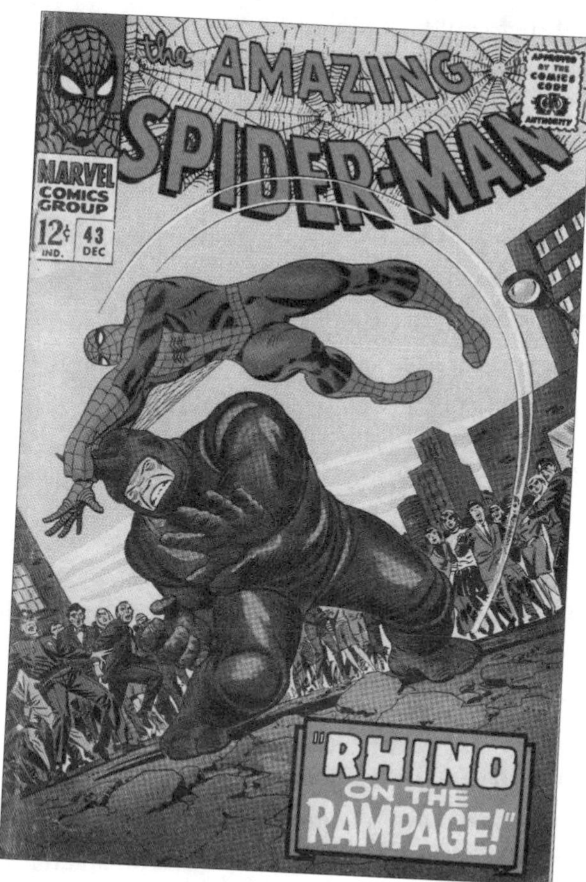

Amazing Spider-Man #43

for Algernon, "Flowers for Rhino" depicts the Rhino undergoing an experiment that gives him a genius-level intellect. Since he's no longer a brutish oaf, Rhino manages to defeat Spider-Man and kickstarts a criminal empire before he loses his passion for living and contemplates suicide. He then reverses the operation and goes back to being the classic, dumb Rhino.

"I tried to stand back and look at this big guy: his thick, thick skin, which suggested a pretty thick head," Milligan said of his story. "I found something both pathetic and noble about him, though he was always portrayed as pretty stupid or thick-headed. I knew and loved the story *Flowers for Algernon* and thought a spinoff of that could be a good way to get under this thick rhino skin, to see another side of Rhino.... The lack of a real back catalogue or history between [Spider-Man and Rhino] gave me more room to tell the story I wanted to tell."[421]

About a decade later, during *Amazing Spider-Man's* "Brand New Day" thrice-monthly publication schedule, writer Joe Kelley wrote a pair of Rhino-centric stories in *Amazing #617* and *#625*. In it, Sytsevich finds true love in a woman named Oksana and plans to retire from being the Rhino. However, a new Rhino emerges and goads Sytsevich out of hiding. During the battle, Oksana is tragically killed and a despondent Sytsevich goes back to his life of super-powered crime. "We took inspiration from [the 2008 film] *The Wrestler*," Kelley said. "He was this old beaten-down guy. We cooked up this story about the old Rhino and what he was going through in trying to do better. It's such a simple story...everyone bought into Rhino not wanting to be Rhino anymore."[422]

In the aftermath of this story, Rhino joined Doctor Octopus's most recent iteration of the Sinister Six supervillain group. He was presumed dead during the "Ends of the Earth" storyline in *Amazing*, but later resurfaced. The character also received some added exposure in 2014, when he had a brief appearance in *The Amazing Spider-Man 2* film, being played by Paul Giamatti. The cinematic version of the character utilizes a robotic-like device that looks like a rhino, rather than being outfitted in grayscale armor.

81 Cloak and Dagger

With their powers that resemble "light" and "dark," Ty Johnson and Tandy Bowen, more popularly known as the superhero duo Cloak and Dagger, have maintained a passionate cult following ever since they debuted in *Peter Parker: The Spectacular Spider-Man #64* in 1982. Created by Bill Mantlo and artist Ed Hannigan, Cloak and Dagger have one of the most socially conscious origin stories in comics. Tandy and Ty met as teenage runaways in New York City before being captured by a chemist who was developing a new synthetic form of heroin to be sold by the underworld boss Silvio "Silvermane" Manfredi. The tandem is part of a larger group of teens that are used as guinea pigs by Manfredi's gang, killing all but Ty and Tandy. Both escape, but in the process, receive strange powers from the drug, and assume the identities of Cloak and Dagger.

Cloak, fittingly outfitted in an ominously-long flowing cloak, is able to make himself intangible and teleport his adversaries to something dubbed the "darkness dimension"—a place that is often described as being cold and desolate. In contrast, Dagger utilizes psionic light daggers that can absorb the opposition's vitality. Her abilities also complement her partner by quenching his thirst for light.

In their first few appearances, Spider-Man works with the raw but powerful Cloak and Dagger in trying to teach them the lessons of great power and responsibility. Initially, both seek to exact brutal and final justice against the criminals who transformed them. But after a few life lessons with Spidey (and a battle against a reanimated robot form of Silvermane), Cloak and Dagger start to resemble more traditional heroes, even if they maintain some shades of gray in terms of their ongoing battle against the illegal drug trade in New York City.

Cloak and Dagger were popular enough to star in their own eponymous miniseries in 1983, written by Mantlo with pencils by Rick Leonardi. The mini performed well enough to justify launching a *Cloak and Dagger* ongoing series in 1985, which published bi-monthly for 11 issues.

Hannigan recalls Mantlo having big plans for Cloak and Dagger from the onset: "Bill definitely intended for them to be standalone characters from the very beginning," Hannigan said. "I was looking forward to it, but after laying out the first issue and actually penciling a couple pages I started to feel a bit restless and burnt out on both the characters and Marvel in general. I wasn't sure I could give the story the artwork it deserved, so I decided to drop it."[423]

While the characters never truly took off as a standalone act as Mantlo envisioned, Cloak and Dagger have both played a prominent role in numerous Spider-Man comic events and elsewhere in the Marvel Universe. They teamed up with Spidey during the jam-packed "Maximum Carnage" storyline in the early '90s and were featured in their own miniseries during 2011's "Spider-Island" event (which reportedly was another trial for an ongoing series). They also appeared in the *New Mutants* and later introduced themselves to a whole new generation of readers by playing a key supporting role in the cult-hit *The Runaways*.

Because of the team's modest, but dedicated following, Cloak and Dagger have often been the subject of rumors for projects going beyond the scope of comics. In 2016, Marvel announced that a live-action Cloak and Dagger television series would debut at some point in the near future on Freeform (formerly ABC Family). Additional details on the series were scant beyond the fact that it would be a "superhero love story" that targets Freeform's ages 14 to 34 demographic.[424] Terry Kavanagh, who scripted a number of

Cloak and Dagger issues when the duo had their own series in the late '80s/early '90s, said the team is "perfectly made for any visual medium, and they particularly lend themselves to Freeform's teen-centric mandate. I actually think they were way ahead of their time.... Urban teens fit well in the Spidey-verse, naturally, and I do think they've been underutilized."[425]

82 The Parker Clones

Ben Reilly and Kaine are Peter Parker's brothers from another... ummm...genetic cloning chamber? Both Ben and Kaine are Peter's clones and played a central role in the 1990s mega-story "The Clone Saga." While the "Clone Saga" remains one of the most controversial and critiqued Spider-Man stories to ever be published—primarily for its absurd length and frequent status quo upheavals that ultimately went nowhere—both clone brothers, especially Kaine, have managed to persevere and become a part of Spidey's mythology.

Ben first appeared (this depends on your point of view on Spider-Man continuity) in 1975's *Amazing Spider-Man #149* by Gerry Conway and Ross Andru, when Spider-Man is forced to fight his own clone, who's been created by the supervillain the Jackal. Peter appears to have survived the battle and dumps his clone's body into a smokestack, where he was never heard from again...until about 19 years later, when a shadowy figure showed up in *Web of Spider-Man #118*, kicking off the "Clone Saga."

Marvel had hoped the "Clone Saga" would return Spidey to its roots by allowing the current Peter Parker, who married his supermodel girlfriend Mary Jane Watson in 1987, to leave the series, while his clone would assume the mantle and become the new (single) Spider-Man. While developing the arcs, two of the "Clone Saga's" chief architects, Terry Kavanagh and Howard Mackie, went back to *Amazing #149* and found the resolution to the clone's story to be riddled with logic gaps. "He dumped his body in a smoke-stack?" Mackie said. "It made no sense. Even EPA regulations back then wouldn't have allowed for there to be a hole up there and an open fire down below."[426]

Upon returning to the comics, the clone was dubbed the "Scarlet Spider," donning an all-red costume with a light blue "hoodie" over it. Tom Lyle, the artist who came up with the hoodie idea, joked that it was meant to be a short-term fix for the character. However, Marvel stuck with it for more than a year due to its popularity and because the "Clone Saga" itself kept getting stretched out beyond its original projected length.[427]

The clone took the name "Ben Reilly" in honor of Peter's Uncle Ben and his Aunt May (whose maiden name is Reilly). Over the course of the "Clone Saga," it becomes clear that Ben has memories of Peter's that extend beyond his "birth" as a clone a few years earlier. That leads to the two undergoing a test (conducted by Ben's close friend, Seward Trainer) that determines Ben is indeed the real Spider-Man. Peter is naturally freaked out by this development, but eventually rides off into the sunset with his pregnant wife, handing the reins of Spider-Man over to Ben and launching the "Spider-Ben" period in Marvel Comics. Ben, in a brand-new costume and a blonde dye job on his hair (so no one from Peter's circle of friends in New York might confuse him with the guy who was supposedly out West starting a family with his wife), was the focal point of the Spider-books for about 10 months. But Marvel got cold feet about its new status quo and killed the character off, revealing him to be a clone (all along) in the process.

Like Ben, Kaine debuted in the "Clone Saga" early on in *Web of Spider-Man #119*. However, Kaine, who was introduced as the first "failed" clone of Peter, was initially cast as a villain and later an antihero. Kaine is tormented by the fact that he is rejected by his "father," the Jackal. His body is covered in scars and he is suffering from a degenerative condition that is slowly killing him. He stalks Peter and Mary Jane, but he does so because in his twisted mind he's trying to protect them from the likes of Ben, as well as other villains like Doctor Octopus (who he kills in an issue of *Spectacular Spider-Man*). "We were looking for a villain who would be specific to the story we envisioned, and we knew it had to be a character who would be a more physical challenge to Spider-Man than the Jackal," Mackie said of Kaine. "We were thinking of Peter and Ben as brothers from the very beginning, so, what if…there was a third brother? What if he was the last in a line of failed experiments? What if instead of being shaped by his pain into a hero he was broken by his pain into a villain?"[428]

Before seemingly dying during the "Maximum Clonage" arc in 1995, Kaine redeems himself with Peter and Ben. Then, for more than a decade following the "Clone Saga," both Ben and Kaine were left untouched by the various creators with the exception of the alternative universe *Spider-Girl* series. However, during the "Brand New Day" *Amazing Spider-Man* initiative in the late 2000s, writer Marc Guggenheim pitched a new chapter in the clones' stories. Thinking that it would make for a compelling tale if someone with "Peter Parker's face" had committed a crime somewhere (and Peter gets blamed), Guggenheim asked to bring back Ben Reilly. When Marvel insisted that Ben remain a puddle of genetic soup, Guggenheim got the green light to revive Kaine.[429]

Following the publication of Guggenheim's "Remember Ben Reilly" arc in 2009, there was a definitive Kaine renaissance. The character made amends with Peter and was seemingly sacrificed by the Kravinoff family and presumed dead again in "Grim Hunt," only to revive again to join the battle against the Jackal and the Spider-Queen in 2011's "Spider-Island." Following that storyline,

Marvel made the unexpected announcement of having Kaine star in his own solo series, *Scarlet Spider*, which lasted 25 issues between 2012 and 2013.

Meanwhile, after years of editorial resistance to resurrecting Ben, in 2017, Marvel finally pulled the trigger and revealed the character as the mastermind of their "Clone Conspiracy" arc. And despite the fact that Ben was initially brought back as a villain, Marvel quickly followed up "Clone Conspiracy" with a new Reilly-centric series, the appropriately titled, *Ben Reilly: The Scarlet Spider*, by Peter David and Mark Bagley.

83 J.M. DeMatteis: The Thinking-Man's Web-Head

When it comes to grim and gritty Spider-Man stories, J.M. DeMatteis is your guy. He's responsible for some of the very best dark Spider-Man tales in the character's history, including the death of Peter Parker's best friend, Harry Osborn; the death of Peter's Aunt May; and "Kraven's Last Hunt," which featured Spider-Man being buried alive for two weeks by one of his villains, Kraven the Hunter.

In other words, lots of bright and cheery stuff.

JMD is notoriously one of comic's more reflective, methodical writers. While he's an old rock 'n' roller at heart—he got into comics after his dreams of being a musician came and went—he's also the kind of guy who cites Russian novelist Fyodor Dostoevsky as an inspiration for some of his superhero stories. His comics tend to be more character-driven than action-packed, and he's also not afraid to use the medium as an outlet for some of his own personal feelings and emotions. DeMatteis's personal struggles were actually a part of the core that fueled arguably his most famous Spider-Man story ever, "Kraven's Last Hunt." JMD had been kicking around his story for years, first starring Wonder Man, and then as a vehicle for Batman. By the time it became a Spider-Man storyline, DeMatteis was in the midst of a divorce. "It was probably great therapy for me to write that story," he said. "I was trying to claw my way back to the light the same way Peter was as he was clawing his way out of the grave."[430]

Born in Brooklyn, New York, in 1953, JMD got hooked on Marvel when he was in junior high school. He got his start as a writer penning music reviews for local newspapers, and eventually *Rolling Stone* magazine, before some negative feedback he received for a snarky review he wrote convinced him to focus more on the creative side rather than the tearing-art-apart side.[431]

He pitched to both Marvel and DC before eventually catching on as a staff writer at Marvel. He scripted his first Spider-Man story, *Marvel Team-Up #101*, in 1981. Within a year, he kicked off a 20-plus issue run writing *MTU*, where he developed his familiarity with all things Spider-Man.[432] He also used his time on the books to showcase his sense of humor with the creation of such wacky heroes and villains as the fur-covered crime boss White Rabbit, and Frog-Man, a guy who dresses like…a frog.[433]

During the same timeframe, DeMatteis scripted *Captain America* with artist Mike Zeck, with whom he would later collaborate on "Kraven." He then moved on to some "smaller" work that actually helped make him more of a name around the industry. He created the graphic novel *Moonshadow* for Marvel's Epic line—the first major American comic to be fully painted, as well as the Doctor Strange graphic novel *Into Shamballa* and the vampire story *Blood: A Tale*. By 1987, it was time for JMD to make something out of that rejected Wonder Man/Batman story. After a lunch meeting with a couple of Marvel editors, DeMatteis cooked up a way to incorporate Spider-Man into his "back from the grave" story. And with Peter's wedding to supermodel Mary Jane in the works, the timing of such a dark story couldn't have been better. JMD first created his own villain for the tale—his own take on Batman's Hugo Strange. But after thinking better of it, he started flipping through a copy of the *Marvel Universe Handbook*, found Kraven the Hunter's entry, and instantly knew he was the guy for his now-legendary story.[434]

After "Kraven's" success, DeMatteis was recruited as the lead writer on one of Spider-Man's core titles, *Spectacular Spider-Man,* with longtime Marvel artist Sal Buscema. One of DeMatteis's first major storylines for *Spectacular* was "The Child Within," which depicts Harry Osborn being haunted by the ghost of his father, Norman, aka the Green Goblin, causing him to lose his sanity and become the Goblin himself. Similar to "Kraven," DeMatteis actually first envisioned "The Child Within" as a Batman story, starring the Dark Knight and his longtime villain Two-Face.[435] But DeMatteis realized the potential of making it a Peter/Harry story, and even used it as an opportunity to explore some of the trauma Peter had experienced when his parents left him (and died) as a four-year-old. "It's great to have two guys punching each other, that's fine, but I call it 'the Big Why?' Why do they do this? Why is this guy trying to run around and shoot Spider-Man? What is there in his past? What's the trauma? What is the psychological twist that made him do this?"[436]

DeMatteis left *Spectacular* only to get asked to become the lead writer of the main Spider-Man book, *Amazing Spider-Man.* JMD was as confused as anyone as to why the "dark" guy was being asked to write one of Marvel's most mainstream titles.[437] Of course, when DeMatteis started on *Amazing*, the years-long arc known as the "Clone Saga" was just kicking off. JMD was initially cynical when the story was pitched to him—which involved Peter's thought-to-be-dead clone returning and staking a claim as the rightful Spider-Man. However, DeMatteis reconsidered and even pitched some of his own ground-shaking ideas, like the death of Aunt

May in *Amazing Spider-Man #400*.[438] He also created the clone-centric *Lost Years* miniseries with John Romita Jr., which followed the tragic adventures of two of Peter's clones, Ben Reilly and the deformed Kaine, before they resurfaced in the modern continuity.

As the "Clone Saga" dragged on (and on and on), JMD left Spider-Man again before the over-stuffed arc was concluded. However, once it had wrapped, he returned to write Spidey for a fourth time on *Spectacular*. With a new Spider-Man status quo to play with, DeMatteis did what he always did: write character-centric stories involving some dark and twisted turns for supporting cast members like Peter's high school bully-turned-friend, Flash Thompson.

As it turns out, DeMatteis wasn't terribly happy with his second stint on *Spectacular*. Despite his love for Peter and his supporting cast, he had reached a natural breaking point with Spidey. He contributed some stories here and there—including a backup tale in 2012's *Amazing Spider-Man #700*—but his days of writing Spidey on a monthly basis were over. And for JMD, that's fine by him: "I've been really lucky with Spider-Man. I've been able to do really everything I've ever wanted to do with that character.... I've explored that character from every angle and it has been a great honor."[439]

84 David Michelinie: Peak Spider-Man

Spider-Man has always been one of the comic book industry's most popular characters. But under the stewardship of David Michelinie in the late 1980s and early '90s, Spider-Man was really, really popular.

The Wilmington, Delaware,-born writer has the distinction of scripting the *Amazing Spider-Man* during the book's heyday in terms of sales. Granted, this time period was incredibly kind to the entire comic book industry, thanks in large part to a speculator bubble that had collectors buying up comics like they were Scrooge McDuck with dollar signs in their eyes. However, Michelinie's contributions to the Spider-Man universe had a lot to do with it too. He got to write the first batch of stories after Spider-Man's alter-ego, Peter Parker, got married to supermodel Mary Jane Watson. He also co-created two of Spidey's biggest villains in Venom and Carnage. Working alongside a trio of superstar artists like Todd McFarlane, Erik Larsen, and Mark Bagley didn't hurt either.

Michelinie actually credits Spider-Man for getting him back into comics when he was in college. He was an avid reader of comics as a young kid but grew out of the medium by the time Stan Lee, Jack Kirby, and Steve Ditko were changing the industry forever. However, when he was 20, he was playing in a rock band when his bass player produced a trunk full of comics. His bandmate started singing the virtues of Spider-Man, talking about how he was an average guy with everyday problems. Intrigued, Michelinie started thumbing through the Spidey comics in the trunk and got hooked.[440]

In the early '70s, Michelinie started working for DC, writing mostly mystery comics. After scripting a number of stories for DC, including the infamous "Death of Aquababy" issue of *Adventure Comics* (Aquaman), Michelinie eventually crossed paths with Marvel's then-editor-in-chief, Jim Shooter. Shooter had been writing *The Avengers*, and he asked Michelinie to script a couple of plots he had come up with. These issues went on to become a part of the epic *Avengers* story, "The Korvac Saga." Interestingly enough, Michelinie had never read a single *Avengers* comic until he scripted that story.[441]

Michelinie would make an immediate mark at Marvel. He created the second Ant-Man (and the character that starred in the *Ant-Man* film), Scott Lang, and, during his first stint scripting *Iron*

Man alongside artist Bob Layton, he wrote one of the medium's most famous stories ever, "Demon in a Bottle," which dealt with Tony Stark's battle to overcome alcoholism. He also created the supervillain Taskmaster, who had the unique ability known as "photographic reflexes" (he could instantly copy any fighting style or use of weapons after witnessing someone else do it).

Around this time, Michelinie had his first interaction with Spider-Man. He was asked to script the second installment of a two-part story featuring the Black Cat in *Amazing Spider-Man #205*. The book's regular writer, Marv Wolfman, had abruptly left Marvel in the middle of the arc. A few months later, Michelinie wrote his first Spider-Man story of his very own, *Marvel Team-Up #103*, which paired Spidey off with Lang's Ant-Man.

Michelinie would have his first semi-regular stint on a Spider-Man book in 1985 when he started scripting *Web of Spider-Man*. At that point in Spider-office history, Marvel's editorial department was attempting to give each Spider-Man book its own distinct flavor and vibe. *Amazing Spider-Man* was the main book, *Spectacular Spider-Man* was dark and gritty, and the *Web of* would feature a traveling Peter Parker/Spider-Man on assignment for the *Daily Bugle*. "It wasn't exactly what I had in mind," Michelinie said. "It took me away from his supporting cast and perhaps the most important part of his supporting cast: New York City."[442]

Still, Michelinie was finally working with Spider-Man and his run on *Web of* gave him an opportunity to start planting storyline seeds that would eventually pay off by the time he got to *Amazing*—like having a mysterious hand push Peter in front of a subway train in *Web of #18* and having that hand's owner turn out to be Venom. Michelinie's *Web of* work even invited some real-life drama for Marvel. In *Web of #20*, Michelinie sent Peter off to Ireland, where the story addressed the very real conflict between Ireland and Northern Ireland. After the first issue came out, Marvel received a bomb threat from someone claiming they were from the

IRA (Irish Republican Army). Michelinie was given the option to rewrite the storyline, but he declined, leading the arc to end abruptly under the pen of another writer.[443]

Michelinie finally made his way over to the main Spider-Man book, but not without more conditions and caveats. As he started on *Amazing*, he was operating under a mandate from Shooter that Peter and Mary Jane were to be married as part of a huge event that would mirror what Stan Lee was writing on the Spider-Man daily newspaper strip. Michelinie "hated it." His original pitch for "The Wedding Issue" was cast aside for something that Shooter wrote himself and Michelinie suddenly had to deal with a plot device that he found unnecessary. But rather than fight it, he decided to "make it work" by depicting Peter and Mary Jane "in a happy marriage," with no bickering or nagging or anything that might turn readers against the relationship.[444]

Very soon after he became lead writer of *Amazing*, Michelinie began collaborating with a young, up-and-coming artist named Todd McFarlane. McFarlane's very kinetic visual approach was an instant hit with readers, and sales on the book started to skyrocket. While Michelinie was certainly happy with the royalty checks that accompanied higher sales, he also sincerely enjoyed working with McFarlane, who he described as a "thorough professional.... His pictures were so interesting and exciting, it made my work better."[445]

It was with McFarlane's help that Michelinie's most famous creation, Venom, made his debut. In *Amazing #300*, Marvel wanted the featured villain to be someone new and exciting. Michelinie had tossed around the premise of bonding the alien symbiote that made up Spider-Man's black costume a few years earlier with someone who hated Spidey. Originally Michelinie had worked up the idea of having a pregnant woman who was driven insane after her husband was killed by a car accident, causing her to miscarry, become Venom, but the editors thought a more traditional, hulking villain would be more appropriate.[446]

McFarlane eventually left *Amazing* to script and illustrate his own series (known as "adjective-less" *Spider-Man*). In his place was another artistic hotshot, Erik Larsen. However, the Michelinie and Larsen union was anything but pleasant. The two started feuding after Michelinie had written a letter to *Wizard*, a comic book industry magazine/price guide, disputing a story in the publication that claimed McFarlane was the sole creator of Venom. Larsen took umbrage with the perceived slight against another artist and wrote a response to *Wizard* calling Michelinie a "clown." "That did not make for a wonderful working relationship," Michelinie said after the fact.[447]

Larsen would eventually leave after *Amazing Spider-Man #350* to be one of the founding members of the independent comic book publisher Image (alongside McFarlane). Following him on pencils was the ultra-talented Mark Bagley, a guy who had dreamed of illustrating Spider-Man since he was a kid. Things between Michelinie and Bagley were far less hostile than they were under Larsen. Together, they created the sociopathic "spawn" of Venom. But Michelinie had started to become increasingly disenchanted with his Spider-Man work. A switch in editors meant Michelinie was doing more event-oriented stories like "Maximum Carnage," which he didn't like. The last straw came when Michelinie's editor suggested he write a storyline where Peter's parents mysteriously came back from the dead. "I had no idea who they were," Michelinie said, and when he asked his editor what the twist was, "He didn't seem to know either."[448]

Still, even with a somewhat lukewarm ending to his tenure, Michelinie remains thankful for the opportunity that led to him writing nearly 100 issues of *Amazing Spider-Man*: "It was a dream come true" and "the highlight of my career."[449]

85 The Mystery of the Hobgoblin

In 1983's *Amazing Spider-Man #238*, Roger Stern and John Romita Jr. introduced the newest masked member of Spider-Man's legendary rogues' gallery, the Hobgoblin. As an homage to the Silver Age–era storyline that introduced the Hobgoblin's predecessor in villainy, the Green Goblin, Stern's original intent for the character was to keep his identity shrouded in mystery as part of a long-simmering plot in *Amazing Spider-Man*. However, little did Stern suspect that the behind-the-scenes drama with unveiling the Hobgoblin would come to overshadow the story itself.

Fans were immediately mesmerized by the Hobgoblin mystery. Depicted as being more calculating and diabolical than the Green Goblin, readers pitched their own theories to Marvel via fan letters and at conventions. But before Stern could script the resolution to his story, he left *Amazing* at issue *#250*. In that comic, after months of misdirection and red herrings, Stern finally started to shine a spotlight on the character he intended to reveal as his sensational new villain. In one scene, an inordinate amount of attention is paid to fashion mogul Roderick Kingsley, a character Stern created a few years earlier while he scripted *Spectacular Spider-Man*. In one panel, Kingsley refers to having a brother that was out of town. While it probably seemed innocuous at the time, Stern, who later admitted he heard "Kingsley's voice" when he first scripted the Hobgoblin, was showing his hand. Roderick Kingsley was our mystery villain.[450]

Not everybody at Marvel agreed with Stern. When the writer announced that he was leaving *Amazing*, his editor and later his successor on the book, Tom DeFalco, asked him to finally come clean about his villain. Stern said it was Kingsley—but with a twist. He wanted to introduce Roderick's brother Daniel, a complicit conspirator in the Hobgoblin mystery. While Roderick and Daniel were not twins, they looked enough alike that Daniel could show up at business meetings with a hairpiece and pretend to be Roderick while his brother flew around New York City on his goblin glider pumpkin-bombing Spider-Man and whoever else got in his way. DeFalco incredulously dismissed the twist as "Roderick Kingsley's evil twin," and, once he took over on *Amazing*, decided to respectfully put his own spin on the Hobgoblin saga.[451]

DeFalco and his artistic collaborator, Ron Frenz, had their own version of the Hobgoblin mystery: Richard Fisk, son of Wilson "Kingpin" Fisk, was the villain. Meanwhile, as a nod to Stern, they intended to make Kingsley the well-coiffed, purple-hooded gangster known as the Rose.[452] To keep readers off-balance, DeFalco/Frenz started to frame *Daily Bugle* reporter Ned Leeds—who was acting increasingly more erratic due to his wife, Betty Brant, having an affair with Peter Parker's high school bully-turned-friend Flash Thompson—as the prime suspect. In another twist, in *Amazing #276*, Flash is falsely revealed as the Hobgoblin. Who else would be able to frame him other than the actual Hobgoblin himself, and who had more incentive to see Flash rot in jail than Ned?

Still, there was yet another wild card in this storyline: Spider-book editor Jim Owsley (now known as Christopher Priest). Various creators have described Priest as being rather hard-headed and combative when he started editing the Spider-books in the mid-80s. He frequently clashed with DeFalco and Frenz over missing deadlines on *Amazing Spider-Man*. During the height of their tensions, Priest pressed DeFalco in front of the comic industry press about the Hobgoblin. In an effort to get Priest to stand down, DeFalco jokingly told him it was Ned.[453] And then that's when things really started to get weird.

Priest fired DeFalco and Frenz from *Amazing*, claiming they weren't timely enough with the book. While the series transitioned to a new creative team, Priest scripted a number of *Amazing* issues

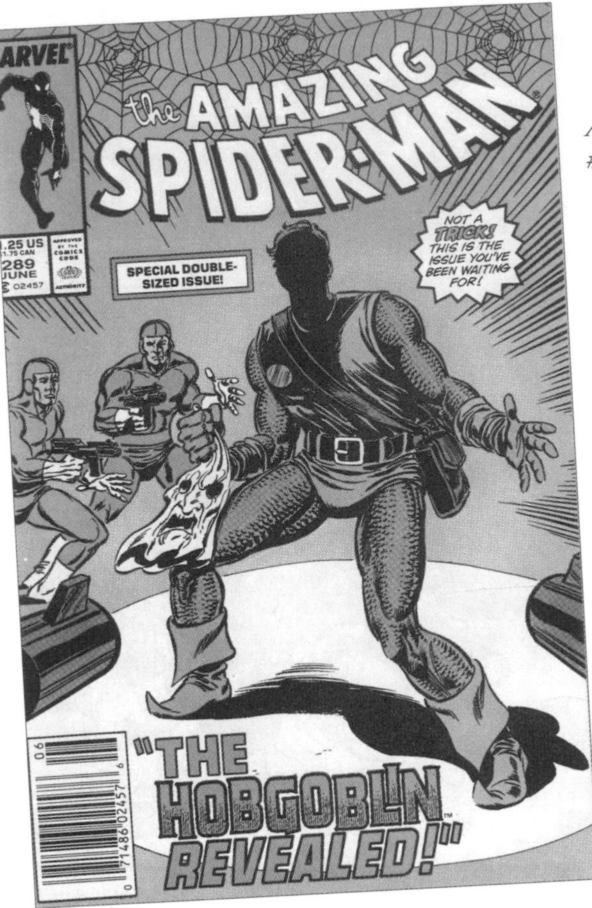

Amazing Spider-Man #289

(dubbed "Gang War") that DeFalco had plotted. In the arc, Priest reveals Fisk as the Rose, while Kingsley is treated as a non-factor. Additionally, Ned acts crazier and crazier, making it obvious that he was going to be the Hobgoblin.

Except, as "Gang War" was being published, the *Spider-Man vs. Wolverine* one-shot, which Priest also scripted, was released and, to the shock of everyone, Leeds was murdered in the comic, meaning…who the heck knows?

DeFalco said after the fact that Priest only killed Leeds to spite him, which sounds childish and petty. But other creators actually have corroborated that story. Peter David, who was Priest's hand-picked writer for the *Spectacular Spider-Man* series during this era, discussed the Hobgoblin mystery with his editor and speculated that, based on all of the evidence, the villain had to be Ned. That's when Priest told him that it couldn't possibly be Ned because he was slated to be killed off in *Spider-Man vs. Wolverine*. "Why would you do that?" David asked. "'To piss off Tom DeFalco,'" David recalled Priest telling him.[454]

So there you go. With pretty much every logical option off the table, the Hobgoblin mystery seemed destined for failure. After "Gang War" wrapped, Priest was supplanted as Spider-office editor by Jim Salicrup, and David inevitably pitched the storyline that made it to print in *Amazing #289*: Ned was the Hobgoblin. The Kingpin would make this startling revelation to Spider-Man. Apparently while Peter and Ned were on assignment in Germany (in *Spider-Man vs. Wolverine*), a rival gang boss sent his hitmen after Leeds. When Peter walked in on Ned's dead body, he had witnessed the aftermath of the Hobgoblin's murder.

"I was satisfied with what I wrote because I was thrust into a situation that I absolutely could not win. It's the most insane project I've ever been involved with," David said. "It was a story that I did because there was absolutely no other way to do it."[455]

Jason Macendale, who had operated for a while as the villain Jack O'Lantern, took over from Leeds as the new Hobgoblin. But after all the twists and turns this story took, the Hobgoblin was used quite sparingly thereafter. However, there was one lone voice in the wilderness that thought it might be fun to update the Hobgoblin saga, referring to it as a "cold case just waiting to be solved"—the character's original creator, Roger Stern.[456]

"It seemed incredibly out of character for Ned Leeds to have been the real Hobgoblin," Stern said, adding that Ned ("not the Ned we knew") wasn't capable of murdering someone as the Hobgoblin did.[457] Stern also objected to the way a couple of random henchmen were able to overpower and murder the Hobgoblin—a man with super-strength. So Stern came up with an idea: what if Leeds had been brainwashed into believing he was the Hobgoblin by the real Hobgoblin, Roderick Kingsley? There was certainly precedent. In an earlier *Amazing Spider-Man* story, a crook named Lefty Donovan is brainwashed into thinking he's the Hobgoblin. After some debate among the powers that be, Stern was given the green light by Marvel to script the three-part miniseries, *Hobgoblin Lives*. Frenz was brought on to provide pencils. And Stern finally got to execute his brilliant twist—two brothers, who are not twins, but look alike, working together to perpetrate one of the biggest criminal enterprises in Marvel Comics history.

Regardless of the story's bizarre outcome, the Hobgoblin is still celebrated today as one of Spider-Man's greatest villains. Kingsley is back to being the guy (though current *Amazing Spider-Man* scribe Dan Slott faked a lot of people out in 2010 when it looked like Roderick had been killed by another rival, only for the dead man to be revealed as...Daniel Kingsley). And he's still being depicted as a master manipulator and escape artist. Just don't ask him to talk about that 10-year period where the Hobgoblin was more of a punchline than a primetime player.

86 Spider-Man's "Brand New Day"

In the immediate aftermath of 2007's controversial "One More Day" storyline, which dissolved Peter Parker's marriage to supermodel Mary Jane Watson, Marvel's hierarchy set off to push Spider-Man comics in a risky, but necessary, new direction. Peter was back to being a swinging bachelor, striking out with women while having problems balancing his superhero and social lives, à la Spidey's earliest days, when he was being written and illustrated by Stan Lee and Steve Ditko. Certain characters from the past were surprisingly resurrected, like Harry Osborn (who had been killed off in a storyline in the early '90s). Others regained a more prominent role in *Amazing Spider-Man's* narrative, like Peter's first-ever girlfriend, Betty Brant, and his high school tormentor-turned-friend Flash Thompson. And a number of new villains were introduced, like Menace, the Freak, and Mister Negative, while the classic rogues (as well as Mary Jane) were temporarily phased out or pushed to the background.

Ultimately, the motivation behind this initiative—which was dubbed "Brand New Day"—was a "back to basics" approach to Spider-Man; i.e., getting back to what made the character so successful (and relatable for casual fans) years earlier. Not only was Peter's marriage to MJ removed from the equation, but so were some of the mystical powers he received during J. Michael Straczynski's run on the book, such as organic webbing and night vision. And Spider-Man's public unmasking in *Civil War* was totally struck from the record, also negating stories involving Aunt May, the Fantastic Four, and others, who at one point knew Spidey's civilian identity.

From a procedural standpoint, the biggest change *Amazing Spider-Man* endured during "Brand New Day" was its publication schedule. Marvel decided to eliminate Spidey's other "B" books, *Sensational Spider-Man* and *Friendly Neighborhood Spider-Man*, in favor of a thrice-monthly *Amazing*. To accomplish the herculean task of creating three issues per month, Marvel employed a team of writers and artists (known as the "Webheads") to rotate over the course of a year, similar to how many creative teams behind episodic television series operate. Overseeing the Webheads was editor Stephen Wacker. Wacker had previously worked for DC as editor of its weekly series, *52*, which meant he had the necessary experience to keep the frenetically scheduled book on time and on track.

One of the keys behind the success of the team format was who Marvel chose as its Webheads. "There were no alpha dogs," said Dan Slott, who has since parlayed his tenure on "Brand New Day" into being the every-issue writer of *Amazing*. "There were no strong personalities or strong flavors. It was like a relay race. Everyone would be there for the team and no one would try to dominate the other guys."[458]

That's not to say it was a bunch of schmoes working on Marvel's flagship character. "Brand New Day" featured such respected creators as Marc Guggenheim (currently a writer for the comic book show *Arrow*), Joe Kelly (who launched *Deadpool* into the stratosphere in the late '90s), and Eisner Award–winner Mark Waid.

Of course, one of the tallest orders for the Webheads was dealing with all the negative fan backlash caused by "One More Day." Guggenheim recalls attending the first summit for "Brand New Day," unaware of the "buzzsaw we were stepping into." But once the plans for "One More Day" and "Brand New Day" became clear, the team set out "not to apologize for 'One More Day,'" Guggenheim said. "We were going to take as much ownership and creative authority as possible."[459]

The Webheads met every few months and attempted to plot out *Amazing Spider-Man* as far into the future as they could. While the team certainly lacked an "alpha" with the star power of a Brian Michael Bendis or Ed Brubaker, many of the Webheads credit Slott as being the driving force behind the initiative. He came up with many of the storyline's core tenets and was generally considered the go-to guy for creativity and positivity. "Dan is the most enthusiastic guy in the room," Kelly said. "He loves Spider-Man, he loves these stories. We all found that enthusiasm infectious."[460]

As "Brand New Day" stretched on, some of the elements that were initially off-limits, like Mary Jane or classic villains such as Doctor Octopus and the Green Goblin, were eventually unleashed, giving the first reappearances of all these characters a special feel. Marvel's executive editor, Tom Brevoort, also emphasized that the team should return to having long-running mysteries in *Amazing*, à la the original mysteries behind the Green Goblin or Hobgoblin's identities in the 1960s and '80s, respectively. As such, "Brand New Day" featured such cryptic arcs as who was the new red-headed antihero Jackpot (who looked and spoke suspiciously like Mary Jane), how did Harry Osborn return from the dead, and who was the new Goblin villain, Menace?

In 2010, after 27 months and more than 100 issues, Marvel finally decided it was time to return *Amazing Spider-Man* to a more traditional production schedule and creative team structure. Slott became the lead writer, with a rotating cast of artists on a bi-monthly schedule. "We've been doing it for almost three years, it was time for something new," Wacker said. "We'd more than proven our point that we can get these things out."[461]

And despite having to overcome some heated fan reactions after "One More Day," Marvel's hierarchy deemed its "Brand New Day" experiment a successful time for Spider-Man and his core book: "About a year or two after 'One More Day,' we would have that one person at a [comic] con who would yell out that they didn't like 'One More Day' and I would respond 'But do you like "Brand New Day" and all the stories that have flowed out of it?'" said Marvel's editor-in-chief, Axel Alonso. "And they would invariably say 'Yeah' and I would say 'Mission accomplished!'"[462]

87 J. Michael Straczynski: Peaks and Valleys

Joseph "J." Michael Straczynski, or JMS, reached some of the highest highs and hit some of the lowest lows during his six-year tenure scripting *Amazing Spider-Man* in the 2000s. The writer's arrival on the book in 2001 was a sorely needed shot of adrenaline for what had once been one of Marvel's flagship books. But his departure from *Amazing*, following the highly unpopular story "One More Day" in 2007, was shrouded in bitterness and controversy.

Born in Paterson, New Jersey, in 1952, Straczynski was an accomplished writer in newspapers, books, animation, television, and film prior to joining Marvel. He's probably best known as the creator of the science fiction television series *Babylon 5*, which ran from 1993 to '98. He also founded his own comic book imprint, Joe's Comics—named after the box of comic books he kept as a kid as his family moved around the country—in 1998.[463]

JMS had long been a fan of comics but claims he never considered working in the medium until his time as showrunner for *Babylon 5*.[464] In 2000, Marvel's now-editor-in-chief, Axel Alonso, took over as the editor of all the Spider-Man titles with the charge of reinvigorating the line with some new blood. Marvel was in the midst of transforming itself following its near-collapse in the '90s after its bankruptcy filing and had been hiring a number of high-profile writers like Hollywood film director Kevin Smith, and rising stars Brian Michael Bendis and Mark Millar. For *Amazing Spider-Man*, Alonso coveted two writers: Grant Morrison, who had established himself as one of the medium's most compelling, if not enigmatic, creators, and Straczynski, who was scripting Alonso's "favorite superhero book," *Rising Stars*, for Joe's Comics.

Morrison had already been pegged to write *X-Men* with Frank Quietly, so Alonso was more than happy to extend an offer to JMS.[465]

Straczynski was paired with an industry vet, artist John Romita Jr. Their first arc together, "Coming Home," was exactly what Alonso had in mind in terms of breaking new ground on Spider-Man. JMS showed no fear about challenging Spider-Man's status quo, introducing new mythology about Spider-Man's origins as well as a new villain, the vampiric Morlun. He also rehabilitated a number of the book's supporting cast members, like Peter's Aunt May, who, after years of being cast as a milquetoast worrywart, was suddenly acting more independent and defiant around her nephew.

Then, in the midst of all of these dramatic superhero stories, *Amazing's* narrative was put on hold for a month in light of the September 11, 2001, terrorist attacks on the United States. Considering how vital New York City is as a character in its own right in the Marvel Universe, the company's hierarchy wanted to use the power of comics to espouse a reaction to the tragedy. Spider-Man, the quintessential everyman hero, was selected as the character to star in this yet-to-be-created story. When Straczynski first received this emotionally daunting assignment, he was lost as to how to proceed. Then, while on the set of one of the shows he created, *Jeremiah*, Straczynski found his inspiration: "I had never written in that style before and don't know where it came from. The whole thing is a prose poem, really," he said.[466]

Another one of Straczynski's contributions to the Spider-Man universe was the reuniting of Peter with his estranged wife, Mary Jane Watson. The couple had been famously married in the '80s, but after a number of aborted storylines that were designed to remove the marriage from the narrative, JMS was left with a "tangled mess" to deal with, if he so chose. Straczynski liked the idea of writing a married Spidey, so he brought Peter and MJ back together. But in doing so, he also opened the door to a larger debate amongst some of Marvel's top editors and writers about what to do about the Parkers over the long-term.[467]

The resolution of that debate was "One More Day," which saw the Peter/MJ union wiped from existence after the couple cuts a deal with the devilish Mephisto to save Aunt May's life in exchange for their marriage. Despite being seemingly pro-marriage a few years earlier, Straczynski was reportedly on board to work with Marvel's editor-in-chief, Joe Quesada, to script "One More Day" as his final arc on *Amazing*. However, when it finally came time for JMS to do the deed and end the marriage, something unexpected happened. Straczynski handed a script in to Quesada that was vastly different from the story they had all agreed upon more than a year earlier. JMS had suggested implementing a retroactive wipe of all the Spider-Man events going back to 1971's *Amazing Spider-Man #98*, including the death of Gwen Stacy, considered one of the watershed moments in comics. Fearing that JMS's treatment would make a gigantic mess of not only Spider-Man, but all of Marvel's continuity, the script was rejected and rewritten by Quesada. Both creators received credit for the story, though Straczynski reportedly asked for his name to be removed from the arc's final two issues. [468]

Following his tenure on *Amazing*, Straczynski stayed on with Marvel to write *Thor* and *Fantastic Four*, but he eventually left the company and continued to write for a broad spectrum of media including, of course, comics. When asked about his tenure on *Amazing*, and specifically "One More Day," JMS is not shy about his unhappiness in how things ended, reaffirming his opposition to the story. "When I'm left to my own devices, I can do what I feel is a competent job," he said in one Marvel post-mortem interview. "When I start to get mandates and edicts written into my ear and am suddenly being pulled into events and crossovers and being yanked one way or the other, I don't do my best work because I can feel the hand on my shoulder. Cases like those are the low-point moments."[469]

88 Spider-Man in Animation (Post-1970)

A Spider-Man animated series may seem like a given these days, but that wasn't always the case. Following the moderate success of the original *Spider-Man* Saturday morning cartoon which ran from 1967 to 1970 (also known as the show with the catchy theme song that starts: "Spider-Man, Spider-Man, does whatever a spider can") kids (and adults) had to wait nearly a decade before the "Webhead" popped up again in animated form. Since then, there have been seven different Spider-Man-centric animated series, with more coming down the pipeline. Here are some quick facts and highlights of each.

Spider-Man: Following the creation of the animation studio Marvel Productions, this eponymously titled series debuted in 1981 and was syndicated for one season with 26 episodes. It was marketed primarily as a pseudo-sequel to the original *Spider-Man* cartoon from the '60s. In that vein, it had a similar cast of characters as *Spider-Man '67*, mostly focusing on how Peter Parker split his time at the *Daily Bugle*, at home caring for his Aunt May, and as Spider-Man.

Spider-Man and His Amazing Friends: Marvel Productions concurrently developed this series in 1981 to air on NBC alongside the aforementioned syndicated *Spider-Man*. As a result, people often consider these two animated series to be crossovers, though *Amazing Friends* ended up being far more popular and culturally relevant. It lasted three seasons (though only 24 episodes) and introduced the world to the superhero Firestar, who is now a mainstay in the Marvel comic book universe. In addition to Firestar, Spider-Man also teamed up with the mutant Iceman in each episode, battling the likes of the Green Goblin, Doctor Doom, and Magneto. Dennis Marks, a producer for the show, said the team-up concept was used for the series because previous Spider-Man cartoons that depicted him as a solo act "had not been a success."[470]

Spider-Man: The Animated Series: Arguably the most popular Spider-Man cartoon, this series was a staple of Fox's Saturday morning lineup from 1994 to 1998. Christopher Daniel Barnes, of *Little Mermaid* (voice of Prince Eric) and *The Brady Bunch Movie* (Greg Brady), was tapped to voice Peter Parker/Spider-Man. The show produced 65 episodes and, similar to the comics, developed many long-running arcs that lasted over the course of a season—an idea that was championed by producer/story editor John Semper. The show's budget was reportedly much larger than previous Spider-Man cartoons, and its exhaustive cast list included nearly every major Spider-Man rogue, love interest, family member, and co-worker from the comics. By the way, for those who are still traumatized by it, Semper says he's "very sorry" he made Mary Jane a water clone and had her dissolve into nothing without ever properly resolving that subplot before the series was canceled.[471]

Spider-Man Unlimited: Fox's 1999 follow-up to the highly successful *Spider-Man: The Animated Series* flamed out rather quickly after losing traction to the era's cartoon fads like *Pokémon* and *Digimon. Unlimited's* storyline was also quite atypical: focusing on Spider-Man's adventures on a "Counter-Earth" alternative universe, similar to some of the stories found in Marvel's trippy "cosmic" comics in the '70s. The show lasted 13 episodes and mostly featured Spidey taking on Venom, Carnage, and a slew of "alternative" versions of villains from Counter-Earth.

Spider-Man: The New Animated Series: After Spidey finally got his successful big screen debut in 2002, a conglomerate of production studios, including Marvel Entertainment and Sony Pictures Television, developed this series to function as a continuation of the stories featured in the film. The series is most notable for its unique animation style; all of the characters were computer generated images (CGI). It also featured a dynamite cast of voice actors, including Neil Patrick Harris (*Doogie Howser*, *How I Met Your Mother*) as Spider-Man, singer/songwriter Lisa Loeb as Mary Jane Watson, and Ian Ziering (*Beverly Hills 90210*, *Sharknado*) as Harry Osborn. The show lasted 13 episodes and aired on MTV.

The Spectacular Spider-Man: This beloved series was influenced heavily by two of the most celebrated comic book runs in Spidey history: the Stan Lee/Steve Ditko issues of *Amazing Spider-Man* and the Brian Michael Bendis/Mark Bagley issues of *Ultimate Spider-Man*. In fact, co-creator Greg Weisman said he read the first seven collections of *Essential Spider-Man* (paperbacks that reprint classic Spidey comics) in preparation for writing the series.[472] As a result, fans were treated to a series that was very true to the comics in terms of its tone and characterization, featuring updated looks at such classic storylines as the "Mystery of the Green Goblin," the "Alien Suit Saga," and "Spider-Man vs. the Sinister Six." Unfortunately, the show was discontinued after only two seasons and 26 episodes when Sony Pictures Television relinquished its rights to producing a Spider-Man animated series back to Marvel.

Ultimate Spider-Man: With the animation rights back in Marvel's hands, this series debuted in April 2012 as part of a larger block of programming on the Disney XD network. With more than 100 episodes produced, it is the longest-running Spider-Man animated series to date. A number of top-notch writers from the comics, including Brian Michael Bendis, Joe Kelly, Joe Casey, and Paul Dini, helped shape the direction of this series, which also leaned heavily on the comics for inspiration. The third season, which was renamed *Ultimate Spider-Man: Web Warriors*, featured alternative versions of Spidey, similar to the "Spider-Verse" storyline from the comics. Season four shifted its focus to Spider-Man and his most famous rogues, the Sinister Six. At New York Comic Con in 2016, it was announced that *Ultimate Spider-Man* would air its last episode in early 2017, with a new Marvel animated Spider-Man series in the works.[473]

89 Electric Boogaloo: *Spidey Super Stories*

For some fans and future creators, their gateway to the world of Spidey came courtesy of the Children's Television Workshop and its weirdly amusing, if not somewhat disconcerting, sketches featuring Spider-Man on the PBS television series *The Electric Company*. "My only exposure to Marvel when I was young was through *The Electric Company*," said longtime comic book writer Marc Guggenheim, who scripted *Amazing Spider-Man* in the late 2000s. "Their Spider-Man terrified me…he went against one guy who gave you the measles."[474]

That last sentence, in a nutshell, describes *Electric Company* Spider-Man. *The Electric Company* was an educational television program geared toward children who had grown too old for *Sesame Street*. The series ran for 780 episodes between 1971 and 1977. Starting in season four, the show featured a three-to-six minute segment featuring a live-action Spider-Man, played by puppeteer Danny Seagren. From the annals of "before they were famous," the "voice of God" himself, Morgan Freeman, often narrated the segments. Demonstrating the series' off-putting awkwardness, Spider-Man never spoke, but rather "word balloons" would appear above his head, along with random sound effects. All of Spider-Man's "fights" were against villains developed exclusively for the show such as Dr. Fly, the Spoiler, and (a personal favorite) the Wall, who had a penchant for disrupting Spider-Man's enjoyment of New York Mets baseball games by causing mischief at Shea Stadium.[475]

In concert with *The Electric Company* segments, Marvel started publishing *Spidey Super Stories* in 1974, an ongoing Spider-Man comic book series geared toward children. Each issue featured a kiddie-fied Spider-Man story, with simpler vocabulary and less-hostile stories involving one of his classic rogues, like Doctor Octopus or Doctor Doom, and then a backup story that was an adaptation of one of *The Electric Company*'s television bits. Jean Thomas, one of the few female writers at Marvel during this era (and ex-wife of Marvel's former editor-in-chief, Roy Thomas), was tapped to script the series. Thomas has credited her elementary school teaching license for landing her the gig, since she had to collaborate often with the Children's Television Workshop.[476]

After 15 issues, Thomas left the series and was replaced by future Spider book editor Jim Salicrup. One Salicrup story that has achieved a cult following is *Spider Super Stories #39,* involving one of Marvel's most nefarious villains, the "Mad Titan" Thanos. Thanos had become one of Marvel's most popular villains. While mainstream Marvel Thanos was often seen courting the physical embodiment of Death to be his girlfriend and threatening to commit mass genocide against the universe, the "children's" version of the character searches for the Cosmic Cube using his "Thanos-Copter" (a goofy-looking yellow helicopter with his name "Thanos" emblazoned along the side).

Years later, Salicrup still has a sense of humor about his unique use of Thanos, claiming that he also used a "kinder, gentler Kingpin" in *Spidey Super Stories* shortly before Frank Miller transformed him into a cold-blooded gangster in *Daredevil.* "As for the Thanos-Copter, let's just say, I needed a simple way for him to get around," Salicrup said, "and I'm a big fan of the Adam West/Burt

Ward *Batman* movie, which featured the cinematic debut of the Bat-Boat and the Bat-Copter."[477]

90 Listen to the *Amazing Spider-Talk* Podcast

If you're looking to hear two passionate Spider-Man fans talk about everything that's relevant to the "Web-Singer's" universe, then look no further than the *Amazing Spider-Talk* podcast, the greatest Spidey podcast on the World Wide Web.

Full disclosure: I might be a wee bit biased in this endorsement, as I am one of the two founders and hosts of this weekly audio series, which reviews Spider-Man comics past and present, interviews creators and editors, and also discusses Spider-Man's role in film, animation, and elsewhere. However, even if I weren't one-half of this dynamic podcast team, which also includes a filmmaker, writer, and jack-of-all-trades named Dan Gvozden, I would heartily endorse this show, which aims to look at the Spider-Man world in a bit of a bigger picture and doesn't resort to only unwarranted praise or relentless criticism of Spidey's comics and movies like some other podcasts do.

The first episode of the show dropped in April 2013 and included a review of *Superior Spider-Man #7–8*. At that point, in an effort to reflect the drastic status quo shift of the comics, the podcast was known as *Superior Spider-Talk*. However, a year later, when the main Spider-Man book reverted back to being *Amazing Spider-Man*, we followed suit by dropping the "superior" adjective and calling ourselves the *Amazing Spider-Talk*.

Demonstrating the show's relationship and rapport with writers, artists, and editors from all eras, *Amazing Spider-Talk's*

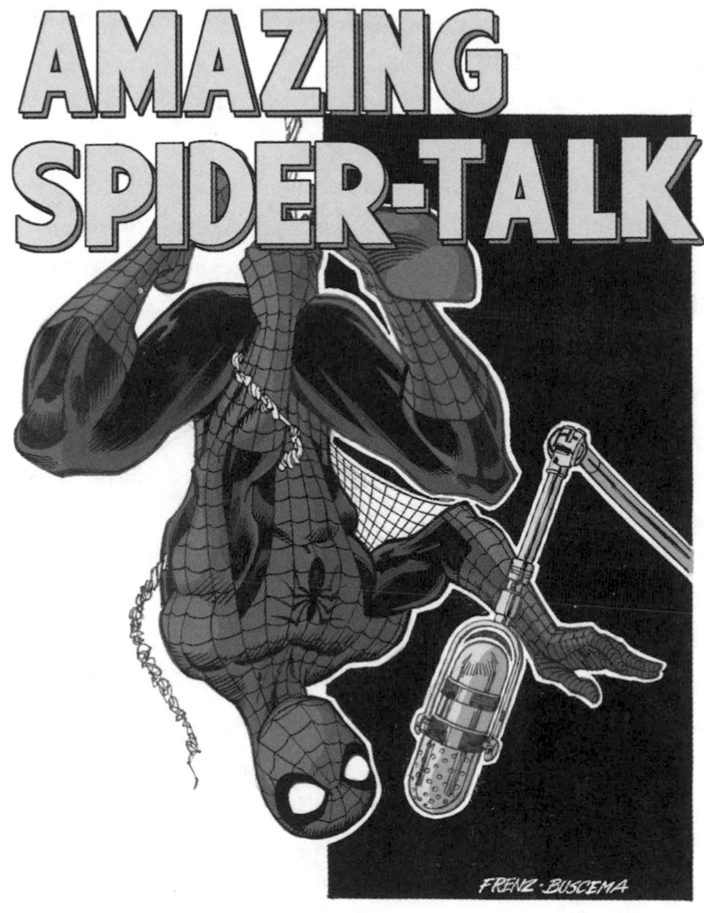

Our amazing logo, penciled by Ron Frenz, with inks by Sal Buscema.

visually dynamic logo, which depicts an upside-down Spider-Man hanging on a web and talking into a microphone, was penciled explicitly for our use by longtime Spider-Man-artist Ron Frenz, with inks by the equally prolific artist Sal Buscema. As such, Frenz has been a frequent guest on the show, where he's given career-spanning interviews as well as discussions about individual comics that he's worked on. Similar interviews have been conducted with such Spider-Man luminaries as Gerry Conway, Tom DeFalco,

David Michelinie, Peter David, Howard Mackie, Joe Kelly, Marc Guggenheim, and J.M. DeMatteis.

But the heart and soul of the show remains our regular discussions about the newly released Spider-Man comics. In these episodes, Dan and I provide listeners with a spoiler-filled dissection of the newest issue of *Amazing Spider-Man*, commenting on the story's structure, characterization, and relevance to classic Spider-Man comics and themes. And, of course, we discuss the comic's artwork and make note of the quality of its visual storytelling, consistency in form, and coloring, and the overall dynamism.

Dan and I conduct similar review segments whenever Spider-Man stars in a major theatrical release. In fact, when 2014's *The Amazing Spider-Man 2* was released, we invited Conway, who wrote the iconic "The Night Gwen Stacy Died" story in the early 1970s (which inspired many sequences in the film), to join us for the discussion.

In addition to reviews and interviews, Dan and I read and answer fan mail and reviews of our own show submitted on sites like iTunes and Stitcher, recap all the major Spider-Man "news" in a given recording cycle, and conduct what we refer to as our "B Book" reviews—short micro-reviews of many of Spider-Man's secondary titles like *Spider-Gwen*, *Spider-Woman,* and *Spider-Man 2099.* These segments tend to drum up a lot of fan comments and reactions since they include "guest spots" from longtime comic book characters, Eugene "Flash" Thompson and Swarm (a super-villain that is actually a reanimated Nazi skeleton made completely out of bees). If all of that sounds absolutely bizarre, you'll just have to download an episode (and subscribe—please subscribe!) to hear it for yourself.

You can download and/or subscribe to *Amazing Spider-Talk* via the show's page on iTunes, Stitcher, Google Play, and YouTube. Episodes are also hosted to stream in perpetuity on www.superiorspidertalk.com. The show offers its Friendly

Neighborhood Spider-Talk Members Club that, in exchange for modest donations, provides "members" with free swag, digital comics download codes, and other giveaways and incentives. You can sign up for the club by visiting https://www.patreon.com/superiorspidertalk.

91 Miguel O'Hara: Spider-Man of the Future

Okay everyone, it's time to fire up your DeLorean and party like it's 2099 (and riff off every other pun/pop culture reference to the future that you can think of). Miguel O'Hara was created by Peter David and Rick Leonardi in 1992 as one of Marvel's flagship characters in its *2099* imprint: a series of reimagined superhero stories that took place more than 100 years into the future in the year 2099.

Marvel's *2099* was a dystopian world (think Ridley Scott's *Blade Runner*) where mega-corporations and the richest of the rich call all the shots, and citizens are addicted to recreational drugs that are marketed as pharmaceuticals (keep in mind, regardless of how ominously familiar this all may sound, *2099* is a completely fictitious universe). Miguel O'Hara was the head of a genetics program at Alchemax, one of Nueva York's (the *2099* nomenclature for New York City) largest companies. He was charged by Tyler Stone, Alchemax's CEO, with developing an army of corporate-controlled super-powered beings. When one of Alchemax's test subjects dies, O'Hara wants off the job until he is blackmailed by Stone into staying. While working on Alchemax's program, O'Hara tests the genetic-coding machine on himself and transforms into a new Spider-Man.

David was charged with developing all of the finer details of *Spider-Man 2099's* universe when he was first hired for the book in the early '90s. "I don't remember exactly which aspects of the *2099* were already part of the initial setup when I came aboard," David said. "I do know, though, that there was almost nothing specific for Spider-Man other than that he was, well, Spider-Man and…an employee of Alchemax."[478]

David thought of some general ideas for a new costume and then sat down with Leonardi, who ran with what became the finished product. David has called it "one of the single best collaborative moments in my life."[479] The writer also wanted to ensure that Miguel was a truly distinct character, so he took every aspect of mainstream Marvel's Peter Parker/Spider-Man and made his *2099* version the "polar opposite." Peter was an orphan, so O'Hara had a mom and a brother. Peter was awkward around girls and O'Hara had a fiancée. Miguel was also projected as being somewhat darker and ethically compromised than Peter, though he never truly crossed the line into antihero territory.[480]

David scripted the series for 44 issues, along with some other specials and one-shots (including a graphic novel where Miguel and Peter cross the time stream and meet each other for the first time) until he quit the book in protest of Marvel's firing of editor Joey Cavalieri. *Spider-Man 2099* was canceled two issues later.[481]

Still Miguel managed to live on, first as a part of the cult hit comic series *Exiles*, and then as a playable character in the popular video game *Spider-Man: Shattered Dimensions*. In keeping *Spider-Man 2099* as part of the collective consciousness, Marvel was able to launch a full-scale revival of the character in 2013–14. That's when Miguel made a much ballyhooed appearance in the *Superior Spider-Man* series, where the character warns the present day Marvel Universe that the fabric of the future was starting to break down because of an over-manipulation of the timestream.

Then, thanks to overwhelming fan response, Marvel announced a few months later that Miguel would star in his very own ongoing series again, with David back at the helm and Will Sliney providing pencils. In the new series, O'Hara travels back and forth between the present-day Marvel universe and 2099 in an effort to change the course of the present and save his future from an even more dystopian outcome. David is not surprised by the character's enduring qualities, but still finds himself "flattered by it. People love the character. It's obvious I did something right."[482]

92 Spider-Girl and Spider-Man's "Spider-Verse"

For years, Marvel prided itself on having one main universe and one straightforward timeline for all of its characters. The multiverse—a hypothetical set of infinite universes, each with their own versions of heroes and villains—were better left to DC, publisher of the landmark miniseries *Crisis on the Infinite Earths* as well as many other tales that dealt with the multiverse. In the Marvel universe, the one exception to that world had long been its *What If...?* series, which featured stories that examined critical moments in Marvel history and how things would change if a certain character or characters acted differently. While these stories were great fun, they were never intended to be anything more than one-shot tales, and these alternative universes and timelines were rarely revisited again.

But over time, attitudes stared changing at Marvel and the company started to transition over to a more traditional multiverse setup, first in the late 1980s with the "New Universe," a new imprint featuring stories that took place in a totally different timeline from the mainstream Marvel one. And later, in the early

'90s, with its 2099 imprint, which took a series of popular Marvel characters like Spider-Man, the Punisher, and the Hulk, and placed them 100 years in the future.

In 1998, Marvel married the premises of the New Universe and 2099 universe together to create Marvel Comics 2—an imprint featuring superhero stories that transpired in both the future and in an alternative universe. And the flagship series in the MC2 universe was *Spider-Girl*, starring Mayday Parker, the daughter of Peter and Mary Jane Parker.

The initial idea for *Spider-Girl* came from longtime Spider-Man writer and editor Tom DeFalco. While DeFalco was working on the infamous "Clone Saga" in the mid-90s, he proposed that Peter and MJ should have a baby. In addition to parenthood being a logical progression for the couple, who had been married for nearly a decade by that point, it was also a means to an end for the Spider-office. One of the primary goals of the "Clone Saga" was to write Peter and Mary Jane out of the main Spider-Man books because there were concerns that they had become too unrelatable to younger readers. The "Clone Saga" would have removed the couple from the equation while Peter's long-lost clone, Ben Reilly, would take over as a "single" Spider-Man. Meanwhile, Peter and MJ would be allowed to gracefully leave the world of comics, so they could ride off into the sunset together and start their family.

However, less than a year later, Marvel got cold feet and reversed track on the storyline. Peter and Mary Jane returned and their child was kidnapped (and presumably killed) by Norman Osborn, who had been resurrected after being killed off in the comics decades earlier.[483] DeFalco was unhappy with the editorial reversal. He believed if Marvel was so itchy to bring Peter and Mary Jane back, the company could have created a series that featured the married (with child) life of the couple.

But that never came to pass. Instead, while DeFalco was scripting issues of Marvel's *What If...?*, he got together with his longtime artistic collaborator Ron Frenz and thought up a one-and-done story about Peter and MJ's daughter, alive and well and 15 years old. As it turned out, she had inherited Spider-powers from her superhero father. Like other *What If...?* stories, the whole thing took place in a separate timeline. And like most other *What If...?* tales, DeFalco had no intention in telling his story beyond that one issue.[484]

Like all stories famous enough to merit their own chapter in a book, "one time only" turned out to be empty rhetoric. Mayday's origin in *What If...? #105* was well-received enough that Marvel's then-editor-in-chief, Bob Harras, proposed an entire line of alternative future books with *Spider-Girl* as the main title, alongside *A-Next*, (a team of future Avengers) and *J2* (starring the son of the Juggernaut). *A-Next* and *J2* both lasted 12 issues. *Spider-Girl*, on the other hand, lasted 100 issues in its first volume, plus another 30 issues in the subsequently released *Amazing Spider-Girl* series, and yet another 11 issues as *Spectacular Spider-Girl* (plus a number of one-shots and miniseries). All told, Spider-Girl went from being a single issue to being a regular part of the Marvel line-up for more than 12 years. The initial series was the longest-running female-centric Marvel comic in the publisher's history.

DeFalco has long owed the success of the series to the fact that there was something infectious about the adventures of Mayday. Similar to the earliest days of *Amazing Spider-Man*, DeFalco's *Spider-Girl* series depicted the tricky balancing act of a bright high school student struggling to use her great powers in a responsible way. Her parents, Peter and MJ, were key supporting characters, along with a mix of brand-new cast members and reimagined, future versions of some old favorites like Kaine, Hobgoblin, and Normie Osborn (grandson of the original Green Goblin, Norman Osborn).

DeFalco has made no bones about the fact that scripting *Spider-Girl* was a personal experience for him. He based a lot of Mayday's interactions with her parents on his niece and her parents. And while longtime artist Pat Olliffe penciled more than 60 issues of the series, *Spider-Girl* also gave DeFalco another opportunity to work with his very good friend Frenz.[485]

Spider-Girl's success also indirectly led to a number of other alternative timeline Spider-Man books to be published—mostly as miniseries and one-shots. Pretty soon, there was a different Spider-Man inhabiting nearly every timeline and universe that Marvel could conjure up: a Spider-Man from the 1930s in *Spider-Man: Noir*; a Spider-Man from the 17th century in *Spider-Man 1602*; and a Spider-Man from India in *Spider-Man: India*. These are just a few of the many Spideys that were created in the years following the launch of MC2.

In fact, there were so many Spider-Men running around the Marvel Universe that, in 2014, *Amazing Spider-Man* writer Dan Slott created an entire storyline about them called "Spider-Verse." In it, the "main" Spider-Man assembles his team from throughout the multiverse to take on the Inheritors, a band of vampiric villains that feed on the life-force of Spider-beings. The storyline is also notable for creating an alternative take on Spider-Woman, where Peter's girlfriend, Gwen Stacy, is bitten by a spider and gains powers. In the wake of "Spider-Verse," Marvel launched its series *Web Warriors*, which ran for 11 issues over the course of 2015–16.

93 The Tangled Web of Spider-Women

In the world of superhero comics, it is not uncommon for a male hero to have a female counterpart. Superman had Supergirl. Batman had Batgirl. So when Marvel introduced a new female spider character in 1977's *Marvel Spotlight #32*, it probably looked like Marvel was following the trend and looking to capitalize on Spider-Man's popularity by creating an analogous character named Spider-Woman. Well, not exactly.

The original Spider-Woman, whose civilian identity was Jessica Drew, was created by Archie Goodwin and Marie Severn with one primary purpose in mind: Marvel's publisher (and Spider-Man's co-creator) Stan Lee caught wind that a rival company was planning to unveil a new Saturday morning cartoon about a female named Spider-Woman. In an effort to beat this company to the punch while also creating a copyright for Marvel to own, Lee charged his staff to introduce their own Spider-Woman. And that's the how Spider-Woman was born (meanwhile, that cartoon series debuted as *Web Woman* in 1978).[486]

Unlike Supergirl or Batgirl, Spider-Woman shared very little in common in terms of powers or origins from her male predecessor. There was no spider-bite, nor was there any web-slinging or friendly neighborhood banter, à la Peter Parker. In Goodwin's origin story, Spider-Woman goes by the name Arachne and is depicted as being brainwashed by the evil criminal organization, Hydra, to murder Nick Fury, the director of the espionage group, S.H.I.E.L.D. By the end of the story, the reader is told that Spider-Woman was created by the cosmic High Evolutionary and was actually an evolved spider.

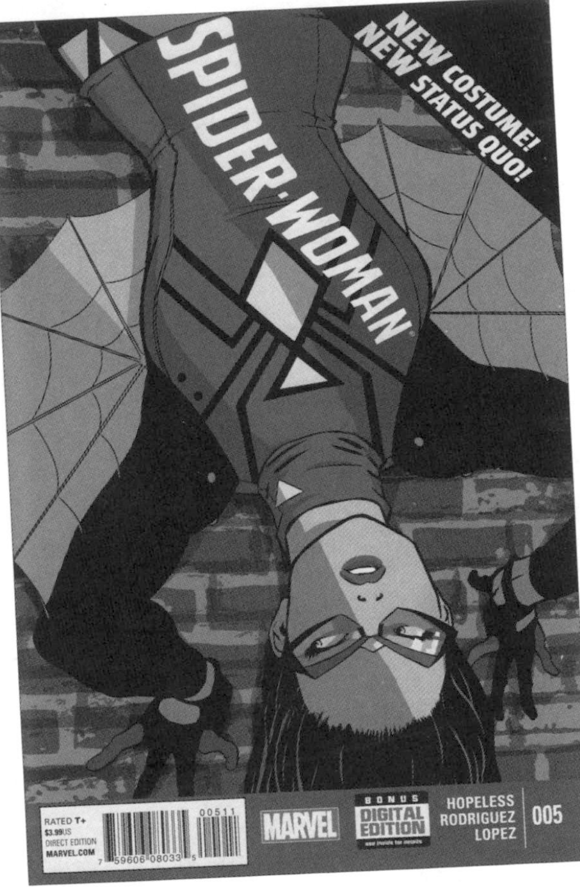

Spider-Woman #5

So yeah, nothing like Spider-Man. *Marvel Spotlight #32* sold better than expected, so rather than treating the character as a one-off, Marvel sought to make some more Spider-Woman stories. Veteran writer and editor Marv Wolfman took over and immediately simplified her origin (what exactly is an "evolved spider" anyway?). First and foremost, Spider-Woman became a human named Jessica Drew, daughter of a scientist who experimented on her and gave her powers after her life was threatened by uranium illness.[487] These powers include superhuman agility, strength, speed, etc. Her most curious power involved secreting a pheromone that makes her attractive to men and repulsive to women. Then again, the tight, spandex costume she wore was probably just as effective as any pheromone.

Jessica eventually got her own book in 1978, which was scripted by Wolfman. However, Wolfman was never happy with his work on the series and left after nine issues. Despite a rotating set of creators, *Spider-Woman* lasted 50 issues until Drew was apparently killed off. Drew would return about a year later, but would fade into obscurity, opening the door for others to assume the mantle of Spider-Woman. The first of which was Jessica Carpenter, who was introduced in Marvel's *Secret Wars* series in 1984 (strangely, she wore a variation of Spider-Man's black suit before Spidey himself got the costume in the miniseries). Carpenter would later join the West Coast Avengers team and fought for various superhero squads like Force Works and the Secret Defenders before her powers were stolen from her and she retired (she would later regain her powers and operate as Arachne before becoming the second Madame Web in the Spider-Man universe).

The third Spider-Woman had a more direct connection to Spider-Man. Mattie Franklin gained superpowers during a ceremony overseen by Spidey's adversary, Norman Osborn, aka the Green Goblin. She made her first full appearance in *Amazing Spider-Man vol. 2 #1*, where she actually impersonates Spider-Man while he was in the midst of one of his patented short-term retirements. She eventually became the new Spider-Woman and got her own solo series in the early 2000s that was canceled after 18 issues. She was later killed off in an issue of *Amazing*.

Drew experienced a revival in the mid-00s with the arrival of writer Brian Michael Bendis at Marvel. Bendis had long desired to write a Jessica-centric *Spider-Woman* series, but after a number of false starts, he instead made her a member of the *New Avengers* team in 2004. Drew became a focal point of a number of major Marvel events written by Bendis, including *Secret Invasion*, where

The Amazing Silk

What if the radioactive spider that famously bit Peter Parker back in *Amazing Fantasy #15* had crawled off and sunk its fangs into someone else? Marvel answered this hypothetical question in 2014 with the introduction of its newest Spider-femme, Cindy Moon, aka Silk.

Silk was created by Dan Slott and Humberto Ramos and played a key role in the big Spider-Man event "Spider-Verse," which saw the Inheritors, a family of vampiric soul-suckers, scour the universe in order to feed (and kill) anyone with spider-powers. In Cindy's origin, readers learn that after she received a spider-bite, she was locked away in a bunker for years in order to protect her against the Inheritors. After Spider-Man rescues her (and inadvertently alerts the Inheritors to her existence), she discovers that her parents and brother have mysteriously disappeared. Her quest to find her family while also adapting to reentering a modernized world, can be followed in her solo series, *Silk,* which is scripted by longtime television writer Robbie Thompson.

she is abducted and replaced by the shape-shifting alien race, the Skrulls. Bendis also played up Drew's street-level/spy sensibilities by often depicting her as a double agent working multiple sides at once.

In 2014, Drew starred in her own ongoing series again—this time as a tie-in to the Spider-Man-led event "Spider-Verse." The series' first four issues connected to "Spider-Verse" before the book got a dramatic shake-up at issue *#5*, including a new status quo, where Jessica quits the Avengers to focus on being a street-level spy. The comic also debuts a more sensibly outfitted costume that plays up her spy abilities while also featuring no spandex. "This is the new Jessica," said Dennis Hopeless, *Spider-Woman's* writer. "She's putting aside the old version of herself."[488]

94 The Amazing Spider-Man Newspaper Strip

By the end of the 1970s, Spider-Man had headlined hundreds of best-selling comics for Marvel. But it wasn't until 1977 that the character managed to coexist alongside the world's top headlines, when *The Amazing Spider-Man* daily newspaper comic strip debuted in syndicates across the United States. Conceived by Spider-Man's co-creator, Stan Lee, and his longtime collaborator, John Romita, the newspaper strip published its first four-panel, black-and-white installment on January 3, 1977, kicking off a still-going, often incredibly weird sub-universe of Spider-Man stories.

Prior to launching the strip, Lee had been getting calls from newspaper syndicate editors for years about writing a daily edition of *Spider-Man*. Unfortunately, Lee could never figure out the most effective way to capture his web-slinging hero in a mere three or four panels a day, and then weave together an episodic story over the course of many months.[489] To solve this problem, Lee thought to treat the strip like a daily soap opera rather than a superhero story. Action scenes would be secondary to "characterization, and on whatever personal problems a superhero might encounter living in a realistic world—in today's world."[490]

It was a sound approach, though one that was met with some resistance from Romita, who signed on to the gig thinking he was going to draw a strip that featured Spider-Man fighting alongside the likes of Daredevil and Doctor Strange. However, "Stan told me a hundred times that newspaper readers didn't read comic books. They were a different audience and they were more interested in Peter Parker's personal life." Romita was convinced the strip would fail within two years, but he was obviously wrong.[491]

In addition to focusing on Peter's personal life, the strip also tried to incorporate stories that were loosely (in some cases, very loosely) inspired by newspaper headlines. In the very first arc, Doctor Doom visits the U.S. per the urging of *Daily Bugle* publisher J. Jonah Jameson to address the United Nations on "law and order" (even then, a popular platform from some politicos). In a storyline in early 1978, Peter falls in love with the beautiful daughter of an international terrorist from a fictitious country. Lee, ever aware of the pop culture zeitgeist, also sought to incorporate visual Easter eggs, such as celebrities like George Burns, Henry Winkler, Mary Tyler Moore, John Travolta, and Barbara Streisand.

The Spider-Man newspaper strip was always meant to be a separate universe from the regular comic book series. However, those worlds collided in the mid-80s, when fans at a convention pleaded with Lee and Marvel's then-editor-in-chief, Jim Shooter, to marry Peter off to girlfriend Mary Jane Watson. MJ was depicted as Peter's primary love interest in the strip, but the couple was broken up in the comics. No matter, Shooter decided the wedding would be a great sales event and, for the first time in history, the two universes were synchronized.

While working on the newspaper strip doesn't necessarily offer creators the same level of cachet as writing or illustrating one of the core Spider-Man books, many have found great joy in being part of this fun little experiment that nobody really expected would last as long as it has. Alex Saviuk, a longtime comic book artist who provided pencils on Spidey titles like *Web of Spider-Man* in the late '80s and early '90s, received a personal call from Lee offering him a job illustrating the Sunday strip in 1996. He has since gone on to provide pencils on the weekday strip as well. "I still have the little cassette tape from my answering machine" when Lee called to offer him the gig, Saviuk said. "Stan said, 'I love your work.… [The strip] doesn't pay that much, but think of the glory!'"[492]

95 Rebooting Spider-Man

Marvel Comics was in a state of disarray in the mid-1990s. A series of missteps and the collapse of the comic book speculator market, which artificially inflated sales earlier in the decade, were some of the reasons behind the company filing for bankruptcy by the end of 1996. On the content side of things, Marvel had outsourced the production of comics featuring some of its key properties, like the Avengers and Fantastic Four, to Jim Lee and Rob Liefeld, two superstar artists that had left the company a few years earlier to join the Image Comics indie "revolution." As a result, these series were rebooted and restarted from scratch as part of the company's "Heroes Reborn" initiative.

Spider-Man was one of the only superheroes that Marvel could still count on (despite the fact that the character was embroiled in the "Clone Saga," a story that, in retrospect, is considered a creative low point for Spidey). Still, by the end of the '90s, the industry was changing and Marvel was looking for ways to drum up interest (and sales) in its comics. Restarting a series with a new "number one" issue was an easy short-term sales fix, so, come the end of 1998, it was officially Spider-Man's turn to get a reboot.

Amazing Spider-Man ceased its old numbering after issue *#441* and *Peter Parker: Spider-Man* (formerly "adjective-less" *Spider-Man*) rebooted at issue *#98*. The other two monthly Spidey books, *Spectacular Spider-Man* and *Sensational Spider-Man*, were canceled. Accompanying the rebooted *Amazing* and *Peter Parker* series was a new miniseries scripted and penciled by superstar creator John Byrne. *Spider-Man: Chapter One* would reimagine Peter's origin story, going all the way back to the spider-bite and the burglar killing Uncle Ben. And in a curious twist, Marvel promoted the series not as a flashback or an untold tale, but as the new official "canon" for Spider-Man.

The premise behind the reboot was a classic Spider-Man conundrum and one that has haunted the character for years. Casual readers were having a difficult time relating to Spider-Man and his alter-ego, Peter Parker. Peter was no longer a student struggling with everyman problems like trying to pay the bills while honoring his responsibilities as a costumed superhero. So the two rebooted books and *Chapter One* were part of a "back to basics" approach that aspired to get the character back to the good old days of lots of bad luck for Peter.

Chapter One was a modest success for Marvel, though numerous fans have gone on to criticize some of Byrne's tweaks of Spider-Man's origin. For example, Peter acquires his spider-powers during a lab explosion, as compared to a quiet, almost isolated moment involving a spider-bite at a science exhibition in *Amazing Fantasy #15*. Otto Octavius got his own powers, making him Doctor Octopus, in the same explosion. Other changes were ultimately inconsequential, but equally confounding, like making two of Spidey's main villains, Sandman and Norman Osborn, biologically related. At least that plot enlightened readers as to why both characters have the same ridiculous Tootsie Roll hairdo.

With *Chapter One* reworking the origin, Howard Mackie, a longtime Marvel writer who had worked on multiple Spider-books during the early to mid-90s, was tapped to script both *Amazing* and *Peter Parker*. As part of the main narrative, Mackie and Byrne had discussed using the Shaper of Worlds, a cosmic entity first created in the early '70s, as a medium to magically transport Peter back to high school, essentially rebooting his life.[493] However, this idea was ultimately scrapped for the more straightforward, "softer" refresh.

Peter's Aunt May, who had been killed off in the comics a few years earlier before she was unexpectedly resurrected, was one of the central figures in volume 2. But other than that, these comics offered a tepid narrative of Peter struggling to balance his personal life and superheroics with nary a mention of clones, children, or any of the other baggage that had been added to his biography over the course of the '90s. "Everyone was feeling the weight of the continuity at the time," Mackie said of the desire to move away from these big status quo–shifting stories.[494]

Except some kind of Earth-shattering upheaval was inevitable. In early 2000, Mackie and Byrne addressed one of the lingering issues that seemingly hamstrung Peter's everyman status: his marriage to supermodel Mary Jane Watson. Marvel failed in its first attempt to remove the Peter/MJ union from the main narrative during the "Clone Saga" (when Peter was going to be replaced as Spider-Man by his clone, the single Ben Reilly), so it was inevitable that the company would try again. In volume two's *Amazing #13*, MJ is presumed dead when her plane appears to explode mid-flight. Marvel had been resistant to making Peter a "widower" since that could have potentially aged him more, but Mackie intended for this plot development to last. However, the storyline was ultimately scrapped a year later when MJ's status was upgraded to "alive."[495]

While many of the storylines and ideas introduced in *Chapter One* and Spider-Man's second volume are rarely referenced today, the reboot set an important precedent for Spidey. Years before comic book companies started rebooting all of their series on a regular basis, Marvel demonstrated that it wasn't afraid to start fresh with one of its longest-running legacy books (though the company did eventually revert back to the old numbers in time for *Amazing's* 500th issue). *Amazing* has since been rebooted two more times and likely has many more re-numberings in its future.

96 The *Untold Tales of Spider-Man*

While the Spider-Man comic book universe was embroiled in the complexities and idiosyncrasies of the "Clone Saga" in the mid-1990s, Marvel, as part of a marketing experiment, starting producing a simpler, easier-to-follow flashback series that placed Pater Parker back in high school. *Untold Tales of Spider-Man #1* debuted in September 1995 as part of Marvel's new 99 cent line, a series of books that were designed to address criticism from readers that comics were too expensive. Many of Marvel's top properties received their own 99 cent books, such as the Avengers and X-Men. However, it was *Untold Tales* that proved to be the juggernaut of the group, outlasting the other series by more than a year.[496]

Most of *Untold Tales*'s success could be chalked up to writer Kurt Busiek's back-to-basics approach to Peter and his supporting cast, along with artist Pat Olliffe's Steve Ditko–inspired artwork that evoked the early '60s. There was certainly no better choice for a nostalgia-filled flashback series than Busiek. He had just scripted the critically and commercially successful miniseries *Marvels*, a love letter to the Silver Age-era of Marvel Comics. Busiek was having a hard time latching on as a writer for a monthly ongoing series, but relished the opportunity to write Spider-Man back when he thought he "worked best," as a teenager. "I wasn't all that wild about the 'Clone Saga,' but I love the early Spider-Man material," Busiek said. "I would have much rather [worked on *Untold Tales*] than written the modern Spider-Man of the time."[497]

Meanwhile, hardcore fans were treated to a feast of deep-cut continuity references, such as a photo of a high school-aged Gwen

Stacy on the desk of police Captain George Stacy, in a story set years before either character had been formally introduced in the original comics. The series also added more to the biographies of many of Spidey's supporting castmates, such as Mary Jane Watson, Flash Thompson, and Betty Brant.

Unfortunately for its fans, *Untold Tales* ended in 1997 after 26 issues. From a financial standpoint, the book struggled to find its footing, both at newsstands and comic book shops. Newsstands preferred to sell two 99 cent books together as "flip books" for $1.99, thus negating the entire point of a cheaper comic book line, and shop owners found they had to move twice as many 99 cent books to make the same profit as a full-price book.[498] Additionally, by the time 1997 rolled around, the "Clone Saga," which had spiraled out of control and was getting universally panned by fans, had ended and Marvel was making an effort to return the main Spider-Man books back to Peter's roots (negating the need for a vintage flashback series).

Still, Marvel and Busiek—who followed *Untold Tales* with very memorable runs on *The Avengers* and *Thunderbolts*, as well as creating *Astro City* for Image Comics—remain proud of what they accomplished with *Untold Tales*. Nearly 20 years after it was published, Marvel collected a giant omnibus of the entire series. And fans are still talking about it with the utmost reverence. "None of the other material that was generated for that [99 cent] program has found anywhere near that kind of an audience," said Marvel's executive editor Tom Brevoort, an editor of *Untold Tales*. "On that level, it was completely successful."[499]

97 Go on Your Own Amazing Chase

In 2011, I launched my personal blog, *Chasing Amazing*, which documented my "quest" to collect every issue of *Amazing Spider-Man*—a lifelong dream I eventually fulfilled in October 2014 after more than 25 years of buying and collecting Spider-Man comics. Considering how expensive and hard-to-find some of these books can be, a question I often fielded from readers was, "How did you manage to collect every single issue?" (The other common question I get, which I'm far less inclined to answer, is "How much is your collection worth?")

To be totally honest, collecting every single issue of *Amazing Spider-Man* was hard. It took a lot of time and energy. If it wasn't something I was totally passionate about, I would have never seen it through to its completion. I guess that's my overarching advice to someone who wants to start their own collection of comics: be 100 percent sure that this is something you want to do, because you have to be doggedly committed to reaching your end game. But in the same vein, always remember that your collection is *your* collection. It's not a competition, and you can set the parameters however you see fit. There's no right or wrong way to do this.

For me, I wanted to own every single issue of the main *Amazing Spider-Man* series, i.e., issues *#1-700*. People would often chide me: "What about the Annuals?" "What about *Spectacular Spider-Man*?" "What about Spider-Man's appearances in other series?"

Those all sound like great pursuits, but that's not what I wanted my collection to be. And don't you believe for a second, after everything I went through to own *Amazing #1-700,* that I would ever believe there was something invalid (or, *shudder*, incomplete) about my collection.

But putting personal philosophy and passion aside, 25-plus years of collecting have taught me a thing or two about buying comics. Here are a few other tips that might come in handy if you find yourself tempted to embark on a similar collecting journey.

Know the Market: Different people swear by different price guides in terms of determining the set value of a specific comic (I was always a fan of the *Overstreet Price Guide*). But like pretty much every consumer product, there are always market conditions and supply and demand to consider. If you're chasing a specific comic, you might want to check how much a copy is selling for on an online auction site like eBay to gauge an acceptable price range.

Know Your Sellers: Sadly, the days of the local comic book shop having a smelly, dank room filled with old back issues of comics (trust me, for a collector, this is sexier than it sounds) are history. Most stores today sell primarily new releases. For back issues, some of the best places to go are online retailers like mycomicshop.com and metropoliscomics.com, online auction sites like eBay and Heritage Auctions, and comic book conventions and smaller shows (where a lot of online retailers will have a physical presence). If you're extra brave, you can also join a collector-centric online message group, where a lot of longtime collectors look to sell or trade comics.

Know Your Grades: It's very rare for someone to find a comic, especially a comic that is more than 50 years old, in "perfect" condition. As you might expect, the more physical damage and wear and tear on a comic, the less it's worth. Professional comic graders use a 10–0 scale (10 being the best) to help determine the value of the comic. There's also a vocabulary of terms that graders assign to each numerical grade value that you should know about. In descending order, those are: Gem Mint, Mint, Near Mint, Very Fine, Fine, Very Good, Good, Fair, and Poor. Please pay attention to these. When I was younger, I got burned buying a stack of "Good" comics online without realizing that "Good" was a relative term and the comics themselves were actually in very shoddy condition.

Set Some Standards: You might think to yourself, *Any comic I buy will be the most pristine copy I can find.* And unless you have the bank account of Mark Cuban, you'll be bankrupt within a few months of starting your collection. In my humble opinion, if you're a person of "normal" financial means, it's okay to buy a "lower grade" copy of an older back issue. Just have some standards. For example, even on some of my "Good" comics (like my copy of *Amazing Spider-Man #1*), I want the central cover image to be as close to flawless as possible. As a compromise, I don't care as much about chipping along the edges of the comics, rounded corners, creases, and "dings" that don't affect the central image, damage of the back cover, and/or off-white/slight yellow pages inside the comic.

If You *Must* Buy at a Convention, Wait Until the Last Day: Sure, San Diego Comic Con and New York Comic Con are must-attend events if you're a fan of the comic book medium, but they're actually a pretty lousy place to buy collectible comics. That's because most of the vendors there are catering to more casual fans and not hardcore collectors. That means you're probably not going to get a fair price at a major con…unless you're there on the last day, when vendors just want to unload as much product as they can. That's when you'll find lower prices or vendors more open to negotiate. As for a simple negotiation tip, sellers are usually more amicable to go lower if you're buying more than one item. For example, if you grab three comics that are cumulatively listed for $60, you can probably offer $50 and save yourself 10 bucks without a fight.

Subscribe to New Issues: Unless the newest comics are not a part of your collection, you're going to want to make sure you don't miss a new issue when it's released. Most comic book stores offer a "pull list" where you can essentially subscribe to a couple of series every month and someone from the store will put those books aside for you to pick up at your convenience. You can also subscribe to many books via mail order by visiting the publisher's website. I've long viewed my pull list as a safety net for my collection because life is unpredictable. Sometimes you get sick, or can't get to the store, or who knows what, and relying on a retailer to carry enough copies for everyone who wants them can be a dicey proposition, especially if a certain comic is "hot." Back in 2009, *Amazing Spider-Man #583* featured a special U.S. election story involving the newly elected Barack Obama. The book sold like crazy. But without fuss or incident I got my "first printing" copy thanks to my mail order subscription.

Protect Your Comics: This should go without saying, but if you're going to invest the time and money into a collection, you need to invest some time and money into properly archiving and storing your comics. That means buying acid-free polybags and boards for individual issues and then either cardboard or plastic boxes to keep your collection together. If you have some more expensive comics in your collection, you should invest in Mylar bags. They're pricier than the poly bags, but they should last you at least 10 to 15 years before you need to replace them. And yes, once you store your collection in a bag, board, and box, you need to keep tabs on it because after a certain amount of time, even properly archived comics start to break down if you don't replace the materials you use to store them. Think of your bags and boards like an oil change for your car: every 3,000 miles you need one, lest you want to roll the dice with your car's engine breaking down.

98 Must Read: "The Kid Who Collects Spider-Man" (*Amazing Spider-Man* #248)

At its core, Spider-Man is a superhero fantasy story about a young man learning how to use his unexpectedly great powers in a responsible manner. But a major reason why Spider-Man has endured for so many years as a character is that there's enough diversity in his stories where readers can latch on to any number of different themes and ideas. "The Kid Who Collects Spider-Man," which appears as a backup story in *Amazing Spider-Man #248,* is one of the shorter Spider-Man stories to have ever been published. But what it lacks in length and pages, it more than makes up for in its power and lasting effect on the reader.

Written by Roger Stern, with art from Ron Frenz, "Kid" tells the story of a young boy named Timothy Harrison who is the world's biggest Spider-Man fan. He has a scrapbook of newspaper clippings featuring Spider-Man and even has a jar filled with bullet slugs that he retrieved from the scenes of various Spider-Man battles with villains. One night, Spider-Man visits Tim (please don't call him Timmy), and treats his biggest fan to a display of his fantastic powers. At first it appears that this story is just an inconsequential, whimsical tale of how young children relate to Spider-Man. With Stern's gift for dialogue and Frenz's classical, Steve Ditko–inspired aesthetic, "Kid" would have been a perfectly acceptable "B" story even without the stunning twist that this story is known for.

However, in the tale's second half, "Kid" evolves into something far more profound than what the reader is initially presented. Tim asks Spider-Man how he became a masked superhero, and Spidey discusses his origin story in *Amazing Fantasy #15* and his one big mistake—not stopping a criminal that he could have easily subdued and how that crook went on to murder someone

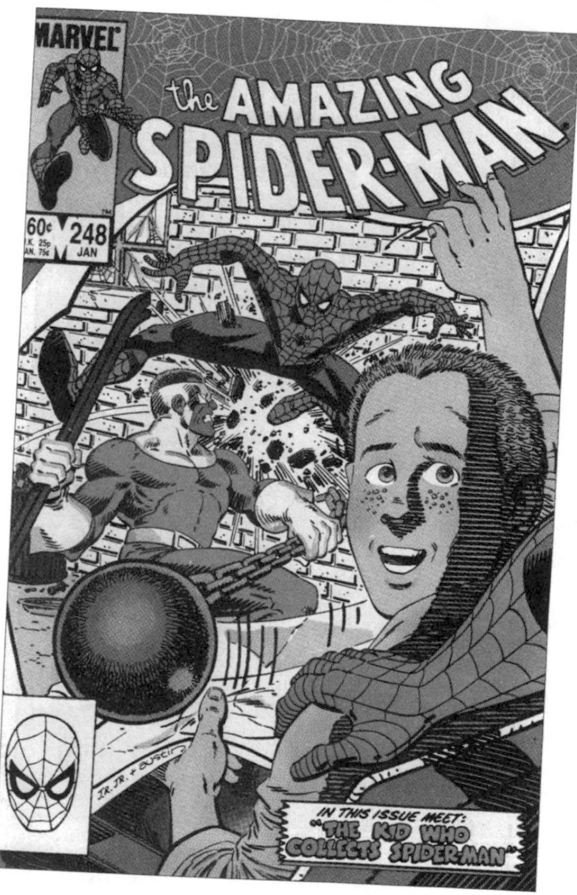

Amazing Spider-Man #248

who "meant a lot" to him. Tim provides comfort to Spider-Man before asking him who he really is. Spider-Man is at first reluctant to reveal his secret identity before dramatically taking off his mask and telling Tim that he is Peter Parker, the photographer who took most of the photos that were found in Harrison's scrapbook. The two then share a very warm moment where Tim promises to honor his secret identity. On the final page is one more emotional whammy: Tim is actually a leukemia patient in a cancer clinic and the doctors have only given him a few more weeks to live. His visit from Spider-Man was essentially his dying wish.

If you're a first-time reader of "Kid" who didn't see that ending coming, whoa boy. Get your box of tissues ready because it's designed to wallop you. And yet the story never becomes overly maudlin or emotionally manipulative because of how true-to-character the comic remains from start to finish.

While many creators over the years have appropriately keyed in on how Peter's guilt over his "Uncle Ben moment" has fueled his desires to be a superhero, Stern and Frenz offer a slightly different spin with "Kid." Peter has nothing to feel guilty over regarding Tim's illness. Tim did not get sick because the Green Goblin knew his secret identity, or because he inadvertently donated radioactive blood to the child. However, Peter is compelled to come to Tim's bedside because of how enormously empathetic he is.

Stern and Frenz understood that even without having a personal motivation, Peter is an enormously caring individual. And because of that, plus his ability to connect to regular folks as Marvel's unofficial "everyman" character, Spidey feels responsible for bringing this dying child a few moments of joy before his inevitable passing. And in turn, the magnitude of Spider-Man's empathy is accentuated by what a realistic and fully formed character Tim turns out to be. Over the span of just a few pages, Stern and Frenz make the reader care about Tim. Tim is warm and caring in his interactions with Spider-Man, but he's also just a kid filled with wonder and delight at the sight of this somewhat strange masked man doing things like crawling on the walls and lifting his bed high in the air.

In addition to the way it captures Spider-Man's personality and his humanity, "Kid" is also an essential read for any Spider-Man fan for its unique form and structure. Critics have often compared "Kid" to a Will Eisner-esque story in terms of its tone and aesthetic. It could almost be mistaken for an indie comic that just so happened to feature one of the most mainstream superheroes in the world. Stern brings the reader into the narration by using a newspaper clipping from a fictitious slice-of-life column called "Conover's Corner." This device initially lends "Kid" its homespun feel before the actual interactions between Spider-Man and Tim elevate it to something far more serious and stirring. "Conover's Corner" then returns to end the story, featuring the tragic reveal about Tim's leukemia.

No critique of "Kid" is complete without praise for Frenz's artwork (with inks from another great, Terry Austin). Frenz has long admitted his adoration for Ditko's earliest Spider-Man visuals, so it's no surprise that they serve as an inspiration for him in this story. However, in addition to paying homage to Ditko, Frenz also adds a layer of warmth and soulfulness that is missing from the early appearances of Spider-Man. While Ditko wanted his Spider-Man to disarm the reader and make him or her uncomfortable with what they were looking at, Frenz clearly understands that the emotional tenor of "Kid" wouldn't work unless there was something physically inviting about Spider-Man in the presence of Tim. The visual where Spider-Man unmasks in front of Tim—Peter emerges from the shadows with a shroud of light around his face—has an almost ethereal quality to it.

"Kid" may not mark a milestone moment in Spider-Man or Peter's life, or the first appearance of a vital supporting character or villain, but it is an essential read all the same. "Kid" is one of those stories that effortlessly captures just how powerful and lasting a comic book story can be.

99 Play with Spider-Man on the Go: Download *Spider-Man Unlimited*

Gamers who are burnt out from the tedium of both endless runners and button-smashing superhero games should check out Gameloft's *Spider-Man Unlimited* game on their mobile devices. Since its initial release in 2014, *Spider-Man Unlimited* is arguably one of the most popular Spider-Man video games ever to be developed, with tens of millions of downloads and counting. And maybe this is just bitterness coming from a Spidey fan who remembers nearly breaking his thumbs playing through the Spider-Man *Maximum Carnage* game on his Super Nintendo in the early 1990s, but *Unlimited* is just plain old fun. It offers players a ton of different challenges to overcome and goals to meet, like defeating a certain number of enemies, collecting items, and boss battles (as compared to other endless runners where the goal is to simply get to the end of the course…also, please don't forget about my thumbs, which this game keeps safe and sound).

The general premise behind the game is that Spider-Man's archenemy, the Green Goblin, has assembled a Sinister Six team of supervillains from a different universe that is conspiring to take over Spidey's own dimension. With the help of some alternate universe Spider-Man characters, Spidey takes on the Green Goblin, as well as versions of such iconic villains as Sandman, Vulture, Electro, Doctor Octopus, and Mysterio.

Available to download on all iOS, Android, and Windows Play devices, the game's developers at Gameloft have managed to keep *Spider-Man Unlimited* relevant with its frequent updates and new additions—especially as it relates to new characters and levels. Unlike previous Spider-Man games (with a few notable exceptions—hello, 2010's *Shattered Dimensions* from Activision),

Unlimited is unquestionably devoted to utilizing some of the main storylines from the comic book universe to drive its narrative. For example, when the *Amazing Spider-Man* series was publishing the multiverse-spanning event "Spider-Verse" in 2014, *Unlimited* made the huge arc, which featured nearly every Spider-Man from every alternative universe and timeline, the focal point of its gameplay. In addition to good ol' traditional Peter Parker, gamers could unlock dozens of alternative Spider-Men, such as Spider-Man 2099, Spider-Man Noir, and Spider-Girl, who could all be leveled-up accordingly by playing and accomplishing certain challenges.

Once "Spider-Verse" concluded in late 2014, *Unlimited* continued to update itself with new players and challenges. When Marvel issued a (much-needed) costume makeover for Jessica Drew's Spider-Woman character in December 2014, the modern-spy aesthetic outfit, designed by artist Kris Anka, debuted in *Unlimited* before making its first appearance in the comics shortly thereafter.

"It has a ton of gameplay variety, a great goal-based structure to accompany its endless running mode, exceptional fan service, and a few ridiculously compelling tricks," wrote Shaun Musgrave in his four-out-of-five-star review for the popular mobile game website *TouchArcade*. "As a huge Spider-Man fan, playing this game is an absolute joy."[500]

100 Make Aunt May's Wheatcakes

You might think the secret to growing up big and strong like Spider-Man is to get bitten by a radioactive spider. That's probably right. But, maybe, just maybe, the other secret is a healthy, well-balanced diet that includes milk, fruit, vegetables, and Aunt May's famous wheatcakes.

What are wheatcakes? Well, they're basically pancakes made with buckwheat and whole wheat flour, instead of regular bleached, all-purpose flour. For comic book fans who also like to play around in the kitchen, 1996's *Untold Tales of Spider-Man Annual* features "May Parker's Famous Wheatcakes" recipe. How did *Untold Tales*' writer Kurt Busiek happen to come across this recipe? "It is a secret I will take to my dying day," he says.[501] Best not to pry, so why not just try this recipe out for yourself to see if eating these will help you outwrestle your Uncle Ben:

Mix Together
1 cup buckwheat flour
1 cup sifted whole wheat flour
2 tsps double acting baking powder
1 tsp baking soda
1 tsp salt

In a separate bowl, mix 2 cups buttermilk and 2 tsps molasses then set aside.

Add to the flour mix:
2 beaten egg yolks
1/4 cup melted butter
buttermilk/molasses mixture

Whip 2 egg whites until stiff (but not dry!), then fold them into the batter gently until blended. Don't over mix!

Cook on a greased hot griddle or frying pan until small bubbles appear on top. Then turn pancakes over and cook until bottom is lightly browned. Serve hot, with butter and maple syrup.[502]

Acknowledgments

I am grateful for the help and support of a lot of heroes for making a book about my favorite superhero, Spider-Man, possible. First and foremost, thank you to my editor, Jesse Jordan, for guiding this project from its infancy; to Triumph for the opportunity and taking a chance on me; to my podcast co-host and good friend, Dan Gvozden, for your endless insights and curiosity into the world of Spider-Man and comics; to the legendary Tom DeFalco, for providing an absolutely amazing foreword to this book and for always being willing to talk shop about "Pete"; and to all of the people who agreed to be interviewed for this book (or who helped set up interviews), including: Axel Alonso, Tom Brevoort, Kurt Busiek, Gerry Conway, Brian Cronin, J.M. DeMatteis, Chris D'Lando, Danny Fingeroth, Ron Frenz, Ed Hannigan, Terry Kavanagh, Howard Mackie, David Michelinie, Peter Milligan, Jim Salicrup, Zeb Wells, and Marv Wolfman.

Lastly, there's my wife and partner-in-crime, Erin, who not only provided moral support during this entire endeavor, but also was a reliable set of eyes and a sounding board as I was writing. I apologize for all the nights I came to bed very late.

Endnotes

1. Lee, Stan; Ditko, Steve. *Amazing Fantasy #15*. New York: Marvel Comics. 1962.
2. Ibid.
3. Tom DeFalco, *Comics Creators on Spider-Man*. London: Titan Books, 2004. p. 12. Print.
4. Pitts Jr., Leonard. "An Interview with Stan Lee," in Jeff McLaughlin, ed., *Stan Lee Conversations*, Jackson: The University Press of Mississippi, 2007. p. 96. Print.
5. DeFalco, p. 13.
6. Bell, Blake. *Strange and Stranger The World of Steve Ditko*. Seattle: Fantagraphics Books, 2008. p. 54. Print.
7. DeFalco, p. 12.
8. Bell, p. 57.
9. Ibid. p. 60.
10. "Library of Congress Receives Original Drawings for *Amazing Fantasy #15*." Online Press Release, April 30, 2008 (https://www.loc.gov/today/pr/2008/08-089.html).
11. Moore, Matt. "Spider-Man's Debut Comic Sells for $1.1 Million." *Associated Press*. March 8, 2011 (http://www.washingtonpost.com/wp-dyn/content/article/2011/03/08/AR2011030803584.html).
12. Dean, Michael. "The Brian Michael Bendis Interview," *The Comics Journal No. 266*, February/March 2005. p. 119.
13. Weiland, Jonah. "The 'One More Day' Interviews With Joe Quesada, Pt. 3 of 5." *Comic Book Resources*. January 2, 2008 (http://www.comicbookresources.com/?page=article&id=12246).
14. Cavett, Dick "The Dick Cavett Show: An Interview with Stan Lee," in Jeff McLaughlin, ed. *Stan Lee Conversations*. Jackson: The University Press of Mississippi, 2007. p. 16.
15. Lee; Ditko. *Amazing Fantasy #15.*
16. Ibid
17. Ibid
18. Slott, Dan; Ramos, Humberto. *Amazing Spider-Man #672*. New York: Marvel Comics. 2011.
19. Lee, Stan; Ditko, Steve. *Amazing Spider-Man #1*. New York: Marvel Comics. 1963.
20. Ibid.
21. Owsley, Jim; Bright, Mark. *Spider-Man vs. Wolverine #1*. New York: Marvel Comics.1987. Print.
22. Bendis, Brian Michael. Bagley, Mark. *Ultimate Spider-Man #4*. New York: Marvel Comics. 2001.
23. *Spider-Man*. Directed by Sam Raimi. Columbia Pictures. 2002.
24. O'Toole, Garson. *Quote Investigator*. July 23, 2015 (http://quoteinvestigator.com/2015/07/23/great-power/)
25. Suid, Murray. "Meet the Wizard of Biff! Bop! Pow!," in Jeff McLaughlin, ed. *Stan Lee Conversations*. Jackson: The University Press of Mississippi, 2007. p. 49-50.
26. Ginocchio, Mark; Gvozden, Dan. "Superior Spider-Talk #14: Spider-Talk and Their Amazing Friends w/Ron Frenz." *Superior Spider-Talk*. iTunes. September 12, 2013.
27. McLaughlin. "Chronology" in *Stan Lee Conversations*. p. xv.
28. Morris, Brian K. "Stan Lee's Amazing Marvel Interview." *Alter-ego No. 104*. August 2011. p. 26-27. Print.
29. Thomas, Roy. "Stan the Man and Toy the Boy: A Conversation between Stan Lee and Roy Thomas (1998)." in Jeff McLaughlin, ed. *Stan Lee Conversations*. Jackson: The University Press of Mississippi, 2007. p. 135.
30. DeFalco, p. 11.
31. McLaughlin, p. xv.
32. Ibid.
33. Ibid.
34. Thomas. "Stan the Man and Toy the Boy: A Conversation between Stan Lee and Roy Thomas." p. 136-137.

35. Murray, Will. "Stan Lee Looks Back: The Comics Legend Recalls Life with Jack Kirby, Steve Ditko, and Heroes," in Jeff McLaughlin, ed. *Stan Lee Conversations*. Jackson: The University Press of Mississippi, 2007. p. 176.
36. Thomas. "Stan the Man and Toy the Boy: A Conversation between Stan Lee and Roy Thomas." p. 138.
37. DeFalco, p. 12.
38. Ibid.
39. Ibid, p. 14.
40. Murray, p. 177.
41. Bell, p. 90.
42. DeFalco, p. 16.
43. *In Search of Steve Ditko*. Ross, Jonathan. BBC Four. 2007. Film.
44. DeFalco, p. 17.
45. Ibid, p. 19-20.
46. Morris, p. 32.
47. Johnson, Dan. "Twenty Years of Wedded Bliss." *Back Issue No. 23*. August 2007. p. 4. Print.
48. Pitts Jr., p. 100.
49. Riseman, Abraham. "It's Stan Lee's Universe." *Vulture*. February, 2016 (http://www.vulture.com/2016/02/stan-lees-universe-c-v-r.html).
50. McLaughlin, p. xviii.
51. Pappademas, Alex. "The Inquisition of Mr. Marvel: On the (surprisingly complicated) legacy of Stan Lee." *Grantland*. May 11, 2012 (http://grantland.com/features/the-surprisingly-complicated-legacy-marvel-comics-legend-stan-lee/).
52. Kay, Janice. "Stan Lee (Playfully) Insults Dan Slott on Twitter." *ScienceFiction.com*. December 28, 2012 (http://sciencefiction.com/2012/12/28/stan-lee-playfully-insults-dan-slott-on-twitter/).
53. Bell, p. 15.
54. Ibid.
55. Ibid, p. 19.
56. Ibid, p. 27.
57. DeFalco, p. 12.
58. Ditko, Steve. "He Giveth and He Taketh Away." *The Avenging Mind*. 2008. p. 19. Print.
59. DeFalco, p. 17.
60. Bell, p. 65.
61. Ditko. "Lifting and the Lifter." *The Avenging Mind*. p. 22.
62. Bell, p. 89.
63. Ibid, p. 90.
64. Ditko. "Creator or Co-Creator?" *The Avenging Mind*. p. 12.
65. Lee; Ditko. *Amazing Fantasy #15*
66. Mantlo, Bill. Buscema, Sal. *Spectacular Spider-Man Annual #4*. New York: Marvel Comics. 1984.
67. Ginocchio, Mark. Gvozden, Dan. "Superior Spider-Talk #15: Spider-Talk and their Amazing Friends w/Paul Jenkins." *Superior Spider-Talk*. January 20, 2014.
68. Douglas, Brad. "Spider-Man Crawlspace Episode 394: Jim Shooter Interview." *Spider-Man Crawlspace*. November 4, 2015.
69. Ginocchio, Mark. Gvozden, Dan. "Superior Spider-Talk #8: Spider-Talk and Their Amazing Friends w/J.M. DeMatteis." *Superior Spider-Talk*. August 28, 2013.
70. Dean, p. 119.
71. Ginocchio, Mark. Gvozden, Dan. "Superior Spider-Talk #31: Spider-Talk and Their Amazing Friends w/Gerry Conway." *Superior Spider-Talk*. March 2, 2014.
72. DeFalco, p. 116.
73. Miller, John Jackson. "Full April 2014 comics sales estimates: Amazing Spider-Man #1 tops 532,000 copies." *The Comic Chronicles*. May 12, 2014 (http://blog.comichron.com/2014/05/full-april-2014-comics-sales-estimates.html).
74. DeFalco, p. 15.

75. Ditko, Steve. "A Mini-History Further Complaints and Influences of the OOs.'" *The Comics! Vol. 14, No. 6.* June 2003. Print.
76. Lee, Stan; Romita, John. *Amazing Spider-Man #39.* New York: Marvel Comics. 1966.
77. Ching, Albert. "Dan Slott on Death, Venom and All Things *Amazing Spider-Man.*" *Newsarama.* February 24, 2011 (http://www.newsarama.com/7110-dan-slott-on-death-venom-and-all-things-amazing-spider-man.html).
78. Pitts Jr., p. 97.
79. Lee, Stan; Ditko, Steve. *Amazing Spider-Man #10.* New York: Marvel Comics. 1964.
80. Trumbull, John. "J. Jonah Jameson: Hero or Menace?" *Back Issue No. 91.* September 2016. p. 37. Print.
81. Ginocchio, Mark. Gvozden, Dan. "Spider-Talk and their Amazing Friends w/ Spider-Man: The Animated Series." *Amazing Spider-Talk.* November 25, 2014.
82. "Have J K Simmons reprise his role as J. Jonah Jameson in the MCU." *Change.org* (https://www.change.org/p/kevin-feige-recast-j-k-simmons-as-j-jonah-jameson-in-the-mcu).
83. "VIDEO: J.K. Simmons Responds To Petition For His 'J. Jonah Jameson' Return In SPIDER-MAN Reboot." *ComicBookMovie.* February 29, 2016 (http://www.comicbookmovie.com/spider-man/video-jk-simmons-responds-to-petition-for-his-j-jonah-jameson-return-a131587).
84. Cavett, p. 16.
85. Lee; Ditko. *Amazing Spider-Man #1.*
86. Ibid.
87. Lee, Stan; Ditko, Steve. *Amazing Spider-Man #26.* New York: Marvel Comics. 1965.
88. Owsley; Bright. *Spider-Man vs. Wolverine #1.*
89. McMillan, Graeme. "Why the Amazing Spider-Man Can't Catch a Break." *Time.* June 27, 2012 (http://entertainment.time.com/2012/06/27/the-ol-parker-luck-why-the-amazing-spider-man-cant-catch-a-break/).
90. Slott, Dan; Templeton, Ty. *Spider-Man/Human Torch #5.* New York: Marvel Comics. 2005. Print.
91. Thomas. "Stan Lee's Amazing Marvel Interview!" p. 6.
92. Tom DeFalco. Phone interview. September 19, 2016.
93. DeFalco, p. 55.
94. DeFalco. Phone interview. September 19, 2016.
95. Bell, p. 89.
96. Ginocchio, Mark. Gvozden, Dan. "Spider-Talk and their Amazing Friends w/Gerry Conway on "Spiral" and Carnage." *Amazing Spider-Talk.* September 9, 2015.
97. Ibid.
98. Scherstuhl, Alan. "The Man Who Killed Spider-Man." *The Village Voice.* January 9, 2013 (http://www.villagevoice.com/arts/the-man-who-killed-spider-man-7177286).
99. David Michelinie. E-mail interview. August 25, 2016.
100. DeFalco. Phone interview. September 19, 2016.
101. Ibid.
102. Ginocchio; Gvozden. "Superior Spider-Talk #31: Spider-Talk and Their Amazing Friends w/Gerry Conway."
103. Ginocchio, Mark; Gvozden, Dan. "Amazing Friends w/ the "Clone Saga" (Howard Mackie & Terry Kavanaugh)." *Amazing Spider-Talk.* September 14, 2016. Web.
104. Tom Brevoort. Phone interview. August 26, 2016.
105. Lee; Ditko. *Amazing Fantasy #15.*
106. Lee, Stan; Romita, John. *Amazing Spider-Man #50.* New York: Marvel Comics. 1967. Print.
107. Marv Wolfman. E-mail interview. September 2, 2016.
108. Lee, Stan; Ditko, Steve. *Amazing Spider-Man #33.* February 1966. New York: Marvel Comics.
109. Thomas, Roy (transcribed by Brian K. Morris). "Stan Lee's Amazing Marvel Interview!" *Alter-ego No.104.* August 2011. p. 9. Print.
110. Bell, p. 91.
111. Ibid, p. 57.
112. DeFalco, p. 30.

113. Ditko, Steve. "The Ever Unwilling." *The Comics! Vol. 20, No. 3.* March 2009. Print.
114. DeFalco, p. 17.
115. Thomas, Roy (transcribed by Brian K. Morris). "A Candid Conversation with Marvel Artist/Art Director Supreme John Romita." *Alter-ego Vol. 3, No. 9.* July 2001. p. 8-9. Print.
116. DeFalco, p. 27.
117. Ibid, p. 28.
118. Thomas. "A Candid Conversation with Marvel Artist/Art Director Supreme John Romita." p. 28.
119. Ibid.
120. DeFalco, p. 29.
121. Thomas. "A Candid Conversation with Marvel Artist/Art Director Supreme John Romita." p. 28.
122. DeFalco, p. 31.
123. Thomas. "A Candid Conversation with Marvel Artist/Art Director Supreme John Romita." p. 29.
124. DeFalco, p. 32.
125. Thomas. "A Candid Conversation with Marvel Artist/Art Director Supreme John Romita." p. 37.
126. Ibid, p. 40.
127. Cronin, Brian. "Top 70 Most Iconic Marvel Panels of All-Time #10-1." *Comics Should Be Good.* September 4, 2009 (http://www.cbr.com/top-70-most-iconic-marvel-panels-of-all-time-10-1/).
128. DeFalco, p. 32.
129. Ginocchio; Gvozden. "Superior Spider-Talk #31: Spider-Talk and Their Amazing Friends with Gerry Conway."
130. Ibid.
131. Ibid.
132. Wolfman. E-mail interview. September 2, 2016.
133. Michelinie, David; Romita Jr., John. *Amazing Spider-Man #290.* New York: Marvel Comics. 1987.
134. Ginocchio, Mark. Gvozden, Dan. "Spider-Talk and their Amazing Friends w/David Michelinie." *Amazing Spider-Talk.* July 24, 2015.
135. Ginocchio; Gvozden. "Superior Spider-Talk #15: Spider-Talk and their Amazing Friends w/Paul Jenkins."
136. Papamichael, Stella. "Sam Raimi Spider-Man 2 Interviewed." *BBC* (http://www.bbc.co.uk/films/2004/07/09/sam_raimi_spiderman_2_interview.shtml).
137. Ginocchio; Gvozden. "Superior Spider-Talk #31: Spider-Talk and Their Amazing Friends with Gerry Conway."
138. Ibid.
139. Ibid.
140. Ibid.
141. Conway, Gerry; Kane, Gil. "The Spider's Web." *Amazing Spider-Man #125.* New York: Marvel Comics. 1973. Print.
142. Ginocchio; Gvozden. "Superior Spider-Talk #31: Spider-Talk and Their Amazing Friends w/Gerry Conway."
143. Ibid.
144. Conway, Gerry; Kane, Gil. *Amazing Spider-Man #122.* New York: Marvel Comics. 1973. Print.
145. Ginocchio; Gvozden. "Superior Spider-Talk #31: Spider-Talk and Their Amazing Friends w/Gerry Conway."
146. DeFalco, p. 148.
147. Michelinie, David; McFarlane, Todd. *Amazing Spider-Man #300.* New York: Marvel Comics. 1987. Print.
148. Ginocchio; Gvozden. "Spider-Talk and their Amazing Friends w/David Michelinie."
149. Ibid
150. Kit, Borys. "'Spider-Man Spinoff 'Venom' Revived at Sony." *The Hollywood Reporter.* March 4, 2016 (http://www.hollywoodreporter.com/heat-vision/spider-man-spinoff-venom-revived-872844).
151. Ginocchio; Gvozden. "Spider-Talk and their Amazing Friends w/David Michelinie."
152. Michelinie. E-mail interview. August 25, 2016.
153. Ginocchio; Gvozden "Spider-Talk and Their Amazing Friends w/*Spider-Man: The Animated Series.*"

154. Stern, Marlow. "Spider-Man Spinoff 'Sinister Six' Is on Ice, Says Director Drew Goddard." *The Daily Beast.* September 28, 2015 (http://www.thedailybeast.com/articles/2015/09/28/drew-goddard-sinister-six-is-on-ice.html).
155. Spencer, Nick; Steve Lieber. *Superior Foes of Spider-Man #6.* New York: Marvel Comics. 2013.
156. Ginocchio, Mark. Gvozden, Dan. "Spider-Talk and Their Amazing Friends w/the Superior Foes." *Superior Spider-Talk.* December 31, 2014. Web.
157. Ibid.
158. Ginocchio. Gvozden. "Superior Spider-Talk #8: Spider-Talk and their Amazing Friends w/ J.M. DeMatteis."
159. Ginocchio. Gvozden. "Superior Spider-Talk #31: Spider-Talk and Their Amazing Friends with Gerry Conway."
160. Bell, p. 15.
161. Lee; Ditko *Amazing Fantasy #15.*
162. Lee, Stan; Ditko, Steve. *Amazing Spider-Man #17.* New York: Marvel Comics. 1964. Print.
163. J.M. DeMatteis. E-mail interview. September 9, 2016.
164. Guggenheim, Marc; Kitson, Barry. *Amazing Spider-Man #574.* New York: Marvel Comics. 2008.
165. Ginocchio, Mark. Gvozden, Dan. "Spider-Talk and Their Amazing Friends w/Marc Guggenheim." *Amazing Spider-Talk.* June 16, 2016.
166. Viscardi, James. "Let's Talk Comics Episode 15—Dan Slott" *Let's Talk Comics.* February 24, 2014.
167. Hickman, Jonathan; Epting, Steve. *Fantastic Four #600.* New York: Marvel Comics. 2011. Print.
168. Parker, John R. "Jason Aaron and Adam Kubert on *Astonishing Spider-Man & Wolverine.*" *Comics Alliance.* May 7, 2010 (http://comicsalliance.com/jason-aaron-and-adam-kubert-on-astonishing-spiderman-and-wolverin/).
169. Stern, Roger; Romita Jr., John. *Amazing Spider-Man #241.* New York: Marvel Comics. 1983.
170. Khoury, George. "The Roger Stern Interview: The Triumphs and Trials of the Writer." *Marvel Masterworks Resource Page* (http://www.marvelessentials.com/features/int_stern_1006_1.html).
171. Lee, Stan; Romita, John. *Amazing Spider-Man #48.* New York: Marvel Comics. 1967.
172. Conway, Gerry; Andru, Ross. *Amazing Spider-Man #128.* New York: Marvel Comics. 1974.
173. Waid, Mark; McKone, Mike. *Amazing Spider-Man #593.* New York: Marvel Comics. 2009.
174. Weintraub, Steve. "John Malkovich Confirms he was the Vulture in Sam Raimi's *Spider-Man 4.*" *Collider.* April 16, 2010. (http://collider.com/.john-malkovich-confirms-he-was-the-vulture-in-sam-raimis-spider-man-4/).
175. Zeb Wells. E-mail interview. August 20, 2016.
176. Wolfman. E-mail interview. September 2, 2016.
177. Henderson, Jeffrey. "Storyboard." *Planet Henderson* (http://www.planethenderson.com/storyboards/#/spiderman4/)
178. Opam, Kwame. "The man who writes Spider-Man talks Marvel's Cinematic Universe." *The Verge.* February 19, 2015 (http://www.theverge.com/2015/2/19/8069257/spider-man-dan-slott-marvel-cinematic-universe-comics).
179. Cronin, Brian. "Comic Book Urban Legend Revealed #15." *Comics Should Be Good.* September 8, 2005 (http://goodcomics.blogspot.com/2005/09/comic-book-urban-legends-revealed-15.html).
180. Superherohype. "*Spider-Man 3* Interviews: Thomas Haden Church." *Super Hero Hype.* April 22, 2007 (http://www.superherohype.com/features/93451-spider-man-3-interviews-thomas-haden-church).
181. Miller, Jonathan. "Spider-Man and Company: The Wide World of Marvel Team-Up." *Back Issue No. 44.* October 2010. p. 38. Print.
182. Ginocchio; Gvozden. "Superior Spider-Talk #31: Spider-Talk and Their Amazing Friends w/Gerry Conway."
183. Wolfman. E-mail interview. September 2, 2016.
184. Ginocchio, Mark. Gvozden, Dan. "Superior Spider-Talk #26: Superior Spider-Man #23 w/Ron Frenz." *Amazing Spider-Talk.* January 20, 2014.
185. Ibid.
186. Johnson, Dan. "Twenty Years of Wedded Bliss." *Back Issue No. 23.* August 2007. p. 3. Print.
187. Ibid, p. 8

188. Ibid, p. 9.
189. Ibid,
190. Ginocchio; Gvozden. "Spider-Talk and their Amazing Friends w/David Michelinie."
191. Weiland, Jonah. "The 'One More Day' Interviews with Joe Quesada, pt. 3 of 5." *Comic Book Resources.* (http://www.comicbookresources.com/?page=article&id=12246).
192. Johnson, Dan. "Black and White and Read All Over: The Spider-Man Extreme Makeover." *Back Issue No. 12.* October 2005. p. 48.
193. Ibid.
194. DeFalco, p. 101.
195. Ibid, p. 102.
196. Khoury. "The Roger Stern Interview: The Triumphs and Trials of the Writer." (http://www.marvelessentials.com/features/int_stern_1006_1.html).
197. DeFalco, p. 102.
198. Khoury. "The Roger Stern Interview: The Triumphs and Trials of the Writer." (http://www.marvelessentials.com/features/int_stern_1006_1.html).
199. Ginocchio, Mark. "The Secret Origin of the Secret Identity of the Hobgoblin, Part 2." *Comic Book Resources.* February 7, 2014 (http://www.cbr.com/the-secret-origin-of-the-secret-identity-of-the-hobgoblin-part-2/).
200. Khoury. "The Roger Stern Interview: The Triumphs and Trials of the Writer." (http://www.marvelessentials.com/features/int_stern_1006_1.html).
201. Richards, Dave. "Sterner Stuff: Roger Stern on Amazing Spider-Man." *Comic Book Resources.* December 10, 2008. (http://www.cbr.com/sterner-stuff-roger-stern-on-amazing-spider-man/).
202. Burgas, Greg. "Comics You Should Own Flashback—*Amazing Spider-Man #229-230.*" *Comics Should Be Good.* March 23, 2008 (http://www.cbr.com/comics-you-should-own-flashback-amazing-spider-man-229-230/).
203. DeFalco, p. 33.
204. Wolfman. E-mail interview. September 2, 2016.
205. Ginocchio, Mark. Gvozden, Dan. "Spider-Talk and Their Amazing Friends w/Ron Garney." *Amazing Spider-Talk.* July 22, 2016.
206. Richards, Dave. "The Ultimate Spider-Decade Part 1." *Comic Book Resources.* November 22, 2010 (http://www.comicbookresources.com/?page=article&id=29554).
207. DeFalco. Phone interview. September 19, 2016.
208. Shaina 411. "Amazing Spider-Man 2 Star Jamie Foxx Talks Playing Electro & His Upcoming Album." *The Source.* May 1, 2014 (http://thesource.com/2014/05/01/amazing-spider-man-2-star-jamie-foxx-talks-playing-electro-his-upcoming-album/).
209. DeMatteis. E-mail interview. September 9, 2016.
210. Lovett, Jamie. "Amazing Spider-Man 2 Exclusive: Marc Webb Interested In Kraven The Hunter As A Villain." *ComicBook.com.* May 2, 2014 (http://comicbook.com/blog/2014/05/02/amazing-spider-man-2-exclusive-marc-webb-interested-in-kraven-the-hunter-as-a-villain/).
211. Ginocchio, Mark. Gvozden, Dan. "Superior Spider-Talk #20: NYCC Spider-Man Writer's Room Edition." *Superior Spider-Talk.* November 3, 2013.
212. Cronin, Brian. "50 Greatest Spider-Man Stories Master List." May 4, 2013. *Comic Book Resources.* (http://www.cbr.com/50-greatest-spider-man-stories-master-list/).
213. Ginocchio, Mark. Gvozden, Dan. "Superior Spider-Talk #8: Spider-Talk and Their Amazing Friends w/J.M. DeMatteis." *Superior Spider-Talk.* August 28, 2013.
214. Van Gelder, Lawrence. "A Comics Magazine Defies Code Ban on Drug Stories," *New York Times.* February 4, 1971. p. 37. Print.
215. Ibid.
216. Van Gelder, Lawrence. Van Gelder, Lindsey. "Radicalization of the Superheroes." in Jeff McLaughlin, ed. *Stan Lee Conversations.* Jackson: The University Press of Mississippi, 2007. p. 27. Print.
217. Manner, Jim. "Cracking the Code: The Spider-Man Drug Issues." *Back Issue No. 44,* October 2010. p 3. Print.
218. Lee, Stan. Kane, Gil. *Amazing Spider-Man #96.* May 1971. New York: Marvel Comics.

219. Van Gelder. "A Comics Magazine Defies Code Ban on Drug Stories," p. 37.
220. Axel Alonso. Phone interview. February 25, 2016.
221. Ginocchio. Gvozden. "Superior Spider-Talk #31: Spider-Talk and Their Amazing Friends w/ Gerry Conway."
222. Scherstuhl. "The Man Who Killed Spider-Man."
223. Alonso. Phone interview. February 25, 2016.
224. Straczynski, J. Michael; Romita Jr., John. *Amazing Spider-Man #36*. Marvel Comics: New York. 2001. Print.
225. Barnes, Julia. "Tough Call Spider-Man." *New York Times*. October 8, 2011. Web archives.
226. Taylor, Robert. Reflections: J. Michael Straczynski, Part I. *Comic Book Resources*. June 26, 2008 (http://www.comicbookresources.com/?page=article&id=16965).
227. DeFalco, p. 231.
228. Richard. "The Ultimate Spider-Decade Part 1." (http://www.comicbookresources.com/?page=article&id=29554).
229. Ibid.
230. Ibid.
231. Ibid.
232. Riseman, Abraham. "Comics Legend Brian Michael Bendis on Guardians of the Galaxy, Sexism, and Making a Nonwhite Spider-Man." *Vulture*. May 1, 2014 (http://www.vulture.com/2014/04/comics-brian-michael-bendis-spider-man-guardians-x-men.html).
233. Viscardi, Jim. "Brian Michael Bendis On Miles Morales Being THE Spider-Man & More." *ComicBook.com*. January 8, 2016 (http://comicbook.com/2016/01/08/marvel-brian-michael-bendis-miles-morales-spider-man-sara-pichel/).
234. Viscardi, James. "Let's Talk Comics Episode 6: Brian Michael Bendis." *Let's Talk Comics*. December 23, 2013.
235. Ibid.
236. DeFalco, p. 231.
237. Viscardi, James. "Let's Talk Comics Episode 36: Brian Michael Bendis." *Let's Talk Comics*. July 21, 2014.
238. Ibid.
239. Ibid.
240. DeFalco, p. 237.
241. Viscardi. "Let's Talk Comics Episode 36: Brian Michael Bendis."
242. Tom Brevoort. Phone interview. August 26, 2016.
243. Viscardi. "Let's Talk Comics Episode 36: Brian Michael Bendis."
244. Bendis, Brian; Michael. Bachalo, Chris. Tan, Billy. *New Avengers #51*. New York: Marvel Comics. 2009.
245. Bendis, Brian; Michael. Quesada, Joe. *Amazing Spider-Man #601*. New York: Marvel Comics. 2009.
246. Grover, Ronald. "Unraveling Spider-Man's Tangled Web." *Business Week*. April 15, 2002 (http://web.archive.org/web/20090510064647/http://www.businessweek.com/bwdaily/dnflash/apr2002/nf20020415_7441.htm).
247. Hiltzik, Michael. "Untangling the Web." *Los Angeles Times*. March 24, 2002 (http://www.webcitation.org/619qthyXd).
248. Grover. "Unraveling Spider-Man's Tangled Web." (http://web.archive.org/web/20090510064647/http://www.businessweek.com/bwdaily/dnflash/apr2002/nf20020415_7441.htm).
249. Ibid.
250. *Spidermania*. von Puttkamer, Peter. Omnifilm Entertainment. 2002. TV Special.
251. Hiltzik. "Untangling the Web."
252. *Spidermania*.
253. Grover. "Unraveling Spider-Man's Tangled Web." (http://web.archive.org/web/20090510064647/http://www.businessweek.com/bwdaily/dnflash/apr2002/nf20020415_7441.htm).
254. *Eight Arms to Hold You*. Sony. *Spider-Man 2* DVD. 2004.
255. *Making the Amazing*. Sony. Documentary. 2004.

256. Ebert, Roger. *Spider-Man 2. RogerEbert.com.* June 29, 2004 (http://www.rogerebert.com/reviews/spider-man-2-2004).
257. Buchanan, Kyle. "Sam Raimi on Oz, *The Avengers*, and Two Huge Movies He Never Made." *Vulture.* March 2013 (http://www.vulture.com/2013/03/sam-raimi-on-oz-and-two-huge-films-he-never-made.html).
258. *Spidermania.*
259. "Sam Raimi: The man behind the web." *Associated Press.* July 2, 2004 (http://www.today.com/id/5263260/ns/today-today_entertainment/t/sam-raimi-man-behind-web/#.WA1lQpgrL-Y).
260. Ibid.
261. Papamichael, Stell. "Sam Raimi *Spider-Man 2* Interview." *BBC.* September 24, 2014 Web archive. (http://www.bbc.co.uk/films/2004/07/09/sam_raimi_spiderman_2_interview.shtml).
262. *Spidermania.*
263. *Making the Amazing.*
264. Papamichael. "Sam Raimi *Spider-Man 2* Interview." (http://www.bbc.co.uk/films/2004/07/09/sam_raimi_spiderman_2_interview.shtml).
265. Trendacosta, Katharine. "Sam Raimi: The Problems With *Spider-Man 3* Were 'My Mistake.'" *io9.* December 31, 2014 (http://io9.gizmodo.com/sam-raimi-the-problems-with-spider-man-3-were-my-mist-1676733026).
266. Papamichael. "Sam Raimi *Spider-Man 2* Interview." (http://www.bbc.co.uk/films/2004/07/09/sam_raimi_spiderman_2_interview.shtml),
267. *Spidermania.*
268. Clinton, Paul. "Tobey Maguire: A thoughtful *Spider-Man.*" *CNN.* May 2, 2002 (http://www.cnn.com/2002/SHOWBIZ/Movies/05/02/ca.s02.tobey.maguire/).
269. Tobey Maguire Biography. *IMDB.com.* Web.
270. *Spidermania.*
271. Clinton. "Tobey Maguire: A thoughtful *Spider-Man.*" (http://www.cnn.com/2002/SHOWBIZ/Movies/05/02/ca.s02.tobey.maguire/).
272. Tobey Maguire Biography. *IMDB.com.* Web.
273. "Tobey Maguire quits *Spider-Man 4*... after new script sends Peter Parker back to high school." *Daily Mail.* January 13, 2010 (http://www.dailymail.co.uk/tvshowbiz/article-1242820/Tobey-Maguire-quits-Spider-Man-4--new-script-sends-Peter-Parker-high-school.html).
274. Johnson, Dan. "Marvel's Dark Angel." *Back Issue No. 17.* August 2006. p. 60. Print.
275. Wolfman. E-mail interview. September 2, 2016.
276. Ibid.
277. Johnson. "20 Years of Webbed Bliss." p. 13.
278. Ginocchio, Mark. Gvozden, Dan. "Spider-Talk and their Amazing Friends w/Joe Kelly." *Amazing Spider-Talk.* September 25, 2015.
279. DeFalco, p. 43.
280. Ginocchio. Gvozden. "Superior Spider-Talk #31: Spider-Talk and Their Amazing Friends w/ Gerry Conway."
281. Ibid.
282. Ibid.
283. "Roy Thomas on Stan Lee." *The Comics Journal No. 44,* January 1979. p. 19. Print.
284. Ginocchio. Gvozden. "Superior Spider-Talk #31: Spider-Talk and Their Amazing Friends w/ Gerry Conway."
285. Arndt, Richard J. "We Were Given the Gift of Serendipity." *Alter-ego Vol. 3, No. 131.* March 2015. p. 32-34.
286. Ibid.
287. Faraci, Devin. "10 Things That Were Changed From The Amazing *Spider-Man 2* Script." *Birth. Movies. Death.* July 14, 2014 (http://birthmoviesdeath.com/2014/07/14/10-things-that-were-changed-from-the-amazing-spider-man-2-script).
288. Aushenker, Michael. "That Other Spider-Man Title ... *Marvel Team-Up.*" *Back Issue No. 66.* August 2013. p. 18. Print.

289. Ibid.
290. Arndt. "We Were Given the Gift of Serendipity." p. 32-34.
291. Ibid.
292. Ibid, p. 34.
293. Ibid.
294. Sacks, Ethan. "Jon Bernthal and Tom Holland made audition tapes together to land The Punisher and Spider-Man roles." *New York Daily News*. March 10, 2016 (http://www.nydailynews.com/entertainment/movies/exclusive-bernthal-holland-teamed-marvel-auditions-article-1.2560381).
295. Ginocchio, Mark; Gvozden, Dan. "Spider-Talk and their Amazing Friends w/Tom DeFalco." *Amazing Spider-Talk*. September 22, 2014.
296. Ibid.
297. Ibid.
298. Ibid.
299. Ibid.
300. Ginocchio; Gvozden. "Superior Spider-Talk #10: Spider-Talk and their Amazing Friends - Tom DeFalco."
301. Ginocchio; Gvozden. "Spider-Talk and their Amazing Friends w/Tom DeFalco."
302. Ginocchio; Gvozden. "Superior Spider-Talk #14: Spider-Talk and their Amazing Friends w/Ron Frenz."
303. Greenberg, Glenn. "When Hobby Met Spidey." *Back Issue No. 35*. August 2009. p. 10-23. Print.
304. Ginocchio; Gvozden. "Spider-Talk and their Amazing Friends w/Tom DeFalco."
305. Ginocchio; Gvozden. "Amazing Friends w/ the "Clone Saga" (Howard Mackie & Terry Kavanagh)."
306. Douglas, Brad. "Spider-Man Crawlspace Episode 15—John Romita Jr." *Spider-Man Crawlspace*. September 2007.
307. Cooke. "John Romita Sr. & Jr.: A roundtable conversation with the talented father and son. Print. p. 19B.
308. Douglas, Brad. "Spider-Man Crawlspace Episode 35—Roger Stern Interview." *Spider-Man Crawlspace*. June 2008. Web.
309. Cooke, Jon B.. "John Romita Sr. & Jr.: A roundtable conversation with the talented father and son." *Comic Book Artists #20*. July 2002. p. 22B. Print.
310. Ibid.
311. Ibid p. 25B.
312. Khoury. "The Roger Stern Interview: The Triumphs and Trials of the Writer." (http://www.marvelessentials.com/features/int_stern_1006_1.html).
313. Cooke. "John Romita Sr. & Jr.: A roundtable conversation with the talented father and son." p. 26B.
314. Ibid. p. 31B.
315. Douglas. "Spider-Man Crawlspace Episode 15—John Romita Jr."
316. Cooke. "John Romita Sr. & Jr.: A roundtable conversation with the talented father and son." p. 24B.
317. DeFalco, p. 38.
318. Lee, Stan; Kane, Gil. *Amazing Spider-Man #90*. New York: Marvel Comics. 1970.
319. Waid, Mark; Kitson, Barry. *Amazing Spider-Man #583*. New York: Marvel Comics. 2008. Print.
320. Howe, Sean. *Marvel Comics: The Untold Story*. New York: HarperPerennial. p. 96. Print.
321. Lee, Stan; Romita, John. *Amazing Spider-Man #69*. New York: Marvel Comics. 1969.
322. Lee, Stan; Romita, John and Kane, Gil. *Amazing Spider-Man #92*. New York: Marvel Comics. 1971.
323. Aushenker, Michael. "Not Amazing, But Spectacular." *Back Issue No 44*. October 2010. p. 57. Print.
324. Viscardi. "Let's Talk Comics Episode 15—Dan Slott."
325. Ginocchio; Gvozden. "Superior Spider-Talk #14: Spider-Talk and their Amazing Friends w/Ron Frenz."
326. Ibid.
327. Aushenker, p. 54.
328. DeFalco, p. 103.
329. Ginocchio; Gvozden. "Spider-Talk #20 NYCC Spider-Man Writers Room Edition."
330. DeFalco, p. 165.

331. Fischer, Travis. "SDCC: Spotlight on Gerry Conway." *Comic Book Resources*. July 31, 2013 (http://www.cbr.com/sdcc-spotlight-on-gerry-conway/).
332. Arndt. "We Were Given the Gift of Serendipity." pp. 35-36.
333. DeMatteis. E-mail interview. September 9, 2016.
334. Richard, Dave. Uncovering Spider-Man's 'The Clone Conspiracy' with Slott & Lowe." *Comic Book Resources*. August 18, 2016 (http://www.cbr.com/exclusive-uncovering-spider-mans-the-clone-conspiracy-with-slott-lowe/).
335. Ginocchio; Gvozden. "Spider-Talk and their Amazing Friends w/Howard Mackie and Terry Kavanagh."
336. Ibid.
337. Ibid.
338. Ibid.
339. Ibid.
340. Ibid.
341. Ibid.
342. Ibid.
343. Ibid.
344. Ibid.
345. DeFalco, p. 145.
346. Ibid, p. 147.
347. Ginocchio, Mark; Gvozden, Dan. "Superior Spider-Talk #12: Spider-Talk and their Amazing Friends w/Jim Salicrup." *Superior Spider-Talk*. September 5, 2013.
348. DeFalco, p. 149.
349. Ginocchio; Gvozden. "Superior Spider-Talk #12: Spider-Talk and their Amazing Friends w/Jim Salicrup."
350. Ibid.
351. Reed, Patrick. "25 Years Ago: Todd McFarlane's Spider-Man #1 Changed the Industry." *Comics Alliance*. June 19, 2015 (http://comicsalliance.com/tribute-todd-mcfarlane-spider-man/).
352. "Todd McFarlane Bio." *Image Comics*. (https://imagecomics.com/creators/view/todd-mcfarlane).
353. Comicbook, Joe. "Todd McFarlane Would Possibly Work With Marvel On Spider-Man Again." *ComicBook.com*. February 6, 2014 (http://comicbook.com/blog/2014/02/06/todd-mcfarlane-would-possibly-work-with-marvel-on-spider-man-again/).
354. Ginocchio; Gvozden. "Spider-Talk and their Amazing Friends w/David Michelinie."
355. Ginocchio, Mark; Gvozden, Dan. "Superior Spider-Talk #9: Spider-Talk and their Amazing Friends w/Mark Bagley." *Superior Spider-Talk*. August 30, 2013.
356. Wells. E-mail interview. August 20, 2016.
357. Ginocchio. Gvozden. "Spider-Talk and their Amazing Friends w/Gerry Conway on "Spiral" and *Carnage*."
358. Viscardi. "Let's Talk Comics Episode 15—Dan Slott."
359. Sunu, Steve. "Amazing Spider-Man Writer Receives Death Threats Via Social Media." *Comic Book Resources*. December 18, 2012 (http://www.comicbookresources.com/?page=article&id=42731).
360. Viscardi. "Let's Talk Comics Episode 15—Dan Slott."
361. Ibid.
362. Levine, Katie. Nerdist Comics Panel #11: Dan Slott. *Nerdist Comics Panel*. August 17, 2013.
363. Viscardi. "Let's Talk Comics Episode 15—Dan Slott."
364. Ibid.
365. DeFalco, p. 177.
366. Ginocchio; Gvozden. "Superior Spider-Talk #9: Spider-Talk and their Amazing Friends w/Mark Bagley."
367. Ibid.
368. DeFalco, p. 180.
369. Ibid.
370. Ibid.

371. Ginocchio; Gvozden. "Superior Spider-Talk #9: Spider-Talk and their Amazing Friends w/Mark Bagley."
372. Ibid.
373. Lee, Stan; Romita, John. Heck, Don. *Amazing Spider-Man Annual #3*. New York: Marvel Comics. 1966.
374. Stern, Roger; Milgrom, Al. *Avengers #236*. New York: Marvel Comics. 1983. Print.
375. Brevoort. Phone interview. August 26, 2016.
376. Ibid.
377. Ibid.
378. Gallagher, Brian. "Marvel's Spider-Man: What did the Sony Hack Reveal?" *Movieweb*. (http://movieweb.com/marvel-spider-man-movie-reboot-sony-hack/).
379. Derschowitz, Jessica. "Chris Evans wants a Captain America cameo in *Spider-Man: Homecoming*." *Entertainment Weekly*. May 26, 2016 (http://www.ew.com/article/2016/05/26/captain-america-chris-evans-wants-cameo-spider-man-homecoming).
380. Riseman. "Comics Legend Brian Michael Bendis on *Guardians of the Galaxy*, Sexism, and Making a Nonwhite Spider-Man." (http://www.vulture.com/2014/04/comics-brian-michael-bendis-spider-man-guardians-x-men.html).
381. Viscardi. "Brian Michael Bendis On Miles Morales Being THE Spider-Man & More." (http://comicbook.com/2016/01/08/marvel-brian-michael-bendis-miles-morales-spider-man-sara-pichel/).
382. Straczynski, J. Michael. Romita Jr., John. *Amazing Spider-Man #35 (vol. 2)*. New York: Marvel Comics. 2001.
383. *Rite of Passage: The Amazing Spider-Man Reborn*. de Lauzirika, Charles. 2012. Documentary.
384. Rea, Steven. "*The Amazing Spider-Man*: Unoriginal but fun." *Philadelphia Inquirer*. July 3, 2012 (http://www.philly.com/philly/entertainment/movies/20120703_The_Amazing_Spider-Man__Unoriginal_but_fun.html).
385. NPR Staff. "Andrew Garfield, Disappearing Into Spidey's Suit." *NPR*. June 1, 2012 (http://www.webcitation.org/686IOrT0Z).
386. *Rite of Passage: Amazing Spider-Man Reborn*.
387. Ibid.
388. Ibid.
389. Pringle, Gill. "Andrew Garfield on *The Amazing Spider-Man*: 'I started to feel the separation of myself from the world – it hit me in a very sad, scary way.'" *Independent*. September 11, 2015 (http://(www.independent.co.uk/arts-entertainment/films/features/andrew-garfield-interview-on-the-amazing-spider-man-i-started-to-feel-the-separation-of-myself-from-10496298.html).
390. McMillan, Graeme. "What to Expect Now That Spider-Man's Back in the Marvel Cinematic Universe." *Wired*. February 10, 2015 (http://www.wired.com/2015/02/spider-man-back-to-marvel/).
391. Ibid.
392. "Sony Pictures and Marvel Studios Find Their 'Spider-Man' Star and Director Tom Holland Cast as the Web-Slinger, Jon Watts to Direct the Next Spider-Man Adventure." Press Release. Marvel/Sony. June 23, 2015 (https://news.marvel.com/movies/24758/sony_pictures_and_marvel_studios_find_their_spider-man_star_and_director/).
393. Child, Ben. "*Captain America: Civil War*: The verdict on Tom Holland's Spider-Man." *Independent*. April 29, 2016 (http://www.independent.co.uk/arts-entertainment/films/features/captain-america-civil-war-the-verdict-on-tom-hollands-new-spider-man-a7007226.html).
394. Siegel, Tatiana. "Robert Downey Jr. and Secret Screen-Tests: How the New 'Spider-Man' Team Was Chosen." *Hollywood Reporter*. June 23, 2015 (http://www.hollywoodreporter.com/heat-vision/how-new-spider-man-team-804569).
395. Stern, Marlow. "How Tom Holland Became Spider-Man." *The Daily Beast*. December 9, 2015 (http://www.thedailybeast.com/articles/2015/12/09/how-tom-holland-became-spider-man.html).
396. Ibid.
397. Douglas, Edward. "Exclusive: Tom Holland Reveals an Interesting Spider-Man Tidbit." *Super Hero Hype*. November 25, 2015 (http://www.superherohype.com/news/359531-exclusive-tom-holland-reveals-an-interesting-spider-man-tidbit).

398. Sacks. "Jon Bernthal and Tom Holland made audition tapes together to land The Punisher and Spider-Man roles." (http://www.nydailynews.com/entertainment/movies/exclusive-bernthal-holland-teamed-marvel-auditions-article-1.2560381?utm_content=buffer6f270&utm_medium=social&utm_source=twitter.com&utm_campaign=esacks+twitter).
399. Ibid.
400. Stern. "How Tom Holland Became Spider-Man." (http://www.thedailybeast.com/articles/2015/12/09/how-tom-holland-became-spider-man.html).
401. Ibid
402. Eisenberg, Eric. "How Spider-Man Totally Changed Black Panther's Role In *Captain America: Civil War.*" *Cinema Blend.* May, 2016 (http://www.cinemablend.com/new/How-Spider-Man-Totally-Changed-Black-Panther-Role-Captain-America-Civil-War-125317.html).
403. Opam, Kwame. "Spider-Man is amazing in *Captain America: Civil War*, but has no business being in it." *The Verge.* May 7, 2016 (http://www.theverge.com/2016/5/7/11612616/spider-man-captain-america-civil-war-marvel-cinematic-universe).
404. Chitwood, Adam. "SPIDER-MAN: Kevin Feige on the Process of Choosing the Reboot's Director and Star." *Collider.* July 1, 2015 (http://collider.com/spider-man-reboot-kevin-feige-on-choosing-director-jon-watts/).
405. Schager, Nick. "FLYING HIGH: Jon Watts on His Bizarre Journey From *The Onion* to *Spider-Man: Homecoming.*" *The Daily Beast.* June 17, 2016 (http://www.thedailybeast.com/articles/2016/06/17/jon-watts-on-his-bizarre-journey-from-the-onion-to-spider-man-homecoming.html).
406. Weiland, Jonah. "The 'One More Day' Interviews with Joe Quesada: Pt. 2 of 5." *Comic Book Resources.* December 31, 2007 (http://www.comicbookresources.com/?page=article&id=12238).
407. Ibid.
408. Ibid.
409. Ibid.
410. Ibid.
411. Ibid.
412. Straczynski, J. Michael; Quesada, Joe. *Amazing Spider-Man #545.* New York: Marvel Comics. 2007.
413. Chapman, Adam. "*Amazing Spider-Man #545.*" *SpiderFan* (http://www.spiderfan.org/comics/reviews/spiderman_amazing/545.html).
414. Slott, Dan; Elson, Richard. *Amazing Spider-Man #698.* New York: Marvel Comics. 2012.
415. Schedeen, Jesse. "Dan Slott Ushers in a New Spider-Man Era." *IGN.* January 13, 2014 (http://www.ign.com/articles/2014/01/13/dan-slott-ushers-in-a-new-spider-man-era).
416. Greenfield, Dan. "The Dan Slott Interviews: A Spider-Legacy." *13th Dimension.* March 26, 2016 (http://13thdimension.com/the-dan-slott-interviews-a-spider-legacy/).
417. Boyd, Jerry. "The House of Ideas Herculean 100th Issues. *Back Issue No 69.* December 2013. p. 12. Print.
418. Straczynski, J. Michael; Romita Jr., John. *Amazing Spider-Man #32.* New York: Marvel Comics. 2001.
419. Slott, Dan. Ramos; Humberto. *Amazing Spider-Man #672.* New York: Marvel Comics. 2011.
420. Lee, Stan; Romita, John. *Amazing Spider-Man #43.* New York: Marvel Comics. 1966. Print.
421. Peter Millgian. E-mail Interview. September 7, 2016.
422. Ginocchio; Gvozden. "Spider-Talk and Their Amazing Friends w/Joe Kelley."
423. Ed Hannigan. E-mail interview. September 3, 2016.
424. Wagmeister, Elizabeth. "Freeform Greenlights Marvel Romance Superhero Series 'Cloak and Dagger.'" *Variety.* (http://variety.com/2016/tv/news/marvel-cloak-and-dagger-freeform-series-1201747907/).
425. Terry Kavanagh. E-mail interview. July 22, 2016.
426. Ginocchio; Gvozden. "Spider-Talk and their Amazing Friends w/Howard Mackie and Terry Kavanagh."
427. Ginocchio; Gvozden. "Superior Spider-Talk #21: NYCC Classic Spider-Artist Edition."
428. Howard Mackie. E-mail interview. September 7, 2016.
429. Ginocchio; Gvozden. "Spider-Talk and Their Amazing Friends w/Marc Guggenheim."

430. Johnson, Dan. "In Our Sights: Kraven's Last Hunt." *Back Issue No. 35.* August 2009. p. 7. Print.
431. Ibid.
432. Ginocchio; Gvozden. "Superior Spider-Talk #8: Spider-Talk and Their Amazing Friends w/J.M. DeMatteis."
433. DeMatteis. E-mail interview. September 9, 2016.
434. Johnson. "In Our Sights: Kraven's Last Hunt." p. 4.
435. DeFalco, p. 164.
436. Ginocchio; Gvozden. "Superior Spider-Talk #8: Spider-Talk and Their Amazing Friends w/J.M. DeMatteis."
437. DeFalco, p. 169.
438. Ibid, p. 170.
439. Ginocchio; Gvozden. "Superior Spider-Talk #8: Spider-Talk and Their Amazing Friends w/J.M. DeMatteis."
440. DeFalco, p. 131.
441. Ibid, p. 132
442. Ginocchio; Gvozden. "Spider-Talk and their Amazing Friends w/David Michelinie."
443. Ibid.
444. Ibid.
445. Ibid.
446. Ibid.
447. Ibid.
448. Ibid.
449. Ibid.
450. Ginocchio, Mark. "The Secret Origin of the Secret Identity of the Hobgoblin, Part 1." (http://www.cbr.com/the-secret-origin-of-the-secret-identity-of-the-hobgoblin-part-1/).
451. Ibid.
452. Ibid.
453. Ibid.
454. Ginocchio; Gvozden. "Superior Spider-Talk #20 NYCC Spider-Man Writers Room Edition."
455. Ibid.
456. Ibid.
457. Ginocchio, Mark. "The Secret Origin of the Secret Identity of the Hobgoblin, Part 2." *Comic Book Resources.* February 7, 2014 (http://www.cbr.com/the-secret-origin-of-the-secret-identity-of-the-hobgoblin-part-2/).
458. Viscardi. "Let's Talk Comics Episode 15 - Dan Slott."
459. Ginocchio; Gvozden. "Spider-Talk and Their Amazing Friends w/Marc Guggenheim."
460. Ginocchio; Gvozden. "Spider-Talk and their Amazing Friends w/Joe Kelly."
461. Douglas, Brad. "Spider-Man Crawlspace Podcast Episode 150: Steve Wacker Interview." *Spider-Man Crawlspace.* September 20, 2011.
462. Alonso. Phone interview. February 25, 2016.
463. Thompson, Chris. "Episode 71—Exploring Joe's Comics with J. Michael Straczynski." *Pop Culture Hound.* January 8, 2014. Web.
464. Ibid.
465. Alonso. Phone interview. February 25, 2016.
466. Taylor, Robert. "Reflections: J. Michael Straczynski, Part I." *Comic Book Resources.* June 26, 2008 (http://www.comicbookresources.com/?page=article&id=16965).
467. Alonso. Phone interview. February 25, 2016.
468. Weiland. "The 'One More Day' Interviews With Joe Quesada, Pt. 3 of 5." (http://www.comicbookresources.com/?page=article&id=12246).
469. Taylor. "Reflections: J. Michael Straczynski, Part I." (http://www.comicbookresources.com/?page=article&id=16965).
470. "An Interview With Dennis Marks." *Spider-Friends.com.* June 2002 (http://www.spider-friends.com/Credits/writers/InterviewDM.html).

471. Ginocchio; Gvozden. "Spider-Talk and their Amazing Friends w/*Spider-Man: The Animated Series*."
472. Amaya, Erik. "LBCC: Cast, Crew Remembers *Spectacular Spider-Man*, Hopes for Return." *Comic Book Resources*. September 29, 2014 (http://www.comicbookresources.com/?page=article&id=55869).
473. Palmer, Roger. "*Marvel's Spider-Man*, an All-New Animated Series, Set to Debut on Disney XD in 2017." *Diskingdom*. October 8, 2016 (http://diskingdom.com/2016/10/08/marvels-spider-man-an-all-new-animated-series-set-to-debut-on-disney-xd-in-2017/).
474. Ginocchio; Gvozden. "Spider-Talk and Their Amazing Friends w/Marc Guggenheim."
475. Weiss, Brett. "Spidey Super Stories." *Back Issue No. 44*. October 2010. p. 23-24. Print.
476. Ibid.
477. Jim Salicrup. E-mail interview. September 2, 2016.
478. Mitchel, Bill. "In-depth: Peter David." *Comic Book Resources*. June 24, 2009 (http://www.cbr.com/in-depth-peter-david/).
479. Ibid.
480. Richards, Dave. "David's Spider-Man 2099 Fights to Reshape the Future." *Comic Book Resources*. March 28, 2014 (http://www.comicbookresources.com/?page=article&id=51762).
481. Mitchell. "In-depth: Peter David." (http://www.cbr.com/in-depth-peter-david/).
482. Ginocchio; Gvozden. "Superior Spider-Talk #20: NYCC Spider-Man Writer's Room Edition."
483. Ginocchio; Gvozden. "Superior Spider-Talk #10: Spider-Talk and their Amazing Friends—Tom DeFalco."
484. Ibid.
485. Ibid.
486. Johnson, Dan. "Marvel's Dark Angel: Back Issue Gets Caught in Spider-Woman's Web." *Back Issue No. 17*. August 2006. p. 58. Print.
487. Ibid. p. 59.
488. Ginocchio, Mark; Gvozden, Dan. "Spider-Talk and their Amazing Friends w/Dennis Hopeless." *Amazing Spider-Talk*. April 1, 2015.
489. Hurd, Joe. "Stan Lee" (1997) in Jeff McLaughlin, ed. *Stan Lee Conversations*. Jackson: The University Press of Mississippi, 2007. p. 127.
490. Ibid, p. 128.
491. DeFalco, p. 39.
492. Ginocchio, Mark; Gvozden. "Superior Spider-Talk #21: NYCC Classic Spider-Man Art Edition."
493. Byrne, John. "FAQ: *Amazing Spider-Man*." *Byrne Robotics*. (http://www.byrnerobotics.com/FAQ/listing.asp?ID=2&T1=Questions+about+Comic+Book+Projects#155).
494. Mackie. E-mail interview. September 7, 2016.
495. Ibid.
496. Brevoort. Phone interview. August 26, 2016.
497. Kurt Busiek. E-mail interview. August 31, 2016.
498. Brevoort. Phone interview. August 26, 2016.
499. Ibid.
500. Musgrave, Shaun. "'Spider-Man Unlimited' Review: The Amazing Ironically-Titled Spider-Game." *TouchArcade*. September 12, 2014 (http://toucharcade.com/2014/09/12/spider-man-unlimited-review/).
501. Busiek. E-mail interview. August 31, 2016.
502. Busiek, Kurt; Olliffe, Pat. *Untold Tales of Spider-Man Annual*. New York: Marvel Comics. 1996. Print.